"A book that deserves to be read."

The New York Times

"His story of the metamorphosis of Little Arthur Arshawsky, the son of poor Jewish immigrants, into Artie Shaw, the mercurial bandleader and idol of American youth, is . . . fascinating. . . . His dissection of the world of hot music–of what makes a fine jazz musician and a fine jazz band–is as good as anything in print. . . ."

The New Yorker

"A completely honest record. . . . The life of a jazz musician in America, revealed here in gripping realism . . . is a fascinating narrative of a contemporary American, an absorbing account of a man's struggle with himself."

Christian Science Monitor

"An honest, moving, and lucid account of the odyssey of one man in search of himself. It radiates integrity. Perhaps its most striking quality is its freedom from pretension, its lack of self-consciousness, its willingness to face truth. . . . *The Trouble with Cinderella* constitutes a fascinating and important cultural document . . . of the struggle of one who has lived the myth of our time . . . the distorting effect of the realization of the American dream . . . his fight to become a real person. Implicit . . . are many lessons from which each of us can profit."

Dr. Robert Lindner, author,
Rebel Without A Cause, The Fifty Minute Hour, etc.

"*The Trouble with Cinderella* is an extraordinary, absorbing, and thought-provoking contribution to Americana. Mr. Shaw's perceptive and literate account . . . point up certain problems of our contemporary values with a sharpness of focus and an awareness of levels of complexity that are not always found in the treatises of our professional moralists. I found it warmly human and I hope it will be widely read."

Vernon Venable, chairman
Department of Philosophy, Vassar College

"This candid, entertaining autobiography . . . yields valuable insights on that fascinating period of American music known as the Big Band Era."

Dan Morgenstern, director
Rutgers Institute of Jazz Studies

"It's all too seldom that someone writes from the inside out about the life of a big-band musician. Artie Shaw has done just that, and at the same time has revealed much about himself."

George Simon

Artie Shaw

THE TROUBLE WITH CINDERELLA

AN OUTLINE OF IDENTITY

ARTIE SHAW

Fithian Press
in association with
Artixo Books
SANTA BARBARA
1992

This book was originally published in 1952 by Farrar, Straus, and
Young. It is reprinted here by arrangement with Artixo Books.

Published by Fithian Press
Post Office Box 1525
Santa Barbara, California 93102

LIBRARY OF CONGRESS CATALOGING-IN-PUBLICATION DATA

Shaw, Artie, 1910–
    The trouble with Cinderella: an outline of identity /
Artie Shaw.
      p. cm.
    Reprint. Originally published: New York: Farrar,
Straus, and Young, ©1952.
    ISBN 1-56474-020-X
    1. Shaw, Artie, 1910–   2. Jazz musicians—United
States—Biography. I. Title.
[ML410.S498A3 1992]   91-48190
                                    CIP
                                   MN

Introduction

IF YOU TAKE a look at the last page of this book you'll see
the lines

> Picardy Farm
> Pine Plains, N.Y.
> December 1950–February 1952

which are, of course, pretty much self-explanatory; and
aside from the bare factual data they provide, there's no
good reason why they should mean anything more to
anyone.

But as I regard them from this particular place and time in
my life I become aware of all sorts of intricate little rustlings
and stirrings deep down somewhere inside myself—a host
of small burrowing creatures sleepily rousing themselves
from a long, dark hibernation. Memories, feelings, all kinds
of forgotten images, crowd and jostle one another as they
surface into consciousness, some sharply painful, others
nostalgically pleasurable, but most of them bittersweet, like
recollections of a long-lost love. Sweet—as I look back on
what I've since come to realize was probably the happiest
and most self-fulfilling period of my life. Bitter—when I
recall the sickening sense of loss I felt on being forced to
sell the place where I thought I had finally reached the end
of my own personal rainbow.

Picardy Farm.... Good God, the emotions those two words evoke. The place where for the first time in my life I had found a real home, a warm sense of security, and a feeling of calm peace of mind. The place where, after almost twenty years of seeking, I thought I would finally get a few things done that I had been hoping to do throughout all those years but had always had to put off for one reason or another, the place where I knew I was now, at long last, going to be able to—

Quickly, I cut all this off. All right, quit that, I tell myself, no time for any of that self-indulgent crap. What's the point, it's all over and done with a long time ago.

Still, I can't quite ignore all those little bells ringing and chiming away down there. Not to mention several big gongs, darkly resonant with all sorts of deep and ominous undertones. Many of the smaller bells tinkle away cheerfully, merry as all Christmases are supposed to be and hardly ever are. (Is there *any*thing, I wonder, that ever turns out the way it's "supposed to"?) As for those gongs? Well. Dismal is a mild word. Frightful? Terrible? Awful? No, not any of those, really. Nauseating, I think, is more like it.

Anybody out there still remember the so-called McCarthy Era? Joe McCarthy, that is. Of course—good old Joe, the sterling Super-American, the man who knew exactly what *Un*-American meant because he knew exactly what American meant and was by God going to see to it that America remained American. It's almost impossible, now, to believe it all really happened—it's more like a weird nightmare, or some fantasy of Lewis Carroll's. There he was, the good Senator, dominating the entire political landscape, an unlikely blend of Fearless Fosdick brandishing a paper club, King Canute single-handedly holding back a vast tidal wave of subversion threatening to engulf us all at any moment, and a pudgy, pasty-faced, balding version of that anonymous little Dutch boy, with one stubby finger stuck in the crumbling dike of democracy. (And now that we've achieved our stunning victories in south-east Asia, any fool can plainly see how truly worthwhile all *that* was. Naturally.)

vi

Well, O.K. I lived through that particular little firestorm. As an invited guest of the House Un-American Activities Committee. The whole shot. And watched the grey pall fall over my entire life as a direct result of having been branded "a controversial figure"—meaning, in simpler and more direct terms, an Untouchable.

Somehow, I've come through it all with a few tattered vestiges of sanity. I *think*. Don't ask me how; I honestly couldn't tell you. Maybe because I'm a natural-born, you might almost say a professional, survivor. Some people are, some aren't. More aren't, I think. Or rather, weren't. And lots of those are long gone, done in by the deadly virus of hatred and intolerance and suspicion and finally downright stupidity that hung over this U.S. of A. like a vast poisonous cloud simply because of the ranting and raving of a handful of witch-hunting lunatics who eventually succeeded in frightening the ordinary common sense out of a bewildered, befuddled, and ultimately brainwashed population. Oh, I suppose it's not all *that* strange, really; it's happened before, and probably will again. Look at Prohibition. Or that more recent Great American Bomb-Shelter-In-Every-Backyard scare. Going all the way back to Salem.

As I say, some of us managed to live through it and emerge pretty much in one piece. Altered somewhat by the experience, naturally; but still hanging in there laughing and scratching away along with everybody else because what the hell is there to do *but* laugh and scratch away with everybody else. As someone has remarked: Life may be hell, but none of the alternatives are acceptable. True, but believe me, chum, it's taken a bit of doing from time to time, just to keep on keepin' on, and while I can't speak for other victims of that particular blight, I'm convinced that the thing that saved *me*, the one thing that kept me going, through it all, was sheer downright orneriness, the fact that I was just too damned mulish to lie down and die to oblige a pack of righteous idiots who believed they'd cornered the market on truth. Besides, I was curious to see what might happen next. Who knows? (I kept thinking) there may be a

vii

sudden outbreak of mass sanity. Hey, don't laugh. It may happen *yet*. Listen, anything is possible.

Well, and so, having just turned forty in that May of 1950 at Picardy Farm in Pine Plains, N.Y., I figured that with any luck at all I had some twenty-five or thirty years left to get a few things done; such as, for example, write three books I was reasonably sure I could handle at that stage of my development, that I felt might be worth writing, and of which this was to be number one. I also had the quaint notion that since I had finally found myself a nice peaceful little haven, I could set myself a rather more human pace than the one I had been keeping for the preceding quarter of a century or so.

No such luck, though. I never did get to spend the rest of my life at Picardy Farm. (Oh, I've tried to console myself from time to time by asking, Who ever has? Rockefeller? Mellon? Dupont? Paul Getty? Howard Hughes? Bernie Cornfeld? Vesco? Ho, ho, ho, I tell myself.) Because as a direct result of the McCarthy plague and its disastrous effects on my life—and for a number of other reasons too complicated and tedious to go into here, some economic, many purely psychological—I was forced to give up Picardy Farm; and as a result of *that*, and also given my particular temperament and complex personal responses to rejection, and so on and so forth (one set of Chinese boxes inside another), I saw no logical reason to go on trying to live a semi-crippled existence here in the dear old Land of the Free and Home of the Everybody-Knows-How-Brave-We-All-Are. So I split out for Europe. And ended up in Spain, of all unlikely places. Catalonia. Just outside of a tiny hilltop village named Bagur, in the Province of Gerona. Where I spent the following five years, after finding a piece of land and building yet another Dream House on the brow of a jagged cape jutting out over Homer's wine-dark sea, and where, once again, I hoped to spend the rest of my days in peace—which of course turned out to be yet another mistaken notion. (Christ, doesn't a man ever *learn*?)

O.K., I'm not about to go into why I left Spain and came

back to the dear old Land of the Free and Home of the Etc. *That* particular version of The Return of the Native is part of a book I'm now in process of writing, and if you can somehow restrain your overwhelming eagerness, I hope to have it ready for publication one of these days. Or months. Or years, more likely, given the pace I write at, compared to which the average snail is an Olympic-class sprinter. (Not that it matters, of course. As the old boy said, all those thousands of years back: Of making many books there is no end. And as I'd put it: It takes me one hell of a long time to write a book; and if you think you can do it faster, just try it, pal, you'll see.)

Getting back to this one. As I've pointed out, I wrote it at a time when I believed I had my life fairly well under control. How naive can you get? But perhaps precisely because of that belief, deluded as it turned out, the book (as I skim through it now) reflects a certain quiet serenity and philosophical detachment. Maybe this won't be too evident at a casual glance, but it's there all right, and I'm pretty sure you'll spot it coming through between the lines every now and again . . .

Apart from the above, there are a few other points that may be worth touching on. The language of the book—the idiom, that is. The use of such words as "hep," for example, which of course is today considered a pretty un-hip term. As the gag goes: "Anybody who says hep ain't hip." Still, that *was* the word back then and I know no good reason why a book shouldn't reflect the period in which it was written, do you?

So—I've left all those things just as they were.

Another point. As indicated in those concluding three lines of the book, I wrote it in a little over fourteen months, working at that aforementioned snail-like pace for about four to six hours every morning, seven days a week, with almost no interruption over the entire period. To say just that, though, is to leave out a few rather important details. (If, that is to say, details of this sort are ever important to anyone except professional trivia-collectors.) The fact is, I had been *trying* to write this book—or one more or less like it—for almost twenty years, off and on, until I finally got down to it for keeps on that December morning of 1950 at Picardy Farm. So, to be perfectly truthful, I should admit that I had probably been unconsciously organizing and sifting much of the material, as well as clarifying and developing a point of view toward it, for some two decades. Maybe even longer for all I know; for who's to say *when* a given book starts to gestate?

Let me tell you a little something about those earlier attempts. The big hangup was that no matter how hard I tried, I simply could not manage to get past the first sentence or two. (Not, by the way, the ones that start *this* book; those came a long time later, after I had been handed The Big Clue to the mystery of not just how to start but, far more important, how to *finish* a book—an altogether different matter.) What troubled me the most, as I look back now, was that I just could not get a *handle* on what I was trying to say. My essential idea, you see (and here we come to what I meant earlier, when I said something about books "worth writing"—because as an *idea* it was sound enough), was to tell what I had seen, done, learned, felt, etc., while living the life of a white jazz musician in the late twenties and early thirties. To tell about it from the inside looking out, that is, meaning from the viewpoint of one who had *lived* it rather than the way it had mostly been written by people who had never personally experienced it and therefore could not possibly write about it subjectively (or really even objectively, come to think about it), let alone with any reasonable degree of realism.

Like most jazz musicians, I was appalled by such woolyheaded romances as, for example, *Young Man with a Horn* (to cite just one example out of many, and not by any manner of means the worst, either) where the central character, Rick Martin, that cardboard cutout of a jazz trumpeter, goes to pieces in a spectacular but utterly preposterous way in his ludicrous attempt to hit some unreachable, impossible, ineffable high note. (*What* note? What *is* this, a parody of that famous old Lost Chord? And what in the world, while we're at it, *is* a Lost Chord? I mean, how the hell does anybody lose a *chord*, for Godsake?) What I'm getting at is that having lived the life, having worked and hung out with most of the top-ranking jazz practitioners, having (as the current jargon goes) paid my dues, I felt it was high time someone who *knew* something about that world were to write about it from some sort of rational perspective.

(At this late date I wouldn't dream of arguing that a rational perspective in itself is any guarantee of a good book. Too often, sad to say, it only serves to guarantee no book at all; which of course may also be something of a blessing.) In any case, it certainly didn't help me any. And God knows, I certainly tried. And tried. And simply could not get started. Until after a time I found myself grappling with a fairly hairy philosophical question: i.e., which is better, to perpetrate a piece of sheer nonsense like *Young Man with a Horn*, or to write nothing at all? In a world of excellent books that no one bothers to read at all, you can see how that little problem might keep a fellow preoccupied for a while. (And all right, maybe I have been coming down pretty hard on that poor little book of Dorothy Baker's. Maybe *Young Man with a Horn* does have some sort of "literary merit"—whatever that means—as a fairy tale, say, as a modern myth, or even as some sort of parable along the lines of a Jonathan Livingston Seagull. And of course the title in itself is surely as good a title for a book about jazz as anyone could ask for, that much must be conceded. But—as an even halfway reasonably accurate description of what it's like to blow a horn for a living in the real world? Forget it.) Anyway ... I finally decided that since there were obviously no other choices available to me at that stage of my life, there was really nothing else for me to do *but* write nothing at all.

All that, though, was mere theory. The hard fact was that I still felt absolutely compelled to write that damned book, still keenly felt that it was "worth writing"—even though I hadn't the faintest notion of how on earth *I* was going to do it when I couldn't even manage to get so much as a start on it.

I was twenty-three at that time (I often wonder, are young people nowadays as innocent as I was at that age?) and had saved up a few thousand dollars working around the New York radio and recording studios, at first as a staff musician at CBS, then as a freelance. With that I bought myself a few scrubby acres near Erwinna, Pennsylvania, in Bucks County, with a ramshackle barn and a dilapidated old farmhouse, where I thought I'd have another go at "that" book of mine. The house had a wood stove and a fireplace for cooking and heat, a well connected to a kitchen pump for water, kerosene lamps for light, and a little two-holer john out back where you could freeze your butt off (I mean *literally!*) on a cold winter morning. But I was happy enough, because what I was looking for was a period of uninterrupted and unharassed time during which I hoped to find the key to unlock the riddle of how to get that damned book written.

No use. After a full year, I found I still could not hack it.

So once again I shelved the project and went back to blowing a horn in those same New York radio and recording studios I'd walked out on the year before. Those were the days before television had reared its schlocky head (not that radio in those days was all that *un*-schlocky). The point is that radio, like television today, was where it was at for the top musicians of that time—"it" being the good pay, the steady work, the decent life in one place (rather than having to go out on the road and hang out in flea-bitten hotels, and all the rest of what went with being a jazz musician back in those pre-Howard Johnson and Holiday Inn days).

And so time slogged on. And wrought its many wonders. Not the least of which was the miracle by which an earnest young cat like me (of all people) was apotheosized into a full-fledged show-biz celeb during a wacky decade or more now known as the Swing Era.

And now A Funny Thing Happened To Me. Having become, as I say, a celeb (which is funny enough, I suppose, and which back then in the mid- to late thirties simply meant having your name appear regularly in Leonard Lyons and Walter Winchell), I found myself coming into contact with other celebs. Some of them writers. Bill Saroyan, for example, to whom I was introduced by Herb Caen in San Francisco around 1940 or so, and with whom I maintained a friendship of sorts for years. Then there was Scott Fitzgerald, whom I met through Bob Benchley when Benchley and I were both staying at the old Garden of Allah, in Hollywood, where I also met Nathanael West, Dorothy Parker, Sid Perelman, John O'Hara, Gene Fowler, and a slew of other well-known writers of that period. Then, a year or so later, I got to know and hang out with John Steinbeck for several months, just after he'd finished *The Grapes of Wrath.* And one night, at the old Stork Club, Lenny Lyons introduced me to Hemingway, with whom I had a long and somewhat boozy talk about life, letters, and even music, of all things, about which he knew a lot more than I had expected (though perhaps "knew" isn't precisely the right word; instinctively sensed and understood as an artist, is probably closer).

And somewhere along the line I met (and eventually developed a real friendship with) Sinclair Lewis. "Red" Lewis, as he was known to those close enough to arrive at a first-name status with him—as I ultimately did, despite my at first almost awe-stricken shyness around him. After all, this was the first American to receive a Nobel Prize for literature, as well as being one of the most brilliant men I have ever encountered—up to then, or since. Yet there we were, playing chess and chatting casually away with each other like old buddies. Who, I would marvel to myself, would have ever imagined such a thing?

My main point in mentioning all this is to lead us to what finally happened as a result of my getting to know Red Lewis well enough to ask him what I now realize was a pretty dumb question.

Came a time when I knew I would be spending several months in one place again. I had rented a spectacular duplex apartment in New York, overlooking Central Park, where I put in a good bit of time daily doing some fairly classy brooding on the subject of "Where Is My Life Heading," while cutting a number of records I had contracted to make for RCA Victor. While I was at that, I figured this might just be a pretty good time to see if I couldn't now, at long last, finally get going on "that" book. That same old book about the jazz world that had been lurking back there in the depts of my consciousness all this time. Except that by now, it would also have something to say about the Celebrity Business (or what I was by then sardonically beginning to think of as "the Artie Shaw business") with which I had had a certain amount of first-hand experience over the previous couple of years or so and about which I felt I had a few hundred thousand pertinent remarks to make.

Well, sir. Once again I ran head-on into a blank wall. If anything, it was even worse than before. (I've long since learned, of course, that the more you know about a given subject the harder it is to figure out precisely what aspect of it you want to write about. Because obviously you can't possibly get it all into one book—a very difficult fact for a neophyte to grasp.) This time, however, out of sheer stubbornness, and finally real fury at my own dumb self, I persisted long enough to squeeze out a couple of paragraphs that didn't altogether nauseate me. (Once again, incidentally, not the ones at the beginning of this book; matter of fact I can't even remember what ever happened to those poor little paragraphs after all this time.)

O.K. Know how long that took? Just two measly paragraphs? Less than half a page?

Would you guess three months? Seems excessive, right? Yes, well, the truth is it took me *over six months*. Honestly, I swear to you.

So, obviously, I had to stop and take stock. What the hell, if a couple of lousy little paragraphs had taken me more than half a year to write, how on earth could I ever expect to finish a whole bloody *book*? Even if I lived to be as old as a sequoia, what was I supposed to *do*, for Godsake, spend the next ninety years on one stupid book? Remember, I was essentially a performer, accustomed to instant feedback from live audiences. And while I was able to conceive of doing a certain amount of work without that feedback (which of course the job of writing demands, since an audience obviously can't tell you anything about a book until after it's been written and published, by which time there's nothing you can do about that one anyway), I couldn't see myself slaving away for what promised to be forever before getting some sort or reaction to what I was hoping to do.

It was a dilemma, all right.

I decided to call my friend Red Lewis—he was living up near Williamstown, Mass. at that time—and laid my problem on him. "How can I ever expect to *finish* a book," I asked desperately, "when it's taken me over six months to do two goddamn paragraphs? Help, Red!"

He laughed. Mercifully, he didn't raise the question of whether the world really needed one more book—to which I would certainly have had no ready answer. Instead, he assured me that this was by no means an uncommon problem among writers, and promised to write me a letter; that way, he said, I would have something to look at whenever I needed to remind myself of certain helpful hints he intended to give me.

Sure enough, a few days later his letter arrived. Here, among other things, is the advice he gave me:

"There are three things you must accept and bear in mind at all times if you really want to solve the problem of how to finish that book of Yours.

"First: Be sure you'll never finish it.

"Second: Be sure that if you ever do, no one will ever publish it.

"And third: Be sure that if by some wild freak of chance both the above do happen, no one will ever read it."

And do you know? That *did* it. Because when I finally sat down at my typewriter, in that December of 1950 at Picardy Farm in Pine Plains, N.Y., I kept repeating those three rules to myself; and somehow they served the purpose of *freeing* me, ridding me of that terrifying self-consciousness that often accompanies the mere act of trying to get a long series of words put down on paper, that strange, almost mystic practice known as writing.

Now, want to hear something really funny? The book actually did get finished, it actually did get published, and people actually *read* it. And even reviewed it—some critics quite seriously. All of that. And then, before it sold out its original editions, it got published all over again, this time in a British edition, and finally even as a paperback. (Not one of those mass-selling jobs, but as a so-called Quality Paperback—which, as I quickly discovered, means one that does *not* get distributed in large numbers in supermarkets, drug stores, airport terminals, and places like that, where books are really sold in quantity nowadays.)

And, so, here it is, after being out of print for almost two and a half decades (longer even than that nap of Rip Van Winkle's), back among us once again. All of which goes to show how wrong even a wise old bird like Red Lewis can be. (Of course, I'm sure old Red knew just exactly what he was really up to when he wrote me that letter.)

Let's see . . . What else? Oh, yes—I mentioned the name Getty a while back. Let me end with a little story about J. Paul Getty and myself.

I happened, for reasons too boring to go into, to be a guest at a very swanky dinner party in London sometime in 1965 or thereabouts, given by an indefatigable American hostess who was busily trying to become the British Perle Mesta. And actually not doing too badly at it either—though, to paraphrase Groucho Marx, what kind of a hostess could it be, come to think about it, who'd have me at her party?

All right. There I was, seated at an elegant Sheraton dinner table, along with twenty-three more people, all of us chomping away at some *cuisine* that was really *haute*. At one point during dinner I happened to overhear someone address the man seated a couple of places away from me as "Mr. Getty." It didn't dawn on me who it was, though, until a few moments later, when I heard our hostess call him by his first name. "Paul." Suddenly a light bulb went on in my head. *Paul Getty?* I peered over at him. Sure enough. J. Paul Getty, by God. The old codger himself. There he sat, munching away, just like any ordinary mortal. Hard to believe. It felt a little like having dinner with the Empire State Building.

Later on, when the ladies went off somewhere to powder their noses, so to speak, and the men went into a room for port and cigars (it's true, we actually did—I *told* you it was a swanky party), I made it a point to go over and have a little chat with him. I was curious to hear what he might have to say to a question I wanted to put to him. After introducing myself, I asked if he minded my asking him something that I wondered if anyone had ever asked him before.

Not at all, he replied, looking at me rather quizzically. What did I have in mind?

"Well," I said, "I wonder if anyone has ever asked you if there was anything you've wanted in the last thirty years or so, that you didn't get?"

He cocked his head to one side, then sort of smirked. "Why, no, I can't say I've ever been asked that particular question before." I could tell it pleased him. It was as though he regarded it as a sort of amusing little game we were playing; nothing important, or profound, but fun in a harmless enough way.

"In that case," I said, "what would you say is the answer, Mr. Getty? *Was* there anything you wanted badly and didn't get?"

He gave that some thought. Finally, "No," he said, "I can't truthfully say there was." He smirked again.

"In other words, sir, there wasn't *anything* you wanted that you didn't get?"

"Yes, I believe that is true. Why?"

"I don't really know," I told him, truthfully enough. "But I find it terribly sad."

"*Sad?*" he echoed. He hadn't expected that. Neither had I, really; I hadn't even known I was going to say it until after I did. He looked at me in some puzzlement. "Why do you find it sad?" he asked.

I phumphered around for a moment, then blurted out: "Well, I guess I find it sad because most of the people on earth have experienced something you apparently never have. Don't you think that's kind of sad?"

He gazed at me for a long moment, his eyes narrowing a bit as he slowly shook his head. His expression changed. A moment later he turned without a word and walked to the far end of the room, as far away from me as he could get.

Well, there's my story about Getty and me. I can't say I'm altogether clear on just what the point of it is, but I'm pretty sure there is a point there, and that it has something to do with this book of mine, one way or another.

Maybe *you* can figure it out.

ARTIE SHAW
November 1978
Newbury Park, California

For Stevie —

In the hope that this may some
day help him along his own road.

Foreword

THE FOLLOWING pages represent a sort of inventory of my attitudes to the life I have known. I have included a certain amount of specific autobiographical material, as documentation. Over a period of some fifteen years I have been living a kind of double life—on the one hand, as a rather highly-publicized "personality" in a profession through which my name has become known to many people who know nothing more about me than the publicity-machine has told them, and on the other, as a man living his life as his inner necessities have forced him to, and trying to make a modicum of sense in a particularly bewildering period of history.

Now that I have put myself down on paper this way, I'm aware that a great many of my present attitudes stem from a rather special set of circumstances in my past. I'm also aware that a great many people may not find them acceptable, or even palatable.

To that I can only answer:

I've stated them as clearly as I can, and as honestly as I am at present able to do. I am in no position to know how different from yours they may be. As corroboration of your own attitudes they may easily turn out to be completely valueless. But as information about how another fellow ticks and what makes him tick that way, you may find them illuminating. . . .

The Trouble with Cinderella

Part I

The Trouble with Cinderella
(an outline of identity)

Part I

"Life's a long headache in a noisy street."

JOHN MASEFIELD
—*The Widow in the Bye Street*

"From every-one of the Four Regions of Human Majesty
There is an Outside spread Without & an Outside spread
Within,
Beyond the Outline of Identity both ways, which meet in
One . . ."

WILLIAM BLAKE
—*Jerusalem*

"If you wish for something, you had better look out, because you may be so unfortunate as to get it."

CHARLES FORT

Chapter One

I'VE BEEN TRAVELING along this highway for quite a while now. Looking back at where I started out it seems to me I've come a considerable distance. Of course there's no way for me to tell how much actual progress I've made. Progress is a word that has no meaning unless you can measure how far you've come in terms of where you want to end up; and I haven't the vaguest idea where I'm heading.

However, it's been an interesting trip so far. Not necessarily a pleasant one at all times but I've kept going because I've been curious as to just where this highway leads.

There have been a few detours along the way. Now and then I've gone off to follow some promising side road; but always in the end I've come back to this main highway again and stuck with it past forks, crossroads, intersections, all sorts of by-ways that might have taken me to some other place than where I am right now.

At the moment, though, I'm in a bad fix. I've come to a dead stop. I'm going to have to make some kind of decision before I can get going again because this isn't like any other place I've been in up to now.

The highway has opened out into a wide space, a sort of hub, with a lot of roads radiating out in all directions like the spokes of a wheel, and I'm stuck with the problem of trying to figure out which one I want to take.

It's a pretty tough decision to make. It may very well be that one of these new roads leads somewhere I might want to go; but I can't tell, from where I stand.

There are no road signs. There are no arrows or any other kinds of markers to give me any clues.

I guess there's not much I can do but stick around and try to puzzle this thing out. "When in doubt do nothing," as the saying goes. Only trouble with that is I can't think of anything much tougher than just that—doing nothing.

Now and then I catch myself thinking it wouldn't be such a bad spot to be in if I had someone else here with me. But if I'm going to be honest about this I suppose I may as well face the fact that there wouldn't really be any use in that either. I've learned by this time that there isn't anyone a guy can take along with him on this trip.

Anyway, how could anyone else help? All either of us could do would be to speculate. The only difference between being by myself and having someone here with me is that this way I've got to try to work it out for myself and the other way there would be two of us each trying to work it out for himself.

Because one thing seems certain. Once you have come to this intersection, this crossroads, this whatever-you-want-to-call-it—once you've come to where you have to leave the main highway and strike out along your own special road to travel to wherever it is you've got to go—once you've come to this point, you're on your own. . . .

Not that there's any rule that says a fellow's *got* to go any place special. Most of us manage to keep ourselves fairly busy just going about the business of keeping alive. The way things are going these days, that alone may turn out to be a pretty neat trick if we can do it. But still, supposing—just supposing, you understand—a fellow happens to feel a little intense about this need to go someplace with this one relatively unimportant life he's got in his hands to live, supposing that—then what?

Oh, sure, I know there are a million and one ways of ducking the problem. The world is so full of a number of things, I'm sure we should all be as happy as kings—and, as Thurber says, you know how happy kings are.

Kings aside, though, there's no doubt a guy could get himself up a list of various distractions that would reach from here to the nearest corner saloon—which, in many cases, it does. This search for distraction can even become a kind of distraction in itself. There's hardly a single institution in our whole society that doesn't amount to some sort of distraction for somebody, somehow, from at least some point of view.

Romain Rolland once wrote:

"There are in life certain ages when there takes place a silently working organic change in a man: then body and soul are more susceptible to attack from without; the mind is weakened, its power is sapped by a vague sadness, a feeling of satiety, a sort of detachment from what it is doing, an incapacity for seeing any other course of action. At such periods of their lives when these crises occur, the majority of men are bound by domestic ties, forming a safeguard for them, which, it is true, deprives them of the freedom of mind necessary for self-judgment, for discovering where they stand, and for beginning to build up a healthy new life. For them so many sorrows, so much bitterness and disgust remain concealed. . . . The common round, anxiety and care for the family for which he is responsible, keep a man like a jaded horse, sleeping between the shafts . . . —But a free man has nothing to support him in his hours of negation, nothing to force him to go on. . . ."

So there we have one type of distraction, a quite common

one. And certainly there's nothing wrong with it as far as it goes. Marriage, family responsibility, all that sort of thing. These are things a fellow can aim at and if he's lucky they'll work out well enough to keep him occupied and busy and on the go all the time, so that the chances are he'll never even have time to stop long enough to ask himself where he thinks he's going in the first place. Of course there is always the possibility that he might wind up in a much worse fix than he'd be in if he'd had to try to make it on his own; but the only way you'll ever know for yourself is to try both ways, and then come to your own conclusions, if any.

One conclusion is pretty certain: no matter how it works out, good or bad or in-between, it'll keep a guy pretty distracted. And that is the big point to get clear about any kind of distraction. Make sure it distracts.

There is another distraction, though, a Great Big One, maybe the chief distraction of all. This one, in one form or another, seems to work for almost everybody. And the strange thing about it is that nine tenths (or maybe ninety-nine hundredths) of the population never do get to learn that it is a distraction at all—which is, of course, its principal value. The fact is that most people never get a chance to examine it closely enough to find out what it adds up to for them, or even whether they really wanted it to begin with.

There are a multitude of names for it. Some call it Success, others think of it as Money, still others call it Love, and in our own Declaration of Independence we have a household phrase referring to it as "the pursuit of happiness"—but when you get right smack down to what this thing really is, you'll find it all comes to pretty much the same old thing—the good old Cinderella Myth once again. Our little friend Cinderella and her ever-lovin' Prince Charming all dressed up and ready to go about their business of living "happily ever after."

The trouble with Cinderella, though, as a working concept

for living what is laughingly referred to as Life In Our Time, is that nobody lives happily ever after.

After what?

Well, let's take a fast gander at what happens to Cinderella. She winds up with this Prince of hers, after a dingy sort of life with a battle-axe of an old stepmother and a couple of beatup crows for stepsisters. In one quick parlay she achieves 1) a Happy Marriage, 2) Wealth, 3) Social Position, 4) Prestige, etc., etc.—all of which, translated into twentieth century terms, add up to a perfect blend of Success (that old thing again) and $ucce$$ (to spell it the way I think makes more sense in this context).

O.K. What do we have now? Cinderella has become a sort of composite portrait of Wally Windsor, Rita Hayworth, Bobo Rockefeller, and the truck driver who marries the beautiful heiress. And of course, as everybody knows, all these people are so happy they can hardly see straight. Naturally. Why shouldn't they be? What more could you ask for? They've *got* to be happy because it figures. They've got everything.

Haven't they?

Well, for all I know, Rita, Wally, Bobo and even the truck driver may all really be awfully damn happy. I guess it depends on what you mean by "happy"—and that opens up a can of peas it would take us a long time to empty. All I know for sure is that this quest for the Cinderella-solution to the problem of working out some sort of reasonable life is just about the most common distraction of all; and while fairy tales may be all very well for the amusement of small children, they are hardly the thing as a steady diet for anyone trying to arrive at some realistic understanding of a world like the one we happen to be stuck with.

As long as most of us persist in thinking in magical terms about such concepts as Success and Happiness it seems to me we're all going to go right on making no sense at all. None of these concepts are static. They don't exist in absolute forms.

Any such ideas are bound to be pretty relative, relative to the people who are out after them, and the time in which they're operating; and as a result they're going to mean not only different things for different people at different times but—and here's the rub—different things even for the same people at different times.

I believe I have as much right as the next guy to set myself up as a commentator on all this, because in a sort of cockeyed way I've gone through some of this Cinderella business myself and I am in a position to make the following report:

It's murder.

This business of catching up with whatever you may have started out after is a little like kissing a buzz saw. Still, there is one thing to be said for it. If it doesn't finish you off once and for all, you can learn a few things from it.

One is that Happiness is not a state like Vermont, where a guy can buy himself a one-way ticket and go and stay as long as he likes. It's neither the state of Vermont nor any other kind of state. It doesn't stand still and wait for you to catch up with it.

Anybody who kids himself by tearing around after it is like a dog chasing a locomotive. As long as the locomotive keeps going he's going to have himself a hell of an exciting time. There's a lot of drama connected with a chase, and any dog who's found himself a nice big locomotive he can tear after is in a pretty good spot. Look at the fun he can have thinking about what he's going to do with it if he catches it. Boy! he can think to himself, I'll rip that old black thing to pieces when I get hold of it. I'll chew it up into little tiny hunks and swallow 'em all up one at a time.

Fine. Just so it keeps going.

But what happens if it suddenly stops?

Now you know that's apt to be pretty rough on this dog. Up to now, he's been having himself a hell of a lot of fun, but what's he going to *do* now that he's got it?

Well, sure, at first he can sniff around at it for a while, and maybe he can try taking a bite out of one of the wheels. Of course that won't work, so then he can even try lifting a leg up against the thing. But there isn't a great deal more he's going to be able to do. And on top of everything else, all the drama and hurly-burly is over. Here he's been, with this big important mission in his life, this enthusiastic chase that's kept him so busy and distracted that he hasn't had time to stop and think about what it's like to be a dog and what there really is for a dog to do with his time—and now, all at once, all that is finished and he's right back where he always was, just a dog after all, and in one sense much worse off than he was before the whole chase started; because now he's got to start in all over again and find something else to keep him busy enough to prevent his being bored to death.

All of which is obvious enough. Nevertheless we keep right on running, most of us. It seems to us, each one of us, one at a time, that in our own particular, individual, unique case it's different. We get ourselves involved in all sorts of mad projects, such as the highly respected process of piling dollar bills on top of dollar bills, like crazy squirrels piling up nuts in a hollow tree, more nuts than they're ever going to be able to eat if they live to be a hundred. The one thing most people never seem to understand is that a guy with a thousand dollars who's miserable because he wants two thousand is not actually any *more* miserable than the guy with one million who suffers from a compulsion to have two million. Sure, one has a lot more than the other, but basically it's the same thing—they're both miserable because they haven't got enough; and while there's no logic in it at all for the one with the million, you'd have one hell of a time convincing *him* of it.

All of which brings me back to our little Cinderella. Why not follow her home, just to see how things are working out?

Her first problem, I suppose, is going to be how she gets along with her new mom and pop, the King and Queen. But of course that's no problem. Because naturally they're bound to be delighted with their son's choice. What more could they ask for? She's a hell of a nice kid, pretty, sweet, modest, quiet—she's got everything. Of course, aside from having very small feet, she's not too well-equipped for the way she's going to have to start living now, but that's only a small matter. She's got a certain amount of stuff to learn about how to behave as a Princess and all that, so she's given a tutor. Let's make the tutor good and old so we won't have to complicate our plot with such possibilities as her liking him and then sometime while the Prince is off killing dragons—well, you know the nasty complications that can arise.

Anyway—Cinderella goes on studying until she's got everything down pat. No more boners pulled on prime ministers' wives, or ambassadors' daughters, or any of these new people she's got to hang around with now. Cinderella is housebroken. Everybody can relax.

All right then, let's assume that along the line Cinderella has a couple of babies. And, again giving everybody the best of it, let's say these kids are just about the most perfect kids anybody ever laid an eye on since kids first started being made. To top it all off, one of them is a boy.

Now let's see what's going on. By this time Cinderella and Prince Charming have been married for a few years—say five or so—and "the first fine careless rapture" is beginning to curl slightly around the edges. Every now and then—with all the good intentions in the world—our little friend Cinderella finds herself a tiny bit bored. She begins to notice certain little things about Prince Charming that—well, maybe irritate is a strong word, but something like that anyway. After all, it *is* possible.

Well . . . Cinderella is looking for trouble. And if she doesn't get wise to herself in a hurry, trouble is exactly what she's going to find. Unless she figures out some way of getting her mind off the subject of—to coin a song title—What Happened to *Romance?*

Of course, she may come out of it all right. Lots of women do, one way or another. On the other hand, there are a number of Cinderellas keeping appointments on a steady five-day-a-week schedule with their neighborhood head-doctors.

You see, another trouble with Cinderella is that her story is apt to fool you if you're on the outside of it. Because one thing is pretty certain: Cinderella herself isn't likely to tell you how things are with her, even if she knows.

"The majority of men employ the first portion of their lives in making the other portion wretched."

LA BRUYÈRE

Chapter Two

THE WAY I GOT STARTED on my own particular quest for the Cinderella-solution is that, like many people, I had to make a choice about what I wanted to do with my life at an age when I knew nothing about either life or myself. There is nothing specially odd or unusual about this in a society in which most of us are forced to make some sort of decision regarding the way we are going to earn a living long before we are equipped to understand what particular *kind* of living will make sense for us individually.

The inevitable result is that most of us wind up our adult lives following our noses along a highway leading nowhere at all. The curious part of all this is that if you were to ask the average guy (whoever *he* may be) how he likes his particular highway, the chances are he'd tell you he had long ago come to the conclusion that the whole thing was a big mistake. But what the hell, he'd probably go on to say, a fellow's gotta make a living some way, so what the hell.

Under these circumstances it more or less follows that while the fellow's *making* that living he's got to find some way of keeping himself from thinking too much about how much he dislikes what he has to do in order to make it; and in keeping himself from thinking about *that* he uses up his time in such a way as to prevent himself from ever coming to grips with whatever it is in himself that stops him from doing what he would have to do to get away from what he hates but must do to make his living in the first place—and so forth and so on, until after a number of years of this deadly routine he ultimately disappears somewhere deep down inside of himself and is never seen or heard from again. A likely enough solution and, in our time, a common enough phenomenon. A sort of death-in-life, and if you happen to believe that zombies are restricted to the West Indies, all you've got to do is take a good long look around, or better still, a good long look deep inside yourself and then ask yourself if this is where you started out to go.

All I can tell you is this: If the answer is Yes, you're a fortunate citizen indeed.

This whole question of aims and goals is one that most people never get the time to examine deeply. Even if they do have the time, it's quite easy to build up an elaborate system of inner defenses against this sort of self-probing. On the whole, it seems easier to go on with present known pain and anxiety than to face the possibility of change and uncertainty.

Speaking for myself, I know this is so. For a number of years, during the course of a fairly hectic life, I have had a great many bouts with myself regarding where I stood, how I'd got there, and how I felt about it. The answers I was able to come up with varied a good bit—depending on my own state of development, the chances I thought I had of reaching the goals I was aiming at, and, of course, the nature of the goals themselves. But as long as they remained vaguely formulated, strongly tinged by my own involvement with the Cinderella Myth, I was unable to do anything very decisive about changing them. Instead, I concentrated harder on achieving my muddled-up objectives. This, with the usual variations, could easily have wound up as The Story of My Life.

Fortunately, however—or unfortunately, depending on the

point of view—a series of circumstances took matters out of my hands.

In the first place, all of a sudden, through a series of unforeseen flukes, I found myself acting out the leading role in my own version of the Cinderella Myth. This, let me assure you, is an extremely curious experience, for it enables a guy to learn a lot of first-hand stuff about this Cinderella broad.

In the second place, right smack in the middle of the second act of this little drama I was starring in, there came along another little drama called World War II, in which I also played a part. Hardly a starring one, of course, but it was a much more difficult part and gave me a much better sense of proportion regarding the role I *had* been playing.

The third circumstance, though, is the one that really did the trick. Coming back to the United States after some fourteen months in the South Pacific as an enlisted man in the U. S. Navy and receiving my medical discharge, I finally met up with a very famous man. Namely Dr. Freud—and although I didn't actually meet up with him personally I was fortunate enough to get into the hands of a doctor who understood the value of Freud's basic principles. What's more, he understood them well enough to avoid undue rigidity about even those which are by now firmly established.

Now it would be absurd to try to give the details of this last experience. Psychoanalysis is such a highly personalized process that it would be impossible for me to explain it in terms meaningful to anyone else. There has, however, been so much irresponsible gibberish written on this subject that I feel it should at least be pointed out that, since the whole thing takes place through the medium of language, no two people are going to go through quite the same experience in the analytic process. No two people have the same connotative response to language—even when they speak the "same" language. Carl Sandburg has a poem called "Elephants Look

Different To Different People." Well, so do words, of course; and once this is clearly understood it shouldn't be too difficult to figure out why no one has yet been able to convey to anyone else exactly how psychoanalysis works. Except through analysis itself.

Therefore, confining myself only to those aspects of it that *can* be discussed objectively—let me assure you that through this process a guy can learn a hell of a lot about himself that he can learn no other way. I found out a great deal about who I am, what I am, how I tick, and what makes me tick that way. I even know now how I want to *continue* ticking from here on in. But that last is a matter I'll take up in its proper place. For the moment, then, suppose we just stay with the first part of what I've learned and see what we can make of that.

"The original self is the self which is the originator of mental activities. The pseudo self is only an agent who actually represents the role a person is supposed to play but who does so under the name of the self."

ERIC FROMM

Chapter Three

EACH OF US has any number of distinctly separate and entirely different "personalities." I state this truism here only because it has distinct bearing on my entire story. For in the course of my professional life as a musician and popular bandleader, my own public personality has undergone a rather startling metamorphosis. Much to my surprise I have seen myself gradually transformed into a composite of all sorts of entirely unrelated qualities, hypoed by the publicity machine into a weird blend of more or less "colorful" characteristics (in the gossip-columnist sense)—to the point where I myself have had considerable difficulty living with this public *alter ego* of mine named Artie Shaw.

I feel I should make it quite clear once and for all that this Artie Shaw fellow has very little to do with me. Although he has supported me for a number of years, sometimes in a manner to which I have not even *yet* become accustomed, still I'd be the last person on earth to tell you I know him. He's a name to me, that's about all, in almost the same way he may be a name to you. There our relationship ends. With one exception. That is, that over a period of time I have now and then come close enough to him to observe him rather carefully. I have seen the way he has behaved, and have even begun to understand some of the reasons for his behavior. But in spite of that, basically he's still pretty much of a stranger to me.

In fact, for the most part, he's caused me more trouble and embarrassment than any other single factor in my whole life. I'm perpetually having people say to me, after a short while of acquaintance, "Why, you're *nothing* like what I thought you'd be." When this first began to happen I used to ask these people what on earth they had expected, or, for that matter, why they should be amazed when these expectations were not fulfilled. I soon learned that in every such instance they were not talking about me at all. Turned out they had been discussing this fellow Artie Shaw. So, of course, as soon as I explained that they'd made a mistake, that I wasn't Artie Shaw at all—as soon as I'd clarified my relationship to this Shaw fellow, everything was straightened out, and from there on we were able to resume on a more normal basis. However, in all honesty, I suppose I'm stretching the word "normal" a bit, for I have also noticed that in such cases people have eyed me in a rather peculiar way—but what the hell, you can't have everything.

There are quite a few variations on the Why-you're-nothing-like-what-I-thought-you-were-going-to-be gambit. I've seen almost every possible type of attitude—ranging all the way from curiosity (as displayed toward side-show freaks) through suspicion (as toward someone who may steal the silver the minute you turn your back) to open and down-right hostility (the kind you'd be apt to show if someone had gratuitously insulted you) and they're all equally hard to take.

So I've finally had to accept the fact that when it comes to dealing with anyone whose name has been highly publicized, all ordinary standards of behavior seem to go by the boards. I wasn't joking a bit when I spoke of curiosity of the kind displayed toward side-show freaks. There have been so many times over the last twelve or fifteen years when I have seen ordinary people behave in the most extraordinary way toward me, that I can only come to one conclusion—apparently there are two kinds of behavior in our society, both perfectly acceptable. One is called "manners," and it operates under ordinary circumstances. The other—well, that's the way you behave with people called "celebrities." Whatever the hell *that* is.

What all this amounts to is that because of this business of having become a "name" I have had to live a kind of double life. "To disregard what the world thinks of us is not only arrogant but utterly shameless," someone once said. I can't say how arrogant or shameless it would be—but I can truly say it is impossible. A man is by no means only what he thinks he is. True, he *should* know as well as anyone else what he is and what he would like to be. But you can't ignore what *other* people think you are and should be and how you should be-have, even though you'd like to. You can't, because they will be constantly exerting subtle pressures on you to behave as they expect you to behave—or, to put it as it more probably is in actuality, they will try to get you to behave as they assume *they* would if they were what they think *you* are.

This is true, to some extent, in all human relationships. But in the case of a highly publicized person, it is true to an inor-dinate degree. Anyone who has been put through the publicity hopper and emerged on the other end as a full-fledged "name" is going to have to accept this state of affairs and modify his subsequent behavior accordingly. For example, he can try to ignore it, behave more or less as he always has, be "himself" as much as possible, and put up with the peculiarities of the new attitudes he is bound to encounter on all sides. Or, taking the opposite extreme, he must somehow succeed in selling himself on the idea that there *is* something different, some-thing special, about himself that sets him apart from others; and this way he will not only stop being bothered by all these peculiarities, but will eventually come to expect them as, after all, only his due.

Either way is some sort of adjustment to a highly abnormal and un-sane (if not downright insane) change in actual environment—for that is what this "name" business entails, at least on the part of the people making up the environment. As to which adjustment is better for which individual, does a fellow *have* a choice?

I strongly doubt it. . . .

" 'The time has come,' the Walrus said, 'to talk of many things.' "

Chapter Four

Now—since I have no intention of setting forth my entire clinical case history, perhaps it might be a good idea to try to narrow things down a bit at this point.

It appears to me that each human being is nothing more or less than the constantly changing end-result of the interaction between his hereditary tendencies and all of the experiences he has lived through. At least that seems to me as good a working-definition as any other. Assuming it to be acceptable then, there is this corollary which should also be acceptable— that there is no way to explain all there is to know about any single human being, yourself or anyone else, for even during the process of explaining, further change is taking place.

This being so, and since we must confine ourselves within some arbitrary limitations for the purpose of any such discussion as this, suppose we start by examining our main theme.

To formulate it as clearly as I can, here it is. I feel that there is a point in Everyman's life when he should take inventory, look back over what he has done with his life up to that point, and then decide whether he wants to continue along the line which has brought him to where he is, or go off into some other form of activity more suitable to his own real needs as a growing, developing human being rather than a cleverly-contrived automaton devised for the purpose of doing the same tricks over and over again. Obviously, this is not easy to accomplish. It takes real self-research. I believe it can finally only be accomplished (in most cases) out of a *conscious*—rather than the more common, quiet, concealed, unconscious—desperation. I know it sounds unduly grim, put that way, but I believe this whole job of self-appraisal and consequent reorientation can only be done out of *the conscious realization that any change—absolutely any change at all—will be an improvement.*

There it is, and as you can see for yourself, there are a number of ways of dealing with it. How, if at all, does a man get to this point? Out of what circumstances, what kind of life-experiences, both inner and outer? Once arrived at this point, furthermore, what can he do about it? How can he change the direction in which he is going? How can he do anything about it at all? And—most important of all—what does he *want* to do, and why does he feel it will be better for him than what he *has* done up to now?

Well, there are as many different answers to all these questions as there are people who might ask them. It is obviously impossible for anyone to answer them for anyone else. All I can do is to give you some idea of the answers as they concern me.

"Life can only be understood backwards; but it must be lived forwards."

KIERKEGAARD

Chapter Five

THE WAY WE BEHAVE is to an enormous extent the way we have been conditioned to behave. As a rule the conditioning has taken place so long ago, under so many forgotten circumstances, and has been accomplished so quietly and subtly, that most of us can never even get more than a slight clue as to why we react as we do to any given element in our environment— even when the environment itself is the most ordinary, commonplace, everyday sort of thing the average man lives with in our society and hence believes to be the only kind that ever existed—that is, if he ever gives it much thought at all.

By way of illustration, I'll go back now and try to trace some of the forces that have caused me to become the person I am.

I was born on the Lower East Side of New York City. For most of the six or seven years I lived there, my parents were in the dressmaking business. All through these years, my mother and father went through a rather hectic period. The family fortunes rose steadily for a time, up to the point where my parents finally moved "the business" out of our home and into a loft where they employed a number of people and started to go places in the world of women's ready-to-wear garments. But in the end the whole thing collapsed with the usual accompanying dull thud; and after a lot of mysterious goings-on having to do with bankruptcy and other such involved matters, they finally decided to move from New York City and start in all over again.

The place they picked for this new start was New Haven, Connecticut. Accordingly, they packed their few belongings, and overnight, without my having much say in the matter, set up their new home and "business" in the new location at an address I still remember, 215½ York Street—a site now occupied by various Yale buildings, numerous unsuspecting students, and a certain amount of carefully-manicured lawn and shrubbery.

At the age of seven, I was enrolled in Dwight Street School in New Haven. From that point on I began to learn a great deal—very little of it, however, having much to do with formal education. In fact, there were two experiences I underwent during the time I attended Dwight Street School, which had as much to do with shaping the course of my life as anything I can think of at the moment.

Until then, I had never given much thought to such matters as being "different" from other kids I knew. As far as I was concerned, kids were kids, some were bigger than others, some were boys, and some were girls. Now, I suddenly had to unlearn any previous notions I may have had about myself and other kids. Because there was this one thing about myself, this "difference" that set me apart.

I learned what it means to be a Jew. . . .

Before I explain how I learned, let me first say that, of course, at this late date I understand many things I couldn't possibly have known then. For example, I now realize that it is practically impossible for any Jewish kid to grow up in the average American town—meaning a more or less predominantly Anglo-Saxon, Protestant community such as New Haven is now and was then—without becoming aware of the fact that he is some curious kind of undesirable alien.

Obviously, this whole so-called Jewish Question is far too

complex to go into at length here. But one thing is certain. No Jewish child, no matter how carefully protected, can avoid at least a few head-on collisions with this thing called anti-Semitism; and as to how any individual child will react, or how hard it throws him and how weird a character-malformation he may develop as a result of his first contact with this particular type of stupidity—well, your guess is as good as any. All I can do is explain how it worked in my own case.

It made a deep and lasting scar which, although fairly well healed by now, still has a tendency to hurt at times, even though I now understand a great deal more about why I got the scar and what it means.

I don't want to overdramatize this thing. I'm aware that the word "scar" has melodramatic overtones. But I can't think of a better word for what I am talking about. I know any number of Jewish people who have this same scar but who try to ignore it by some variation on the I'm-a-Jew-and-proud-of-it theme; but that won't work for me. There is no more sense in that than there is in being proud of being blonde or brunette, tall or short, blue-eyed or brown-eyed. All anyone can do about this whole ridiculous primitive manner of categorizing people into in-groups and out-groups is to try to be as adult as possible about it. Certainly there is nothing wrong with the honest admission that it would be far more convenient to be a member of the in-group, if such a thing as choice were possible, which in this instance it obviously is not.

Incidentally, since this whole thing is a pretty touchy matter, please note that I said "more convenient" rather than "better." And anyone who reads something outré into that, or fails to agree with it on a simple objective basis, could do much worse than to have a good look at his own real inner motivations and the guilt-feelings out of which they may stem. For no one but a masochist or a fool goes around deliberately looking for pain and trouble.

In any event, getting back to myself and my own subsequent

reactions to this sudden unprepared exposure to The Facts, let me give you some indications of the effect produced on me.

I said before that it was anybody's guess how any one kid might react to the circumstance of running head-on into the problem of anti-Semitism. All *I* could figure out was that there must be something about me that was different, alien, strange, and (worst of all) undesirable—that is, from other kids' point of view. I'm sure I wouldn't have recognized the word anti-Semitism if I'd tripped over it. I had no idea what the words "kike" or "sheeny" meant, for I had never heard them before. As for being called a "Christ-killer"—all I can tell you is that up to that time the word Christ had never been used in my presence except as something I vaguely recognized as a "swear-word." However, I did sense quite unmistakably that these terms, as they were applied to me by kids at school, were designed to hurt, to give pain and humiliation; and even though the words themselves had no meaning at first, there was a quality in the tones and expressions of the kids who used them against me that caused me to revise the old adage about Sticks and Stones, out of a new realization that names not only could, but did, hurt a great deal.

So that at the relatively early age of eight I became somewhat introverted, slightly withdrawn. Along with this I began to develop methods of coping with these attitudes, this new shyness which had been thrust upon me. I drew into a little shell, a coat of armor of outer toughness, inside which I tried to conceal my feelings. In other words, from the moment I realized that my being Jewish was something to be jeered at for, called names for, or hated and excluded for—from that moment on I was no longer the same kid I had been before. And not only not the same kid, but changed in a certain, specific way, in a way that I don't believe could possibly have occurred otherwise.

To put it as bluntly as I can, I believe in all honesty and with as much awareness as I can bring to bear on it from where

I stand right now, that this one lesson had more to do with shaping the course and direction of my entire life than any other single thing that has happened to me, before or since.

As a kid of seven or eight, I remember going through a brief phase of wondering what I could do about it when I grew up; until I finally recognized that this was one thing where nothing at all could be done. At that point I had to resign myself to what even at that age I knew to be the plain truth: that for no reason I could understand, and certainly through no choice of my own (for how could there have been a choice when I had not even been aware of an issue?)—there I was, a Jew, whatever that meant, and, whether I liked it or not, a Jew I would remain for the rest of my life until the day I died.

So it may not have been merely accidental that along about that time I discovered a thing called reading. Not the kind you do at school. That was "lessons." This kind of reading was altogether different and could be done for entertainment. I used to read anything I could get my hands on, whether I understood it or not. And one day, when my uncle—who was a house painter—came to our house on York Street and brought me a whole barrelful of old books someone had given him on one of his jobs, I became a reader in earnest.

Later, I'll explain how this reading habit ultimately led to a completely new set of values. How, oddly enough, through that new set of values, I got into the band business, and eventually shoved and climbed my way to the top of that little dung-heap. But first let me give you the details of these two early educational experiences I have so far only touched on in general terms.

The earliest one has to do with one of my first discoveries, and the subsequent acquirement of a hated nickname which stuck to me for as long as I stayed in the school where I was originally tagged with it.

"Every baby has to discover more in the first years of its life than Roger Bacon ever discovered in his laboratory."

BERNARD SHAW

Chapter Six

ANY KID GROWING UP on the Lower East Side of New York City is apt to find himself playing with lots of kids with long, foreign-sounding names. There were all kinds of kids and all sorts of names. Romanoff, Liebowitz, Caffarelli, Esposito, Schechter, Wiecznowski, Anzelowitz, Fiorito, O'Clanahan, Borazybski, to say nothing of Arshawsky. That last was my name. You see, there was nothing particularly strange about it, as names went in that neighborhood. It was long, but then so were many of the others. In that part of New York City the peculiar names were names like Smith, Jones, Robinson—and even at that we were all so accustomed to names of any and every kind that we sort of took them for granted. Anyway, at that age a kid is usually Izzy, Jakey, Mikey, Sammy, Willie, or Joey, so what difference does it make what his last name is?

Fine. Until we moved to New Haven.

The first day I went to school I ran smack up against a curious phenomenon. When I told my name in class some of the other kids laughed. I couldn't understand what they were laughing at. For some strange reason it appeared that they were laughing at me, although I couldn't figure out anything I had done to cause it. It gave me a funny feeling. And when the teacher turned and scolded the kids who were doing the

[27]

laughing I felt even worse. I couldn't understand any of it, neither the laughter nor the reason for it, nor, for that matter, what the kids were being scolded for. All I knew was that it set me apart in some curious way; and I didn't like it.

I'm quite willing to concede that there is nothing so very tough to take about an incident like that. But I was an only child, this was a new school, I was shy and embarrassed about my strangeness and the new surroundings, so the whole thing became exaggerated in my mind. As a result, I felt even more shy than a kid ordinarily does under similar circumstances.

But after a few days everyone seemed to get used to the fact that my name was a good bit bigger than I was; and in time the joke began to wear thin. Everything might have ended up fine except for something else that happened around that same time.

The playgrounds and schoolyards I had known back on the Lower East Side were paved with cement. Up until this incident, I don't remember ever having consciously seen an ant or an anthill. Insects, yes—cockroaches. Also, occasionally bedbugs. We'd had those in the tenement houses we lived in, and I had become familiar enough with that sort of animal life to take it in my stride as part of the normal order. But then this thing happened one day, and although it is altogether a trifling incident when you come right down to it, it had a devastating effect on me—one I couldn't truly tell you I'm completely over to this moment.

We were all out in the schoolyard one day, during recess. As I remember it, I was moping around near the fence, minding my own business or doing whatever a seven-year-old might be doing when he's by himself. There were some bigger boys playing ball over in another part of the schoolyard, but I was paying no particular attention to them until I suddenly heard something smack against the fence near where I stood. I looked over and saw a baseball rolling along the ground. At the same instant I became aware that they were shouting at me to throw the ball back to them.

Eager to prove myself of service to these bigger boys, I tore after it. And right then was when the whole trouble began.

For as I bent over to pick it up, I saw a most astonishing and incredible sight. There in the sandy ground, right beside the ball, was a small, roughly circular mound with a tiny hole in the center of it. And swarming in and out of this little tunnel-like hole were hordes of shiny black creatures. In other words, an anthill.

Now this may not seem especially startling to you, but for me it was an astounding discovery. I had never seen anything like it before. In fact, I would not have had any idea of what it was at all, except for one thing. In one of the schools I had attended on the Lower East Side I had once seen a cross-sectional diagram of an anthill. For some reason it apparently made a strong impression on me at the time, for now as I saw the real thing I remember distinctly being reminded of the diagram, which, up to then, I had dismissed as something unreal, something "in a book" but not true. A child is quite apt to come to such conclusions unless he has some way of making a connection between things he encounters in books and those he runs up against in real life. The discovery of this anthill was one of the high spots of my young and rather bewildered life up to that time.

Well, what do you do when you make a discovery of this much importance? Archimedes leaped up out of his bath and went running down the street shouting, "Eureka!" I did the equivalent. Completely disregarding the ball I had started to pick up, I began yelling at the top of my voice, "Hey, fellas, come here! Lookit what I discovered! Hurry up!"

This was my form of Eureka! and I believe to this day that I had more legitimate reason for excitement than even Archimedes did, for I had no way of knowing how long these tiny creatures were going to hold still for inspection, and I was justifiably anxious to have everybody view my discovery. It was my first really important contribution in this field and I felt quite as proud of it as old Galileo could have when he first viewed the moons of Jupiter through his brand-new telescope. In fact, despite the rather disastrous debacle this whole incident ultimately turned out to be, I'm *still* fairly proud of it as my first pure scientific observation; and if you happen to think it's easy, well, let's see you go out and make a discovery of your own.

Naturally, anything important enough to break up a ball game must be pretty damn important, so it wasn't more than a few moments before I was surrounded by a whole slew of kids, big and little, all staring down intently at where I was pointing. I began hollering again for them to "lookit what I discovered," continuing to point down at the tiny mound of sand.

Somehow, though, they seemed unimpressed.

"Don't you *see* it?" I finally yelled impatiently. "*Look*it! An *ant*-hole!"

Still no reaction. Nothing at all. Only a numb silence.

Looking back at it now I can see that what I then thought was their denseness was actually nothing more than stunned astonishment. Obviously, none of these kids was able to figure out what the hell was going on. All this intense excitement, this whole big stink I was raising, must have seemed absolutely crazy to them. What was it all about? An anthill? What was so exciting about an anthill? How could they know why it seemed so important to me? And how could I possibly have made them know?

All I could do was to keep on repeating myself, over and over like a cracked record, out of some desperate need to get the idea across to these strange kids who for some reason were unable to grasp the significance of what I was showing them. I went on yelling and pointing down at the anthill until somewhere along the twentieth time I'd repeated my formula of "Lookit what I discovered! An ant-hole!" I began to sense that the effect I had anticipated was missing fire somehow.

All at once I heard a guffaw. In another moment they were all roaring at me until they were doubled up with it. There was no doubt that I had made some sort of contribution, although definitely not the kind I had intended. To this day there has probably never been such a yak in the Dwight Street schoolyard.

Charlie Chaplin once told me of a childhood incident in which his serious attempt to recite a poem resulted in an entire classroom's bursting into laughter at him, and said that he thought the incident had been one of the decisive factors in setting him on the road to becoming a comedian. In my case it worked out quite differently.

To me it was horrible, unendurable, unbelievable. I could not accept it. I was shattered.

But they went on laughing and laughing, and presently they began to repeat mockingly, "*Look*it, fellas *look*it! Lookit what I discovered, an *ant*-hole!" The whole yard rang with it. After a while, one of the ballplayers, a bigger, older boy, reached down, picked up the ball, put his heavy shoe on the anthill and ground it into the sand, and said, quite loudly and distinctly, "Holy Mackerel! Lookit what *he* discovered! A goddamn ant-hole!" The scorn and contempt in his voice was withering enough, but then came the real killer, the crusher, the "most unkindest cut of all." "Columbus!" he muttered disgustedly as he stalked off, "—a regular Columbus!" And the rest of them took it up:

"Columbus Arshawsky, Columbus Arshawsky, Columbus Arshawsky!"

It began to swell into a loud chorus. It went on and on, all over the place, and I stood there and I suppose I must have started crying, for the whole thing began to go dim and blurry and unreal and I couldn't believe anything that had happened or was happening and it seemed forever that I stood there with all those kids dancing and shouting and circling round and round me, yelling and jeering in a loud, unending, insane chant.

"Columbus Arshawsky, *Columbus Arshawsky*, COLUMBUS ARSHAWSKY!"

—Until finally, eventually, somehow or other, the whole crazy nightmare came to an end when the bell rang for the end of recess and we all had to troop back into school. . . .

I have told this anecdote only for one purpose, and that is to make a small point about the whole matter of discrimination. In this instance, of course, the ridicule heaped on me for having made My First Important Discovery In The Field Of Natural History would probably not have been one-hundredth as painful if it had not occurred in an already existent context of strangeness. In itself the Columbus nickname was nothing to feel bad about. It was only that I had by then developed a sore spot about names in general. Now, this Columbus business was more than I could take. The whole thing came to a climax shortly afterwards, when a few of the bigger boys decided to put me through the following ordeal.

"Hey, Columbus, come here." This from the same boy who had given me my nickname in the first place, whom I by now hated. I didn't know whether I hated him more for having given me the name, or for having ground "my ant-hole" out of existence.

"What do you want?" I asked apprehensively, going over to where he stood with a group of smirking admirers.

He had a red face and sandy hair, as I distinctly remember him even to this very moment, and there was a beefy look to him. He leered at me and said, "Somebody told me you say the Lord's Prayer every morning with the rest of the kids—that right, Columbus?"

"Sure I do,"—and I looked around at the circle of grinning

faces, wondering what all this was leading up to, wishing I could somehow get away from them.

" 'Sure I do,' he says," he mimicked, looking around for approval from his audience. " 'Sure I do.' " Turning to me once more, and in a loud and threatening voice—"Well, listen, Columbus, you cut it out, right away, if you know what's good for you—you hear me? Because we don't want no goddamn Christ-killers saying the Lord's Prayer around here, see? Go on home and say your lousy kike prayers, and keep your dirty sheeny nose out of other people's prayers, you hear what I'm telling you?"

I was numb with fright. He went on like that, and then pretty soon the others joined in, until the whole affair began to build itself up to a hysterical pitch, a small mob insanity. And perhaps not so small at that, for the next thing I remember is running down the street away from the crowd of shouting boys, running blindly and in a wild panic, anywhere, just running as fast as I could, to get away from the sound of the voices yelling at me, and hurling all sorts of strange, incomprehensible words at me; but before I could get away I had occasion once more to remember the jingle about sticks and stones, for there were a few of them who apparently were in fairly good practice when it came to throwing a stone.

The stones hurt some; but this was one time when the names hurt far more. And I know that before I got home that day I sat down on a curbstone and tried to figure it all out; but there was no way I could find that helped me to understand it. That was when I came to the realization that there was something terribly wrong with me, that I was "different" from these other kids, and that for some reason I was this strange kind of creature called "Jew" (and now "kike" and "sheeny" and "Christ-killer" as well) and that there was absolutely nothing I or anyone else could do about it as long as I lived, for this was not a thing that could be changed, as most things could be, when you "grew up" and "became a man."

And since we're on the subject of how a kid can react, and the kind of pain and suffering a kid can go through because of a thing like this I've just described, here's one other thing you might think about:

I've been told any number of times that there has been great progress made. But somehow I find it difficult to believe. Maybe it's just naiveté on my part. But it seems to me that when a disease like this can reach such proportions as we've seen it reach *within the past two decades*—when some *six million human beings,* men, women, and *children,* are murdered, raped, tortured, experimented on like guinea pigs, herded together like cattle (but not treated like cattle because cattle are valuable property), gassed, burnt in charnel ovens, thrown like dead dogs into lime pits, branded and made into hideous skeletonlike caricatures of human beings, before finally being "mercifully" permitted to die and put an end to the whole miserable sport—when all this can take place before our eyes and you can still to this very moment find any number of well-fed, prosperous citizens going around thinking to themselves, and quite often saying right out loud (for it's a free country, isn't it?) that after all Hitler was right about one thing anyway—that same old puke-making one thing—well, I ask you, what is a guy supposed to think and feel? I don't believe you'll have any great difficulty in understanding a very small amount of mild bitterness. To say nothing of a slight disgust at the idea of having to be a member of a species which can behave the way it quite often does and yet continues to call itself "human"!

I am not deluding myself with any notion of making any Great Contribution in this matter of minority persecution. Bitterness and anger, justifiable or otherwise, cannot help much, practically speaking. Certainly there is good and sufficient reason for both bitterness and anger. I have had my share of both these emotions. But I know they're no use. In fact, I have even seen them work to the detriment of those who use them in the fight against this disease; particularly where they lead victims of discrimination into their own measures of discrimination against those who discriminate—an even more subtle form of discrimination, a kind of counter persecution, inevitably doomed to failure as a method of dealing with the evil. Minorities cannot afford to blind themselves in their fight against persecution. No man can last long as a fighter if he's kidding himself that he can afford anger—and if you don't believe that, ask any professional.

No, I'm afraid emotion alone can do no good. It can be of use, but only when harnessed to some form of organized activity. And in dealing with the problem of persecution and discrimination against minorities—as in dealing with a mad dog—the less confusion, the more effective the manner of dealing and the more possible the ultimate solution.

I would be the last to make any predictions as to how, when, or even if, this thing can ever be licked. There are times when I wonder if anything is ever going to help much.

One thing, though, can be said with some certainty: there are no easy, short-cut answers. For if this were an easy matter to work out there would have been some noticeable progress made a long time ago. And as George Moore once said, "If books did good the world would have been converted long ago."

Most sensitive people must feel a certain amount of guilt nowadays. Since we are all in pretty much of a mess, it seems to me only natural that if we think about it at all we have to hold ourselves, each one of us, at least partially accountable for the mess. For it is, after all, our own mess. We, collectively, as a species, made it.

Of course, I am not intimating that any one of us has had a great deal to do with the making of it. For we are each only one two-billionth or so of the population; and that's hardly a very big percentage. Nevertheless we can at least face our own inadequacies, and those insecurities each of us lives with, which have stopped us from realizing and meeting our own responsibilities as human beings in helping to clear up the mess.

So that, in a sense, what I'm doing here could be called my own small attempt to discharge an obligation. My own personal obligation to the world I live in, if you want to be fancy about it. If not fancy, let's put it this way: I feel we all have an obligation to try to do something about the way things are with us, and this is the best way I can figure out for myself.

There are all sorts of functions; and pointing out evil is one more function—the old gadfly principle. Even pointing out things that have already been pointed out by innumerable people at innumerable times throughout history. As a matter of fact, I believe that the only time a fellow has the right to *stop* pointing out is after the evil ceases to exist. For that is when the job is over—if such a job as the pointing out of evil can ever be finally finished.

"For life is tendency, and the essence of a tendency is to develop in the form of a sheaf, creating, by its very growth, divergent directions among which its impetus is divided."

HENRI BERGSON

Chapter Seven

LET'S GO BACK NOW and pick up a little thread I dropped, where I first brought up the subject of how I started reading, and let me explain how, one thing leading to another, it finally came about that a kid who originally took to reading books as a means of escape should end up in a vortex of exhibitionism like the band business.

It was a zigzag path indeed, the various interacting processes that brought about the curious metamorphosis of a shy, introspective little Jewish kid named Arthur Arshawsky into a sort of weird, jazz-band-leading, clarinet-tooting, jitterbug-surrounded Symbol of American Youth during an entertainment era characterized by the term "Swing."

I'm trying to be quite objective about this sea-change that took place. It would be simple enough to tell the facts that led to the creation of a publicized symbol called Artie Shaw (which, as I've indicated, is nothing but a label for a commodity—in the same way any label is nothing more than a brand name, rather than the commodity itself, whether soap or canned goods or what-have-you). However, that is not the point. The only part of my story that has any real bearing on the main theme we started with has to do with the inner

[37]

processes that shape us, and how these inner processes interact with outer pressures.

This whole attempt to arrive at a set of meaningful general conclusions is, of course, the explanation for my having gone at such length into the question of discrimination and anti-Semitism. The point is, my strong reactions to that particular disease gave rise to all sorts of repercussions in my subsequent development, and because of these early pressures I underwent certain inner changes resulting in tremendous drives toward conflicting goals.

What were these goals? Well, here we are again with our little friend Cinderella—or $ucce$$, and you can take your choice of symbols, for they both add up to the same thing. But—and it's a big "but"—along with the strong drive toward this one goal, there was an even stronger drive toward escape, surcease from pain. I had an enormous need to *belong,* to have some feeling of roots, to become part of a community, all out of a terrible sense of insecurity coupled with an inordinate desire to prove myself worthy. Worthy of what? What difference does it make? For present purposes, it would be correct enough to say that I was still operating out of an old childish desire to prove myself worthy of being included by those kids who had originally excluded me back there at Dwight School—for it ought to be quite obvious by now that those early experiences, even though repressed and hidden away and, in fact, even completely forgotten, had become an important factor in my make-up and were still operating and shaping me into the kind of person I ultimately *had* to become.

So that, whatever happened to me, however it affected me, and whatever the results, I can only state that none of it was entirely accidental. It was no accident that I read a good deal. It was no accident that I got into music in the first place. It was no accident that I wound up as a bandleader. Of course, there were many later incidents which also played their part. But without an already existent preconditioning *along certain specific lines* these same incidents that have had such far-reaching effects on me might otherwise have passed right over my head with no effect at all—just as there have no doubt been any number of things which have occurred in my life that have had little or no meaning for me, but which would have had enormous effects on anyone conditioned in such a way as to be sensitized to *those* particular occurrences.

For instance, let me tell you the following little story, as another example of the sort of thing that played an important part in shaping the specific zigzag path I have followed.

This took place when I was about twenty.

Now up to that time I had continued with my reading habit, or vice, whichever you prefer. As I grew older I learned that there were different kinds of books, some better than others, but, having quit school in my second year of High School, I had no orientation, no way of determining which books were going to be which kind. So I did the best I could, which was to read anything I could get my hands on, good, bad, or indifferent.

As I went on in the music business and worked my way from one band into another, I ran into a fellow who played piano and had been to college, who told me about a writer named Dreiser. Since I considered this fellow an authority in matters of this sort, I ran right out and bought up all the Dreiser I could find in the town where this happened. At that time I was nineteen, I believe.

Well, by the time I got off the Dreiser kick he had started me on, I had read everything Dreiser had written up to that point. I liked what I read. But I still had no conception of a literary tradition, or that while Dreiser had, and will doubtless continue to have, his place in that tradition, he is by no means the whole of it.

In fact, the whole subject of books was pretty well jumbled up in my mind. I was vaguely aware that these books of Dreiser's were somehow "different" from most of what I had read up to then. But I could not have explained in what way they were different—nor would I have understood, at that time, even if someone had tried to explain it to me.

But now, to show you what I mean when I talk about one thing leading to another, look what happened. A while later, when I got to New York City and was trying to find a job to keep me there, I ran across a jingle in some magazine in which there was some reference to what the writer called (as I vaguely remember it now) the Big Three in American literature. One of the three names was Dreiser—Hemingway and O'Neill, I believe, were the others. That became another orientation point for me.

After plowing my way through all the work of these other two members of America's "Literary Big Three," I began to regard myself as a rather well-read lad. As far as I was concerned, these were the important men in American letters, and having read everything the three of them had written—what else was there left for me to do? That was that, and, having no idea of where to go from there, I went back to my original haphazard manner of picking up stuff to read wherever I found it.

At the time this took place, I had finally managed to get set in New York. I had kicked around from one job to another, till I wound up working as a staff musician at the Columbia Broadcasting station.

There was a clarinettist working at CBS, at the same time I was there, whose name was D'Isere. He was a tall, gaunt, strange-looking man of about forty, and not the sort of person you'd be apt to overlook, particularly if you happened to find yourself working in the same orchestra with him.

Not that we worked together often. He was a member of the symphony orchestra, while I was in what was called the dance band. However, from time to time all the musicians on the CBS staff were combined in one large clambake—an alleged musical program called The Columbians. During rehearsals, I began to take notice of this D'Isere fellow's odd habit of carrying his clarinet case inside a battered old brief-case bulging with papers, periodicals, and all sorts of form-idable-looking books. This, combined with his reserved, aloof, and dignified manner, led me to believe that here was the man who could help me with my literary problems. I asked some of the other musicians about him and they confirmed my general impression. Accordingly, one day after one of these rehearsals, I went up to him and had my first talk with him.

I wanted to ask his help, I said, since I had heard from other members of the orchestra that he knew all about books; and what I wanted him to do, if he could spare the time, was to make me up a list of foreign authors—since I had already read all the important English ones! (Somehow I was unable at that time to make the distinction between American authors and English ones—after all, I must have reasoned, if I gave it any thought at all, English is English, isn't it?)

I must say one thing for D'Isere. He was quite kind, and unquestionably a man of great tolerance. For when I made that amazing statement to him he did not demolish me then and there. All he did was to smile down at me patiently (but not nasty-patiently) and ask me if I was *sure* I had read *all* the important English writers.

And he went on to name what seemed to me an interminable string of names, all of which, I gathered, were people who had written books in English and were apparently pretty im-portant. As a matter of fact, I remember distinctly that this was the first time I had ever heard the name Shakespeare used in such a context. And I can also vividly recall my shock when I realized that this man was intimating a most peculiar thing indeed—that Shakespeare was a writer, along with other writ-ers, and that he could be read for pleasure!

Well, before he finished his list of names, he had mentioned just about every English author of any importance at all, I guess, beginning with a fellow named Chaucer and continuing on down through, as I seem vaguely to remember it, another fellow named Faulkner. I needn't tell you how grateful I was to hear—among all these others I had never even heard of before—the names of the three American authors I *had* read. Aside from these three, the rest was a total blank as far as I was concerned.

All I can tell you is that with each author he named I felt myself growing smaller and smaller. By the time he'd ended, and stood there still smiling down at me I believe I'd have had no difficulty walking erect under his shoe.

I don't actually remember how I finally got away from him, but one thing I do know. From then on, for quite a long time, I avoided him as much as possible; for, ignorant as I may have been about books, I knew enough to be embarrassed about my ignorance.

But there was one thing that came out of this encounter. From that moment on I had determined on a course of action.

I had made up my mind that before I left that job I would have read myself to the point where I could again go up to this man and speak with him on equal terms.

Perhaps this all sounds silly now—but there was nothing silly about it for me at the time. The upshot of it was that at that point I became a reader in earnest. During the ensuing year I went at this business of soaking up books with a persistence and determination and dogged tenacity that still astonishes me when I think about it. About a year or so later I walked up to D'Isere and said, "I'd like to have another talk with you about books one of these days if you get the time, Mr. D'Isere."

He must have sensed what was going on. For he smiled and said, "Why, certainly. Let's have lunch one day this week and we can talk."

We had lunch and we talked. And I came away vindicated. I don't mean that I had read everything, or even that I knew a great deal about what I *had* read, but I did know at least where I stood in regard to knowing, and what to look for in order to find out what I wanted to know.

Where did all this leave me?

Well, although I had no clear idea of it at the time it happened, and, for that matter, wouldn't have been able to do much about it if I had, the truth is that from the day I had lunch with D'Isere I began to live two separate and completely different kinds of lives. One had to do with the music I played, through which I continued to pay the rent and so on. The other—and this was for me by far the more important life— had to do with a thing called learning.

I went on reading and reading—this time, however, with a plan. After a time I enrolled for several courses at Columbia University—extension courses, since I had neither the time nor the necessary credits to enroll as a regular student—and through these courses I was able further to directionalize the pattern and scope of my reading.

About that same time, also, I had built up a strong enough reputation around the radio and recording studios as an instrumentalist, so I quit my staff job at CBS and became a free-lance musician. This gave me more time for study, and I went at it as grimly as I had during the year I was preparing myself to "talk on equal terms" with D'Isere.

Just in passing, I must say that he was of the greatest possible help to me throughout this whole period. We had become good friends by the time I left CBS. I was very fortunate in running into a man like that at that particular time, for he was able to give me a great deal of guidance and encouragement when I needed them very badly. As I learned after knowing him a while, he was indeed quite a fellow. Just as an example of the sort of thing he busied himself with in his spare time, he was a fine Latin scholar, and, under the pen-name of Joseph Gavorse, edited and wrote the introduction to the Modern Library edition of Suetonius' "Lives of the Twelve Caesars." Besides being an excellent clarinettist and a Latin scholar, he wrote, printed, and bound various books of Greek myths, one of which, each year, he prepared in a de luxe edition, illustrated in color by such artists as Ernest Fiene. The first copy of each such edition went as a birthday present to his son, who lived somewhere out of New York City with his mother. The rest of each of these editions were sold to defray the cost of making up the edition in the first place—so that, in all, the entire project added up to nothing more than an elaborate birthday present from father to son. I hope the son appreciated the labor, effort, energy, good taste, and talent that went into these little presents, for it was quite a job to prepare each one. I know, for I occasionally lent a hand during some phase of the preparation—in binding or setting up the type or on some other chore connected with the job.

Meanwhile, in between radio commercials and staff recording sessions, I kept on working at my self-education. Gradually I began to make some sort of progress, although never as much as I felt I should, for I was always extremely impatient. D'Isere, with his calm advice, was probably the only influence in my life at that time which kept me from going off the deep end altogether. There was far too much to learn, and I was acutely aware that there was never going to be too much time to learn all I felt I had to know. However, chiefly because of his quiet reassurance and gentle but nonetheless critical help, I was able to maintain some sort of balance. I owe him a lot, and I wish he were around now so I could tell him how much he meant to me during that whole period of my life. I was always awkward and quite inarticulate with him when it came to talking about anything outside of books and writing and things along those lines; and now that he's dead I don't really see what I can do to make up for this lack on my part except this small passing tribute I am paying him— which he will not even be able to see. . . .

At any rate, after a certain amount of this kind of vicarious participation in The Literary Life, it was inevitable that I become interested in how all this stuff I was reading had got written in the first place. Who were these people who did the writing? Why did they do it? What made a man want to become a writer? And, of course, how did a guy go about it— how was it done?

In order to learn some of the answers to these questions, I enrolled for more courses. This time, short-story writing courses, courses in playwriting, etc. And at that point, having done what many other people have done, before and since— which was to confuse the desire to read with the ability to write—I decided that the only thing I needed was time, in order to turn out a stream of literature of my own making.

Please believe me, this was quite serious. I realize how naive I am making myself sound. The truth is I was naive enough then for any three or four people.

At that same time I had already arrived at certain negative conclusions regarding the way I was earning my living. The stuff we played around the studios could scarcely be called music—all it was was another advertising gimmick, and since I had not set out to become a salesman, either of soap or cereals, I decided abruptly (and, as it turned out, prematurely) to make a complete break and go off to try to live my life along new and entirely different lines more in keeping with these new values and interests I was beginning to formulate for myself. That these values and interests (to say nothing of my ability to carry them into any realistic effect) had by no means yet jelled—that this whole welter of confused notions which was seething and boiling inside me had not yet even come close to settling into any semblance of a clear-cut purpose—that I had by no means achieved even a vague articulation of a point of view regarding not only myself but my life (both of which I felt I wanted to write about)—all this I had no way of knowing, since I had not yet had time to find out.

I found out soon enough. As soon, in fact, as I was able to

put my plan into effect and go off and try to make a start as a writer.

However, before explaining what I found out, how I found it out, and what I then figured out to do about it, I think I should go all the way back so I can explain where I stood as a musician at the time I've just been writing about—and also how I had got there, and why, at the age of twenty-three, I was so anxious to get out of a business in which I had already served a rather arduous apprenticeship. . . .

Part II

The Trouble with Cinderella
(an outline of identity)

Part II

"*Out of such trivialities are vocational preferences born. . . . The ideal way to discover what our own preferences are, and whether they are superficial or really fundamental, would be to be given the opportunity of seeing all the inside workings of the occupation we have selected.*"

ARTHUR GILBERT BILLS
—*The Psychology of Efficiency*

"*All life is an experiment. The more experiments you make the better.*"

EMERSON—JOURNALS

"We ain't what we wanna be, and we ain't what we're gonna be—but we ain't what we wuz."

SOUTH CAROLINA MOUNTAIN PROVERB

Chapter Eight

IT WAS DURING the same year in which I had learned my sociological catechism that I had my first brush with The Muse. This was a sporadic and rather hectic affair. My mother somehow got it into her head that I had to learn to play the piano. Where she picked up this curious notion I have no idea. What I do know is that before she was finally defeated in her no-doubt praiseworthy objective, I was so completely disgusted with music that it's a wonder I ever got back to where I was even willing to listen to any of it again, let alone decide to go into the music business as a way of making my living.

The principle difficulty, I suppose, was the method of teaching. I was never able to fathom the reasons why I should have to spend my afternoons after school in what seemed to me quite likely to develop into a lifelong tussle with some character named Czerny, with whom, in practically no time at all, I found myself not only bored out of my wits but downright fed up. No one ever took the trouble to explain to me why I should spend hours on end racking my brain and torturing my fingers with what only seemed to me a meaningless and utterly ridiculous kind of exercise, entirely unrelated to anything in which I had the slightest interest. I remember asking both my mother and the young lady who was engaged to initiate me into these mysteries, a straightforward question —a question which can be summed up in a single syllable— "Why?"

The young lady's answer was so admirably filled with logic and rationality that I had no idea what in hell she was talking about. As for my mother's answer, while I was at least able to understand it I was never willing to accept it. For all *that* came to can be summed up in *two* syllables—"It's nice."

I tried, of course, to get her to explain to me exactly what was *nice* about it. In the end, the best I could get out of her was that the piano had cost a lot of money and the least I could do would be to learn how to make it into an object which had some sort of functional, rather than purely ornamental, value.

Well, I went on with this nonsense for some time—until I reached the age of ten. All that time I managed to sustain a quiet but determined rebellion against this unwarranted intrusion on my private life. Ultimately my single-minded determination to rid myself of this nuisance once and for all prevailed; after which I was finally allowed to go on back to my customary ten-year-old pursuits, such as they were.

Naturally, under such circumstances as I have just described, I had no difficulty at all in promptly forgetting anything I might just accidentally have learned about music or piano-playing. The whole thing amounted to no more than a rather painful inoculation which didn't take; and to this day the best thing I can remember out of that entire musical experience is that I was once given a quarter by some middle-aged lady for playing a piece called *Träumerei* in a way that no doubt would have caused the composer a few uneasy moments had he been present. I was willing to concede that the quarter was more than ample payment for my dubious services in playing that one piece; still, after weighing against it the

endless hours of irksome and meaningless finger exercises I
had had to go through to earn it, I became convinced that
there must be some easier way to make a quarter.

That took care of the piano, my piano lessons, and my musical education for the time being.

In the meantime we moved out of York Street and, the family fortunes having by then dwindled down to near-invisibility,
took a cheap railroad flat over on Grand Avenue. There I was
able to find myself a whole new set of pursuits. There was a
gang of congenial kids living in the vicinity, many of them,
like myself, second-generation children of immigrant parents;
and with this gang I took up such interesting and educational
pursuits as stealing, fighting with similar gangs from nearby
neighborhoods, and other pleasant juvenile delinquencies. Our
stealing was more for entertainment than profit. We used to
go into the Five and Ten Cent stores, spread out among the
various counters, pilfer what we could, and then meet outside
and compare notes to determine which of us was the most
skillful. This was a game that made sense to me, and I remember that I used to rank right up there near the top when
it came to this sport. Also, I remember being caught once.
A contemporary who had secretly joined some sort of civic-
minded group called The Up-Boys met me as I was leaving
Woolworth's Five and Ten with a pocketful of assorted valu-
ables and asked me what I had managed to get that day.
When I proudly showed him my loot he signaled one of the
store detectives who had been standing nearby. I was taken
by the arm and propelled into the office of the manager of the
store.

All sorts of hell took place after that. My parents were noti-
fied and I was subjected to a number of indignities. The kid
who had turned me in was caught shortly thereafter by our
gang and given the full Hollywood treatment for stool-
pigeons as approved by any Humphrey Bogart movie you
may care to mention.

This idyllic life, however, did not continue for long. My family moved once again, this time into a "nicer" neighborhood, over on Orange Street near Grove, and here we stayed until I graduated from grammar school and started my first year at New Haven High School—known as Hillhouse High by those who attended, which I reluctantly did.

I was thirteen years old when, toward the end of my freshman year at Hillhouse, I discovered a new form of entertainment and amusement. At that age I had developed into a lonely, withdrawn, overly bashful kid, with few friends and a tendency to keep pretty much to myself. The original shyness engendered in me by some of my early Dwight Street School experiences had crystallized into a general introspective set. My life had fallen into a pattern which had very little to do with any of the normal social aspects of high school life. I went to school, meaning I put in the requisite amount of time involved in attending classes and so on—but I was actually no part of it. By that time my feeling of being an alien, an outsider, an out-group member, had become so much a part of my whole attitude toward life that I was unable to integrate myself with any school activities outside of those I was forced to take part in.

Even in those, I felt somehow set apart. There was still that business of my name. There was always the matter of having to spell it out, whenever I was asked to give my name for any reason at all. And always, whenever I gave this information, I used to watch out of the corner of my eye for any sign of ridicule, to which, by then, I had become extraordinarily sensitive.

I am aware that this was an inordinate reaction on my part— but there it was. These were the attitudes I had been taught by the life I had known up to then, and I can't see to this day how a kid can be expected to feel or know anything contrary to what his own experiences have caused him to feel and know. It would have done no more good to have tried to change these attitudes in me by telling me "the facts" about them than it does to explain to a sufferer from migraine the "fact" that his migraine is not a "real" headache or that it is only psychogenic, a result of tension and anxiety. For either way the headache is there and it still hurts just as much. And it will continue to hurt until other experiences have substituted new, healthy attitudes for these "false" ones—whether you're dealing with migraine on the part of an adult, or a psychological feeling of estrangement and isolation on the part of an adolescent.

Now, why do I tell all this in this part of my story, when I am supposed to be telling about how I got into the music business? What has all this to do with music in the first place?

In my own case, a great deal.

For this is the subjective story of how I got into the business—these are "the facts" through which I became the kind of kid who was ready for what happened next. In other words, I was already conditioned toward some big change, I was· looking for some quick way out of a life that was daily becoming more and more intolerable to me. I had already figured out what I wanted out of life, and I know right now that it would have made little difference to me how I got it, just so I did get it. Any notion of morality I may have had at that time of my life could be expressed in pretty much these terms: What difference does it make how you get what you're after, as long as you get away with it? Which, looking at it from where I now stand, seems to be close enough to Emerson's famous dictum that "The only thing that keeps the average man honest is the fear of being caught."

So that, instead of turning out to be a musician, I believe I might very well have become a fair specimen of a juvenile delinquent—and perhaps not only juvenile at that. Given my philosophical outlook, my cynical attitudes toward life as I had known it, plus the goals I had already set up for myself, I was in no mood for any long-range plan involving such activities as schooling or training of the sort necessary for the average profession.

I was looking for a short-cut, a quick way out.

There were four little things I had determined I wanted out of life. These four little things I had fixed my sights on were, in almost any order at all, a) Money, b) Success, c) Fame, and d) that old blue-bird Happiness. Recognize the formula? Naturally, our little Cinderella friend, of course, complete with magic thinking and all the usual trimmings. Well, why not? There are plenty of so-called grownups tearing around chasing their tails in this futile pursuit, so it shouldn't be too hard to understand how a kid of thirteen might be doing the very same thing.

There were, to be sure, several minor problems connected with my accomplishment of the above aims. But I soon found a way to overcome any obstacles. There are many different kinds of weapons a fellow can choose from in his own personal fight against the world. Having grown up in the midst of the John Held era, I chose the weapon which appeared to me to hold forth the best chances for helping me to accomplish my desires in a hurry—a saxophone.

The idea first occurred to me during a vaudeville show at the old Poli's Palace Theatre on Church Street in New Haven, Conn. I used to attend these shows quite frequently. Despite the fact that I was supposed to be solving such abstruse algebraic problems as how much X might owe Y if Y worked Z hours for him for 3 days at A, B, or C dollars per hour, I somehow was unable to whip up any enthusiasm for these arcane matters. I therefore did the only sensible thing a boy of thirteen can do under such circumstances. I played hookey. To while away the time, I began to make illicit excursions into the world of theatre as exemplified by these vaudeville shows at Poli's Palace. In the beginning, there was a slight difficulty in regard to the matter of admission. I had no money and would not have dared ask for it at home. In the first place

there wasn't enough money around home for this sort of friv-
olous stuff, and in the second place there was no way I could
have accounted for the need for this money at a time when
I was supposed to be pursuing my alleged education.

However, after a short time, I got to know my way around
Poli's Palace so well—side entrances and back—that the price
of admission became nothing more than an abstract academic
question. From then on in I became a fairly regular patron, if
not a cash customer, of Mr. Poli's.

As I remember them, most of those vaudeville acts were
scarcely designed to interest a kid of my age and predilections.
Nevertheless I was fascinated by them. They gave me a
glimpse into a new and utterly different kind of fantasy-
world. I used to stare at those people up there on the stage,
singing, dancing, laughing, joking; but of course I was far too
shy to imagine myself up there in any of these capacities.

Then one day I saw an act through which I conceived the
idea that there might be a niche for me in that gilded, tinselled
world.

The thing that distinguished this act was the small orchestra
accompanying it, which sat right up there on the stage—unlike
the regular theatre pit band of Poli's Palace, to which I had
never paid a great deal of attention. These stage musicians,
though, were something entirely different. I watched them
with rapt and breathless interest, staring at them with a wild
surmise. The clincher came when, along toward the middle of
the act, one of the musicians, all dressed up in a blue-and-
white-striped blazer, came down to the footlights, knelt down
on one knee (looking sharp as a tack and rakish as all get-out
to me as I sat entranced in my stolen seat), and played a tune
named *Dreamy Melody* on a shiny gold saxophone.

Well-sir—that did it.

Suddenly it popped into my addled head that if I could
manage to get hold of one of these complicated-looking gadgets and learn to play the thing, I too could be doing what this

lucky fellow was doing. At the time, it seemed to be the ideal version of any Good Life I could imagine. For what could be better than to be traveling around the country with all those beautiful chorus girls, making several thousand dollars a minute for doing nothing but wearing a blue-and-white-striped blazer, looking sharp as the aforementioned tack, and causing lovely blatting noises to come out of a gleaming, glittering, glistening, golden gadget with mother-of-pearl keys stuck all over it? I don't remember owning a blazer at the time, but I probably figured I could manage to get hold of one somehow —I don't believe it even occurred to me that a guy could play one of these instruments dressed any other way.

But getting hold of a saxophone turned out to be a lot tougher than I had imagined in my first burst of exuberance. My mother, when I broached the subject, had never even heard of a saxophone. I managed to explain what it was, and, once I was able to convince her that saxophones were supposed to have some vague connection with music, the idea of my playing one was not too repellent to her. She did fire off one last shot, though—that since I was at last becoming interested in music, well, there was that piano still sitting there in the living room after all the money it had cost, doing nobody any good at all. But I stuck to my guns—or rather my saxophone—and after a few days I succeeded in winning her over.

My father, though, was of a different mettle. To begin with, he had been against the idea of buying the piano at all, and after I had quit the thing, he never did tire of pointing out to my mother how right he had been in the first place. This naturally did not make for tranquil domestic relations; and as a result of the constant bickering about the piano, the cost of my "musical education," and the fact that in the end, no one, including myself, had got anything at all out of the whole business—as a result of all this, music was a sore subject with him.

Also, like my mother, he didn't know what a saxophone was;

but, *un*like my mother, he made it quite clear that he not only did not *want* to know but would bat me over the head if I insisted on continuing to talk about some damn-foolishness (or, as he put it, in Yiddish—*mishugas*) which could only wind up with the spending of more hard-earned money on further impractical and nonsensical whims. And when my mother finally managed to get through to him for long enough to make him understand what we were talking about—when he heard what this new-fangled gadget of a saxophone *was*—there was an explosion that came close to blasting the whole idea to hell and gone, and me right along with it!

In time my mother and I managed to prevail, by bludgeoning and cajoling him into a surly resignation of sorts; but even at that he fought the good fight and was vanquished only after several miserable weeks of entreaty, pleas, stormy weeping scenes, and threats (on the part of my mother, for I was scared as hell of him), and every conceivable sort of promise (on my part) of the way in which the acquisition of this instrument would benefit everyone concerned.

Even then the battle was not yet won. He had become resigned, but he was a long way from active cooperation; and cooperation was something he could not, and mulishly would not, be coerced into, in spite of more threats, more tears, and all the combined hell and high water either my mother, or I, or both of us, could produce. Finally, however, something *had* to give, in this tussle between the irresistible force and the immovable object. We wound up with a compromise.

The compromise was this: as soon as my high school term was finished I was to get a job during summer vacation as errand boy at a grocery store run by a friend of my parents. That way I would earn the forty dollars I needed for the second-hand Saxophone Of My Dreams, which, at the time of this decision, reposed peacefully and silently in its purple-plush-lined, imitation-leather case in the window of Wrozina's

Music Shop over on Centre Street, opposite—fittingly enough —a police station.

At a salary of four dollars per week, I put in ten weeks at Gorn's Delicatessen Store on Orange Street, after which, there being no further need for me to continue in the neighborhood distribution of food supplies, I guzzled down one last free bottle of Delaware Punch, promptly severed all connection between myself and Mr. Gorn without even a slight pang, and tore over to Wrozina's Music Shop. I handed over the money, gathered up my precious submachine-gun—pardon me, I mean saxophone—and tenderly lugged it home.

From that day on I was on my way. Where I was going, how it would wind up, what it was going to be like when I got there—none of this mattered in the least.

I knew where I wanted to go, this saxophone was my carfare, and all I had to do now was to learn what to do with it in order to get what I wanted.

I guess I was about as happy right then as I ever expect to be. For if ignorance is bliss—right then I had it; and I don't suppose, no matter how hard a fellow tries, he can ever get back to his original ignorance again.

There have been plenty of times since then, when I would have given a great deal to be able to feel the way I felt that day when I brought home that beatup old saxophone. There have been times when I've had some pretty good moments here and there along the way; but I guess there's no way to top your first really good moment.

"If there is an advantage in self-instruction, there are also great disadvantages, especially the incredible amount of labour necessary. This I know better than anyone else."

JEAN JACQUES ROUSSEAU

Chapter Nine

THERE ARE ALMOST as many cockeyed ideas extant about the saxophone, and the ease with which one of these gadgets can be mastered, as there are about psychoanalysis or the music business. The saxophone is just as difficult to handle as any other instrument, if a man wants to learn to play it well. Maybe even more so, since it is a relatively new member of the family of musical instruments and therefore still in a sort of probationary period, so far as so-called legitimate music is concerned; with the result that in order for it to be accepted at all it almost follows that the average performer on the saxophone ought to be even better, if anything, than the average performer on one of the more standard, traditionally acceptable instruments.

Another important factor is that, with the saxophone—particularly at the time when I first got together with mine—there have been almost as many methods of teaching as there are teachers. And last, but not at all least, since the instrument itself is a sort of bastard composite, being made of brass but played by means of a reed, it has never been quite settled, outside of jazz bands, whether it is, properly speaking, a brass or a reed instrument; although where it has been used by such composers as Prokofiev, Ibert, Vaughn Williams, Milhaud, or, for that matter, even as far back as Verdi, the tendency has been to classify it as a member of the reed, or woodwind, family.

None of this was of the slightest concern to me, however, at the time when I first tackled the only problem that really interested me about this new toy of mine. I had only one real mission for the moment, and that was to figure out somehow what I had to do to play a tune called *Dreamy Melody*.

My first day at home with the instrument was spent in this effort—to the sullen despair of my father who was home out of work, the usual state of affairs during that period.

After several days of unremitting toil and trouble, while it is true that I had learned to produce certain eerie and at times astonishingly unexpected sounds on this new gadget of mine, even I had to admit to myself that these noises bore at best only a wishful resemblance to anything that could be called *Dreamy Melody*, or, for that matter, any other kind of melody. Only someone with an even more vivid imagination than my own could have possibly accused these noises of being music. So next day I went back to Mr. Wrozina's musical emporium with a strong beef.

Fortunately, Mr. Wrozina was a patient man with a mild disposition. We had no difficulty in arriving at what seemed to me a fair enough arrangement. I was to get five free lessons from Mr. Wrozina's head salesman, after which I would be on my own.

Two of those five lessons were all I ever took, for I was now fourteen years old and in far too great a hurry to bother my head with anything other than learning which keys to press down to make which noises. Having learned that much, I was ready to get on to more pressing matters. My teacher, a fellow named Henry Hill, was peculiarly insistent on my having to learn to walk slowly up and down various scales before embarking upon any sudden ambitious musical hundred-yard dashes. Under the circumstances, given my already-well-developed hatred for scales of any kind (remember my brush with that Czerny guy?), there was nothing for me to do but to quit my formal musical training and go on back to my original idea of working out for myself any remaining problems of how to make this possession of mine behave so as to sound remotely like some kind of a musical instrument.

There is no point in going into all the horrible details of what went on during the ensuing weeks. Anyone who has ever had the bad fortune to live in the near-vicinity of a musical neophyte—especially a neophyte who happens to be wrestling with a saxophone—will understand what it must have been like. The entire neighborhood, individually and collectively, raised bloody murder. As for my poor father—the less said about that, the better. Even my mother, indulgent as she always was, and personally involved as one of the original sponsors of the whole unfortunate affair, was just barely able, by what must have been a determined stoicism, to maintain a grim silence. I suppose she had made up her mind to see this thing through somehow, just as she might have lived through any other kind of plague if she were forced to do so, and, being a woman with a robust constitution, she managed to survive where a lesser woman might easily have collapsed under the strain.

However, *Labor omnia vincit improbus,* as the old boy said, and as time went on I began to overcome some of my difficulties, if not those of my "captive audience."

Eventually I learned to play (?) not only *Dreamy Melody* but several other popular tunes of that era, and after a couple of months or so I made my first public appearance as a virtuoso. All dressed up in my best suit (with knickers, for I was not yet allowed to wear long trousers), and sporting a brand-new red and yellow polka-dotted bow tie so big it looked like the kind of ribbon you put around the neck of a house cat, I stumbled out onto the stage of a little neighborhood theatre during one of those weekly Amateur Night shows, and there gave out with what I fondly believed to be a version of a lively little classic entitled *Charley My Boy*. The audience went wild—with hilarity, as I'm certain now; but at the time I simply took it for granted that they were displaying their natural good taste and consequent enthusiasm for my musical ability. And, madly enough, despite (or possibly because of) the fact that the pianist in the pit started off in one key and I in another, and that we never did manage to get together until practically the very end of the whole ridiculously exuberant performance (by which time it didn't matter any longer anyway)—nevertheless, to my own astonishment, to say nothing of what the pianist must have felt, I won first prize—five dollars!

Five whole dollars, just for playing one song!

You can imagine what this must have seemed to me, after having had to put in a whole week at Gorn's Delicatessen (during the preceding summer) in order to earn four dollars.

Needless to say, my proud presentation of this vast sum of money at home had considerable effect on the domestic status of the saxophone as well as myself. As a result of my proven ability to earn money with this tricky plaything, my father began to observe my so-called musical activities with at least a grudging tolerance. He was a practical man, with an earthy, peasantlike approach to money; having long since undergone the first-generation immigrant's disillusioning discovery that the sidewalks of the United States are definitely *not* paved with gold, he had developed a grudging and cynical respect for anyone who had mastered the knack of picking up a dollar by any means whatsoever. As far as he was concerned, a buck was a buck, *gelt* was unquestionably the only *welt* he knew, and I don't think I'm seriously distorting his point of view when I say that it probably would not have made the slightest difference to him whether a fellow made money by playing a saxophone or by robbing banks—except that he probably would have favored the latter method in my case, since it would not only have undoubtedly produced a lot more immediate ready cash (which we all could have used) but would have kept things a great deal quieter around the house.

Still, noisy or not, after this episode he began to accept the saxophone (or the "blower," as he always called it) with something other than his hitherto rather jaundiced attitude. I remember one evening when some of his cronies were over for the weekly pinochle game. To my amazement he asked me to bring my saxophone into the room where they were playing and give them a rendition of my "five dollar song." He was never able to remember the name of it, or, for that matter, of any other tune he ever heard me play.

When I had finished playing for him and his pinochle-playing buddies, he turned to them and said, "You see?"—speaking, as he always did, in Yiddish, "Five dollars the boy gets for playing this—you hear it absolutely free." Then he laughed, but with more sarcasm than humor, turned his head to look at me as if he were seeing me for the first time and couldn't quite understand who or what I was, shook his head in wonder, and finally said: "*America gonniff*"—which meant something along these lines, so far as I could determine it: Very well, then—if people are stupid enough to pay good money to listen to crazy noises coming out of a blower, let them do it, but don't expect *me* to take it seriously, because I know better.

But his troubles and bewilderment—as far as my saxophone and I were concerned, at any rate—were soon over. For shortly thereafter, he packed up, left my mother and me in New Haven, and set out for California with the nebulous idea of establishing himself out there and later sending for us. Actually, he and my mother had not been getting on at all for a number of years, so this was simply a sort of ruse to break up their marriage once and for all. It is even conceivable that my saxophone was the last straw, the one little push he needed to make the break. Whatever it was, he went off and that was the end of him as far as my mother was concerned. They never bothered to get a formal divorce, but their marriage was over and neither of them ever saw the other again.

I went right on practicing, grimly and determinedly. Although I can now afford to look back at it with a certain amount of humor, it was no laughing matter with me at the time. For this instrument was the first thing I had been able to discover that seemed to offer a way out of a life I hated. This saxophone was my Magic Lantern, my Open Sesame! to a new life—my way of achieving status, earning a living, getting away from a place where I had so far only been taught to feel like an outcast, a despised underdog, a Pariah.

I went at it daily for as much as six or seven hours, and then quit only because my teeth ached and the inside of my lower lip was ragged and cut from the constant pressure of the mouthpiece and reed. I had not yet formed an *embouchure*, strengthened the necessary muscles, which would have eased the pain somewhat. I continued in spite of that, learning slowly, the hard way, through constant starts and retracings, fumbling toward one thing and then going back and unlearning what I had laboriously learned; slowly working out my own trial-and-error method, all the while listening to recordings of professionals on our old battered hand-crank phonograph—until it was a question of which would give out first, my lower lip and my teeth (which were fortunately strong), or the patience of everybody living within earshot (which was wearing dangerously thin).

Along about the end of the first few months I began to feel the need to spread out and get myself some broader experience, to do some ensemble playing in addition to the limited solo efforts I had been busying myself with up to then.

At that stage of my musical development I couldn't find any orchestra that would be willing to have me as a gift. So I did the next best thing. I teamed up with another high school lad about my age, who, no doubt for his own misguided reasons, had learned to produce several lugubrious chords on the banjo. Through my one experience in winning first prize at the Amateur Night performance, I had learned that there was a regular little Amateur Night circuit, handled and booked by a man named Johnny Goggins, an agent of sorts, with an office in the same building as Poli's Palace. I had been told about this man by another amateur performer with whom I had talked for a moment before going out onto the stage that first time, and now I went to see Goggins to inquire about the possibilities of getting some bookings for our newly-organized saxophone and banjo duo.

Goggins consented to put us in with a couple of other of his "amateurs"—a term which I now began to discover had many shades and degrees of meaning. For these were what I can only call, for want of a better name, "professional" amateurs. During the course of the average Amateur Night, the level of performance was apt to go so low that it ceased to be even funny—which made it pretty low indeed. In order, therefore, to keep the customers amused and prevent them from becoming so bored as to break up the joint, or walk out and never come back again, various theatre managers resorted to professional "amateur" acts supplied by Goggins. In this way the customers were given an occasional performance which was at least not *too* bad (although plenty bad enough to avoid undue suspicion as to the amateur status of the performers). The "amateur" performers received five dollars or so apiece, Goggins pocketed the difference between what he got from the theatre managers and what he had to pay out for his acts, and, presumably, everybody was happy.

In the course of the next few weeks my banjo-playing partner-in-crime and I appeared in ten or twelve such semi-black-market Amateur Night shows. Now and then we even traveled as far afield as Meriden or Waterbury. All this was fine, as far as it went, but after a short time I looked ahead and saw that it was only a question of how long it would take before we had made the complete round of the circuit—after which it would obviously be impossible for us to play any return engagements without giving away the whole skullduggery. Although we were managing to make a few dollars, this was leading nowhere at all so far as My Career was concerned.

What I needed, still, was work with an orchestra. And, since I could not beg, borrow, or steal my way into any orchestra I knew of, I started to look around school for other kids who played instruments and might be willing to join me in forming a little orchestra of our own.

I took to attending the Saturday afternoon dances at Hillhouse High School and hanging out around the bandstand. I was far too bashful to have ever learned how to dance. So I spent my time listening critically to the amateur band that played for these dances. I used to stand over to one side and sneer to myself at the way the saxophonist played certain songs which were part of my repertoire; but inwardly I was green with envy at his being in a band that was at least able to get a dance to play at.

Sooner or later, it was inevitable that I should run into other aspiring orchestra musicians. I can't remember exactly how it happened but eventually I teamed up with three other twisted lads who had the same general idea about forming an orchestra; and at that time musical history of some sort was made. For, if this was not the *best* four-piece dance band that had ever come along in New Haven, it could at least claim the distinction of being close to the worst.

We called ourselves the Peter Pan Novelty Orchestra and oddly enough managed to get ourselves engaged here and there. We got eight bucks a night, two bucks apiece, playing at occasional linen showers and weddings held by members of our immediate families and those of their friends and acquaintances who could be bludgeoned into hiring us. After hearing us play, some of them actually had to be threatened before they would pay us anything at all, let alone the eight bucks we demanded for our earnest efforts to make the night hideous.

Incidentally, throughout the entire life of this musical aggregation, the matter of leadership was never fully or firmly established. There was a lad in the outfit who played fiddle, and to the bitter end he maintained that the only proper leader for any orchestra was the fiddle-player. I, on the other hand, had several objections to this theory. In the first place I had no great appreciation for either the fiddle or the way he played it. In the second place the name of the orchestra was my idea. Somewhere along in my youth I had learned to draw a picture of what purported to be Peter Pan. Having painted it on the front of our drummer's bass drum, I thought it only fitting that we name the orchestra after this piece of undying art. Where the word "Novelty" came from I still have no idea. I suppose it must have sounded classy to us. Or something. At any rate it came to have meaning enough, for it was always an unquestionable novelty if, at the end of any engagement, we managed to get paid without too much of a squawk.

Anyway, we eventually contrived a rather ingenious method of settling the knotty problem of who the leader would be. It was simple enough at that, as all Great Ideas are.

The only actual difference between the leader and any other member of the orchestra consisted in the fact that the leader was allowed to stand up. And since neither the piano player nor the drummer was *able* to stand up while playing, that left only the fiddle player and myself. The way we finally worked it was this: if the engagement was procured by the fiddle player he was allowed to stand up and be leader for that night—if the engagement was mine, I got to stand and be leader. On any other job we got, through either of the two other members of the band—well, that night *that* member was the leader, but since he *couldn't* stand up and lead and still continue to play, we *all* played sitting down.

I still have a very warm place in my memories for the Peter Pan Novelty Orchestra. For although I had no way of knowing it at the time, I was never going to have as much fun playing in any orchestra again. More money, yes. More musical experience and kicks, unquestionably. But more innocent, simple pleasure—which is, after all, one of the things a fellow ought to be able to get out of playing music—and more downright fun, even in spite of the struggle to settle who was allowed to stand up and lead, I have never had since and never expect to have again. Not as a musician anyway. . . .

"The greater part of progress is the desire to progress."

SENECA

Chapter Ten

DURING THE SIX OR SEVEN MONTHS the Peter Pan outfit
stayed together we were occasionally engaged to play at functions where we were required to furnish a five- or six-piece
band. On such occasions we would get hold of some kid out
of one of the other amateur dance bands around town. It didn't
matter much what instruments we added, for nothing would
have made us sound much better; however, at such times we
were at least a good deal louder than usual—and I guess that
was the whole idea in the first place.

Sometimes we'd hire my old banjo-playing sidekick of the
Amateur Night circuit. When we could we would also get
hold of a trumpet, although these were scarce. Halfway decent
brass men were in such demand that as soon as any trumpet
player was even able to hold his instrument properly he had
little difficulty getting into the ranks of the professionals,
which entailed joining the musicians' union and consequently
not being permitted to work with amateur bands like ours.

We, of course, had to remain strictly nonunion in order to
get any work at all. It wasn't that we had anything against
joining the union. Far from it. We'd have been only too happy
to get in. But in the first place we couldn't afford the twenty-
five dollar initiation fee each of us would have had to lay out
to become a member; in the second place, since we weren't

good enough to demand the union minimum scale for our services, joining the union would have meant not playing at all. As I said, two bucks apiece was all we got—and even at that, not always without a scuffle—whereas union scale for the same work would have run somewhere in the neighborhood of ten or more dollars per musician. And since we knew damn well we didn't have a chance to get up into those stratospheric financial brackets, we let well enough alone and continued to scuffle around for our regular two bucks per night rather than nothing at all. Besides, we all wanted—and badly needed— the experience.

However, since we occasionally hired some of these other musicians from similar groups, it was only natural that these groups reciprocated by hiring one of us from time to time. And since most of these had their own nucleus of three or four instruments, which almost certainly meant that they had their own piano player and drummer—and since our fiddle player was by no means a budding Heifetz or even a Joe Venuti— that left only myself.

As a result, after several months I began to build up a small reputation in local amateur dance band circles. I worked around town with lots of these little groups, lugging my saxophone from one festive occasion to another—weddings, small local dances, lodge benefits, various charity affairs, all sorts of functions where the finances were too low to warrant the services of professional musicians.

Meantime, my playing was improving. All this practical experience was doing me a lot of good. In addition, I kept on practicing like a madman at home, listening to one record after another and patterning my style first after one and then after another of the various recording saxophonists of that era. And not only saxophonists but any other instrumentalists from whom I could pick up some little trick. In time I began to develop a sort of eclectic style of my own and was able, after

a while, to improvise well enough to attract a little attention
—still, of course, only on an amateur level.

By now I had learned enough to have developed a vast
respect, practically a downright awe, for professional musicians. On nights when I wasn't working, I took to hanging
out on the corner of Orange and Court Streets, hiding in the
darkness of a store entrance across the street from the seduc-
tively-lighted local dance hall listening to one of New Haven's
leading dance bands, Johnny Cavallaro's orchestra. In those
days this band was made up of some of the best professional
musicians in town. The name of this local dance hall, incidentally, was the Cinderella Ballroom!

So things went for a while. I continued to improve, and
ultimately I must have become fairly good, for after some six
or seven months, I was "discovered." Here's how that happened.

One night, while playing with one of the little amateur
outfits I was now working with three or four nights every week,
I noticed a fellow standing down in front of the bandstand
listening intently, and occasionally grinning appreciatively at
something I played. I had no idea who he was, but he seemed
to grin at the right times, mostly at some little phrase I had
copied from one of the records I was constantly cribbing stuff
from. I figured he must know something about music. But I
was too occupied to pay much attention to him and after a
while he disappeared. It was just as well for me that I didn't
know who he was, or I'd probably have been scared stiff
and unable to play anything at all. He was nothing less than
one of those exalted personages for whom I had conceived
such awe and respect—a professional musician.

His name was Dave Yudkin, he played the drums, and he
occasionally substituted for the regular drummer in Johnny
Cavallaro's orchestra, that same band I had listened to for so
many nights from my little hideout across from the Cinderella
Ballroom.

I learned all this when he came back to pick me up after we had finished that night's stint. I was packing my saxophone into its case when he showed up again and told me who he was. I was so impressed that I stopped and stared at him, forgetting my saxophone, forgetting everything but the fact that this fellow had, for some peculiar reason, come back to talk to me.

After a few minutes he said, "Come on, kid—you're coming with me."

It was after twelve-thirty A.M. I stared at him in bewilderment. "Where?" I asked.

"Up to the Cinderella," he said calmly.

"The Cinderella—Ballroom?"

"That's right. Come on, hurry up. I just came from talking to Cavallaro,"—to me, at that moment, he might just as well have told me he had been talking to God!

"You did?" I said.

"Sure I did," he said impatiently. "Come on, let's go—you're going to make an audition for Cavallaro's band."

"I'm going to—*what?*"

"You heard me. Johnny Cavallaro," he said. "Come on, come on—hurry up—pack your horn."

I was speechless. I was scared out of my wits. But you never saw a kid pack an instrument into a case as fast as I did.

At the Cinderella Ballroom, Cavallaro's band was just finishing its last dance set of the evening. Hearing that much, I was even more scared, if that's possible, for, heard up close, these musicians seemed to me to be the absolute pinnacle of professional perfection. Most of them were men of twenty-five to thirty. And to me, the ease with which they handled their instruments, the completely relaxed manner in which they all went about their business up there on the bandstand—all this was simply too much. It was frightening.

I stood over to one side, gaping at them, until they were through. After they finished and straggled off the bandstand I waited around, not knowing what to do with myself. I was panic-stricken at the thought of having to go up on the same bandstand with such musicians as these.

Presently, my "discoverer" came back, and a few seconds later we were joined by Cavallaro himself. At that time Johnny Cavallaro must have been in his late thirties, which seemed to me pretty elderly for a musician—for I had just turned fifteen. He was rather stout and very dark-skinned, with jet-black hair and a gleaming white grin.

We were introduced by my sponsor—although introduced is hardly the word. What Yudkin said was, "Here's the kid I told you about, John."

I was staring at Cavallaro as if he were some sort of supernatural phenomenon—which indeed, to me at that moment, he was.

He grinned at me and said, "Hello, kid." His manner was completely casual. He didn't seem to realize that this was probably the most momentous occasion of my entire life.

I mumbled some reply, and he chatted with Yudkin and me for a moment. Then, suddenly becoming brisk and businesslike, he turned and said, "Well—you all set?"

"I—uh—guess so."

"O.K. Get out your horn and let's go." While he called the musicians together, I hurriedly unpacked my saxophone and awkwardly climbed up onto the bandstand.

Since Cavallaro played banjo and never led his own band, Si Byers, the fiddle player, acted as conductor-leader. Byers called out a tune now. As the rest of the men got out their parts, they glanced over at me with amused curiosity. Nobody bothered with any introductions. I fumbled around in the pile of saxophone parts trying to find my part for the tune Byers had called out, but I was so numb that my fingers would scarcely work. Eventually Byers himself helped me find it and spread it out on my music stand. I stared at it, hardly seeing it.

Actually it was nothing but a stock arrangement—the kind of simple printed orchestration put out by publishers of popular music in order to get their songs played by bands which cannot afford their own arrangers. But to me, at that moment, it looked formidable enough to spell out the word "doom" rather than whatever the title of the tune was.

The plain truth is that, although I had learned something about playing my instrument and had even begun to develop a fair degree of improvisational skill, no one had ever bothered to inform me that I should also try to learn something about sight-reading. In the amateur groups I'd been playing with there had never been any necessity for it, since none of the other members of these groups could read at sight either. Our method had always been to go over and over our parts, even with the simplest stock arrangement, until we were all familiar enough with them to try putting them together. If any of us had ever had to sit down cold and play some piece he had never seen before, the result would have been something pretty fearful.

And "fearful" is a good enough description for the result of this first attempt of mine to read a piece of music at sight. Naturally, I couldn't make it at all. After the first few bars I was hopelessly lost. I floundered along, trying to fake my way through, but it was no use. The rest of the men were so embarrassed for me that they didn't look up from their parts. Somewhere in the middle of the first chorus Byers stopped us. He asked me if I'd like to try it again, but I knew it was out of the question. I shook my head. I felt terrible.

The men were all quite nice about it. No one made any comment at all. But it was plain that Cavallaro, who had been standing down in front of the bandstand, had already begun to lose interest. I couldn't blame him. I was ready to call it quits myself.

However, my friend Yudkin was not willing to give up. I suppose, as the fellow who had brought me there in the first place, he felt involved. He spoke up and told Cavallaro that as long as we were all there he might just as well get some idea of how I played when I was on my own. "What the hell, John," he concluded optimistically, "the kid can always learn how to read, can't he? Why don't you listen to him play some jazz?"

"All right," Cavallaro finally said. "What do you want to play, kid?"

I named some tune and, without a word, the piano player went into a short introduction—four bars or so. The drummer and bass player fell in with him. This time, although I was still plenty scared, I was on familiar ground.

I played three or four choruses in a row, and by that time I guess I must have been going along pretty good, or anyway not too bad, for some of the men in the band, who were not playing, began looking over at me with approval. Cavallaro himself was staring intently at Byers, as if to try to get his reaction. I went through most of my little home-made bag of tricks and, while it may not have been right up there with the best examples of *le jazz hot* being produced in that pre-Swing era, nevertheless, after I finished, I saw Byers give a slight nod in Cavallaro's direction. Yudkin, too, seemed to be quite happy about the whole thing. He stood there looking from me to Cavallaro, grinning all over his face as if to say, "See what I mean?"

When we were all through, the rest of the musicians got off the bandstand and began to wander off, smoking and talking among themselves. No one said anything to me. I got off the bandstand and started to pack my saxophone in its case. Out of the corner of my eye I could see Cavallaro talking to Yudkin, who seemed to be arguing with him about something. I couldn't tell what they were talking about, for they were off at the other end of the bandstand. After a while, about the time I had finished putting my instrument away and closing the case, they both came over to where I waited apprehensively to hear what decision had been made.

"Well, kid," said Cavallaro, "I think I could use you all right —but first you'll have to learn to read. . . . Think you can do it?"

I could hardly believe what I was hearing. "You mean you'll put me in your band if I learn to read?"

"That's right," he nodded.

"Boy, oh boy!" I burst out. "Just give me a month or so, will you, Mr. Cavallaro? Will that be quick enough?"

He gave me that grin of his. "Think you can do it that fast, hey?"

That *fast?* Was he crazy? To get into that band, I'd have been ready to learn to do a standing-sitting-one-and-a-half-with-a-triple-twist from the top of the Cinderella Ballroom roof into a thimble of sawdust! That *fast?* A whole month?

"Just you wait and see," I said. "I'll be back in a month, don't forget."

I grabbed my saxophone case, tore out of there, and ran like crazy all the way home. . . .

I don't know quite how I did it. All I know is, that if I had worked hard before that, from now on I went at it like a little demon. And in just about one month from that night I again presented myself at the Cinderella Ballroom.

This time I made it.

Next day Cavallaro took me over to the local headquarters of the musicians' union, where I went through my formal examination and found that it was fairly easy stuff after all. Cavallaro then advanced me the initiation fee and in a few minutes they handed me my brand-new union card. The next thing I had to do was to get outfitted. The band wore dinner jackets at work—although anyone who ever called a "tuxedo" a dinner jacket around that band would undoubtedly have been brained on the spot—so I had to get one of those, too. My first tuxedo was a number we picked up for twelve-fifty in a second-hand clothing store. It could hardly be said to have fitted me very well, and it had a bit of a shine here and there, around the back of the coat and the seat of the pants. But to me it looked breath-takingly beautiful. For not only was it my first tuxedo but it was my first pair of long trousers as well.

I was a professional musician. . . .

*"The chief wonder of education is that it does not ruin every-
body concerned with it, teachers and taught."*

HENRY ADAMS

Chapter Eleven

AT THIS POINT I ran into a fairly big snag—the little matter
of my High School education. I was now earning between
thirty and forty dollars weekly on the Cinderella Ballroom job
alone. And occasionally, when the band went out of town to
play at some nearby college or fraternity dance, I got as much
as fifteen dollars a night. To me as a kid of fifteen it seemed
a pretty large sum for doing something I would have been delighted to do for nothing!

However, I was staying up till two or three in the morning
some three or four nights a week, and the net result was that I
had to do most of my sleeping at school.

During the next few months I suppose I *must* have heard my
various teachers say a few words now and then. It is even possible that I may have soaked up some small amount of "education" through the process of osmosis. I have a hazy memory of
sitting dazedly through classes in French, Latin, Geometry,
Ancient History, and so on. The one thing I remember most
distinctly, though, is the amazingly soporific effect of the voices
of my various would-be instructors.

Obviously, there was no way of keeping up with both my
music *and* my schooling. I was ready to quit high school right
then and there. My mother, however, would not hear of it.

For a while I tried to oblige her by continuing to attend classes; but within a few months it got to the point where I would walk into a classroom, sit down at my desk, and almost immediately doze off. Given these circumstances, it is pretty obvious that I was unable to learn very much.

The fact is, the whole idea of high school seemed to me about as remote from what I did want to learn as anything I could imagine. Who had ever heard of a professional musician, a fellow earning as much as forty dollars a week, going to high school and studying Cicero? Of all the preposterous ideas!

In the end I worked out a simple resolution to this conflict. Actually, it pretty much worked itself out for me. All I had to do was to get the lowest possible grades in every subject I was supposed to be studying. This feat had to be accomplished for two months running, after which there was nothing further for me to do in the matter. According to a rule of Hillhouse High School in those days (and a damn fine rule it seemed to me at the time), after such a brilliant scholastic performance, the authorities were forced to request my resignation from their educational program.

I was only too glad to comply, but my mother would not have it. She was a small dark-haired woman with lively brown eyes and a ready smile, but she could be quite forceful when she had to be. When she heard about this sudden lack of interest in my academic future on the part of the New Haven High School authorities, she marched me right back into the office of the principal himself, and, after several minutes of her eloquence, it was decided I should be given "another chance."

There was nothing I wanted less on earth. But I had to go back once more to Cicero, *et al.*

All it meant, of course, was one more wasted month. For this time when I received the same remarkably low grades, I was really out. And this time even my mother, indomitable woman that she was, had to accept this state of affairs.

From then on there was nothing to prevent me from pursu-

ing the only education I was at all interested in. I could practice all day long and play all night long, if that was what I
wanted to do. And that was what I did want to do. You never
saw a kid go at anything in your life the way I went at that
horn of mine; and, although I can't say how much "natural
talent" went into all this work, somehow I kept improving.
Also, about this same time I bought myself another instrument,
a straight-model soprano saxophone, built along the lines of a
clarinet but played just like any other saxophone. On my new
job it became necessary for me to "double" and since I could
not play the clarinet, this soprano saxophone was the next best
thing.

That gave me something else to work on. As I say, there was
no fundamental difference between this new instrument and
the one I already had—at least not so far as the fingering was
concerned. However, this one had a smaller mouthpiece and
reed, and therefore, required a slightly different *embouchure*.
Eventually, I learned how to handle the new addition to my
little arsenal, and I was all set for a while.

Around this time I began to get jobs now and then with
other professional bands around town besides Cavallaro's.
There was Eddie Wittstein, who booked pick-up bands on what
was called "society work." There were the Yale Collegians,
a fairly good little college dance band, who were not above hiring an occasional outside, professional, noncollegiate "ringer"
like myself. The Collegians were headed by a fellow named
Les Laden, and included another saxophone player named
Rudy Vallee. With this sort of occasional job, as well as my
steady work with Cavallaro's orchestra, I kept pretty busy
during that fall and winter, managed to make a fair weekly
sum of money, and traveled all over New England.

Meanwhile I was painfully acquiring the beginnings of another and totally different kind of education, some of it having
very little to do with music but quite a bit to do with growing
up, or at least learning how to handle the problems of a fifteen-

year-old working on a more or less equal economic basis with a group of older men.

I eventually picked up a certain amount of worldly wisdom— or what passed for it with these guys—mostly through hazing and crude practical joking, for which I was a fairly natural butt. Generally this sort of thing would take place in the car we all went in on the way to some out-of-town job.

One of the men would say to Cavallaro, whose car it was and who did all the driving on these jaunts, "Say, John, when are we working at Webb Inn?"

John would make some vague answer and then there would be a spirited discussion as to whether that was the right night or not. I would begin to worry about why I had not been informed about this particular job. After a while, some of the men would begin to expatiate on the beauties of this place, this "Webb Inn"—and I would ask, "Where *is* Webb Inn?"

At which everyone in the car would join in a loud chorus, "Up the spider's ass!" General hilarity invariably followed.

There were numerous variations on this meager theme. Such as Egg Road Inn—which, of course, turned out, on inquiry, to be "up the chicken's ass." It took me quite a while to learn to keep my mouth shut and never ask questions about anything that did not directly and immediately concern me—and even at that I still kept on putting my foot into it for some time.

This hazing was by no means confined to the car. There were several times on the bandstand when I became the victim of another, and to me far more humiliating, type of humor.

For instance, I have already mentioned that I had begun to develop a little style of improvisation of my own, largely eclectic. However, in jazz music there are certain things that are not done. These have nothing to do with skill or technique, but come under the head of "corn," a vaguely defined but distinctly recognizable way of playing. At that stage it was only natural that some of the musical tricks I picked up should turn out to be pretty bad. The result was a good bit of humor for everyone concerned except myself.

There was one phrase in particular, that I had picked up from some record I had heard, which I used to fit in here and there whenever I was giving out with a bit of *ad lib* playing. Every time I played it I would notice the rest of the men in the band eying each other with a peculiar look on their faces, as if I had just done something pretty damn clever. I was convinced I was giving them quite a kick, so for some weeks I continued to sneak this phrase in wherever I could. Until one night Si Byers, the fiddle player who stood in front of the band, turned on me as I went into the phrase, and snarled, "For Christ's sake, cut out that corn, will you?"

For the first time I realized why the others had looked that way whenever I'd played that bit. Apparently Byers had been in on it all the time too, but that night he must have been just plain tired of the joke.

I managed somehow to keep from bursting into tears of rage and humiliation, and, of course I never did play that particular phrase again. But there were a number of such lessons to learn, and in the course of learning to distinguish the differences between what is jazz and what is "corn," I had to learn also how to keep my feelings to myself. The one thing I knew for sure was that, so far as any of these older colleagues of mine were concerned, anger or tears would have been just about the biggest joke of all.

I don't mean to sound as if I now have any bitterness toward any of those fellows. I don't at all. But at the time it was going on I felt pretty awful about it. Looking back at it now, of course, it's hard to blame them. They meant no real harm. They were only amusing themselves and I guess I was a pretty amusing kid to have around. Anyway, one way or the other, through all this stuff, I began to learn a little about what was what.

And with it all I was also beginning to acquire the only real "talent" I know anything about—the talent for self-discipline. In one way at least, the humiliation that followed anything silly I did, either musically or otherwise, acted as a painful but terribly effective brake on any tendencies I might have had to let things slide and go along as I was. It also gave me a strong competitive drive, a terribly urgent need to keep working at what I was doing until I simply *had* to learn something about it. All my early out-group conditioning, plus this direct competition with older and more experienced men, combined to channelize all my waking (and perhaps even some sleeping) energies into an overwhelming need to prove my validity, to be accepted on the basis of my skills. What else could I do as a fifteen-year-old thrown into contact with these older men for most of my time?

As I think about it now, it must have been a very lonesome life I was leading in those days. However, since I had already developed the introspective set I have already spoken about, it didn't bother me as much as you might imagine. I had a lot to learn, I was busy learning it as fast as I could, and as for the rest—well, I guess I just didn't think about it very much.

Nevertheless, it must have had its effect on me, whether I let myself become aware of it or not; for otherwise what happened next couldn't have happened.

During that first year after I had joined Cavallaro's band, we went off to Bantam Lake, a small summer resort near Litchfield, Connecticut, where we were to work for the entire season, playing six nights weekly at the little dance hall jutting out into the lake. Here the first of a series of stormy episodes with my employer took place.

On this particular occasion, one of the men in Cavallaro's band decided it would be a good idea to teach me something about the manly art of boozing. Up to that point I had never tasted any liquor.

There were only seven men in the band and we all shared a pretty good-sized cottage. Since I was the junior member of the outfit I had to sleep on a cot in the living room. One Sunday afternoon, a few of my co-workers were sitting around the living room with a bottle of Prohibition rye and a case of home-made beer. They were apparently settling down for a nice quiet Sunday afternoon of gentlemanly boozing. Having no special interest in that particular form of recreation, I decided to go over to the dance hall where I kept my instruments, and do a spot of practicing. In the beginning I had tried to do this in the cottage but the others had raised a big stink about the noise.

As I started to leave, one of the men called over to me, "Hey, how's about having a shot, kid?" He was grinning and holding out the bottle of rye. I tried to make some excuse to get out of this awkward situation, but in a moment the others started ribbing me. Suddenly I decided to show these guys I was not such a baby as they seemed to think I was. I made up my mind to prove right then and there that I could handle a drink as well as the next guy, and force them to let up on me for a while.

They were drinking "boilermakers." I gulped my rye down and chased it with a big slug of beer, the way they were doing. After that I guess I had a few more but I can't remember exactly what happened, for shortly afterwards I must have passed out.

That was the end of me for that day.

Cavallaro was away that afternoon and apparently didn't even come back to the cottage before going to work. No one else bothered to wake me. When I finally did come to, it was dark outside. For a few seconds I had no idea where I was. I got to my feet in a daze and hunted around the cottage to see if I could find anyone. Then I looked at the clock and my heart almost stopped beating. Nine-thirty!

That meant the band had already been at work for an hour and a half!

I lost my head and began to run barefooted down the cinder

road toward the dance hall. All I had on was the bright red bathing-suit I had been wearing when I came into the cottage that afternoon. But I wasn't thinking of anything but getting up on that bandstand as fast as I could.

On Sunday nights a movie was shown, beginning at eight o'clock and generally ending around nine-thirty. Then there would be a short intermission, long enough to clear the benches from the dance floor, after which the dancing would begin immediately and continue till twelve-thirty, which was Sunday night closing time. During the movie the orchestra would play quietly, just enough to kill the sound of the projector and lend some sense of underscoring to the movie itself. For those were the days before movies became audible.

I finally arrived at the dance hall, all out of breath. To my great relief I saw that the movie had not ended yet and that the place was consequently still in semidarkness. I stealthily threaded my way through the audience, climbed onto the bandstand, took up my saxophone, and got ready to bluff it through somehow. I hoped I might get away with no more than a mild reprimand from Cavallaro. I was sure that when he heard the full story of how I had come to oversleep, he would bawl out the guys who had been responsible, and I would be forgiven.

When the lights went on at the end of the movie, and Cavallaro got his first look at me, there I was, all dressed up in that wild getup. His eyes popped. Then he let out a howl of rage.

During the roar of laughter that went up, first on the bandstand, and soon spreading out over the whole dance hall, he grabbed his banjo like a huge club and came after me. With him chasing me, I tore across the dance floor, ducking between customers and hurdling benches all the way out the door, while he brandished his banjo over his head and threatened loudly to smash it over mine if he ever caught up with me. I have no doubt he would have kept his word if he had been able to, but luckily I was a fleetfooted kid. I managed to keep out of his reach until I got out to the end of the short pier alongside the dance hall. At that point I had no other recourse but to hop into one of the rental rowboats, swiftly cast off, and drift a few yards offshore. From there I pleaded as eloquently as I could that it hadn't been entirely my fault.

No use. He raved on like a crazy man for a while; but finally, apparently not quite mad enough to take the risk of throwing his banjo at me and having the thing fall into the lake, he went cursing back to the ballroom. Eventually I got back to the pier without oars, but for the rest of the night I carefully stayed out of Cavallaro's sight.

I don't remember where I slept that night. Certainly not at the cottage, where he could have got hold of me. The next day, when I came back after having given him what I considered sufficient time to have heard the whole story and cooled off a bit, I was informed that I was through, fired, *kaput.*

Nothing I could say or do would make him change his mind. I pleaded and begged, but with no effect at all. He told me, some months later, that he had only been trying to give me a little scare. However, I had no way of knowing that at the time. I was so filled with a sense of blind outrage when none of my colleagues would bear out my assertion that they had been partially at fault in getting me drunk in the first place that, acting out of fear of Cavallaro and anger at having been made the victim of an injustice, I accepted my dismissal and made it stick by running off.

In fact, by the time I stopped running, I had covered quite a distance. All the way from Bantam Lake, Connecticut, to Lexington, Kentucky, then part of the way down through Florida by way of Tennessee and Georgia, and finally, at long last, back home to New Haven again. This was only the first of many such professional Grand Tours I was to make as I grew up in this business I had somehow got into at an age when most kids are just going through the painful-enough experiences of the average adolescent and trying to fit themselves for some sort of "normal" life.

The one thing I am positive about is that any kind of "normal" life was just about the furthest thing from my thoughts at that stage—whatever the phrase "normal life" might have meant to me anyway.

All I know is that I was running like mad, not only away from "normal life" but from everything connected with the only life I had ever lived or known about. Whatever I may have been like at the tender age of fifteen—I don't believe the word "normal" would cover it. . . .

"I wonder . . . whether it is possible for an individual who has never had a problem—if there are any individuals like that— to have any significant insight into the problems of individuals who do have serious problems."

Chapter Twelve

WE NOW COME TO A PART of my story I would be glad to skip over entirely. However, since it had a direct influence on almost everything that has taken place in my life from that time on, it is important that I include it. Anyway, I now realize that, given the particular environmental forces that had shaped me into what I had become at fifteen, it would have been impossible for me to have behaved in any other way than I did.

Anyone who lives in an abnormal way will inevitably develop abnormal attitudes—until he arrives at a clear enough evaluation of the nature of his conditioning to enable him to substitute healthy attitudes for his original unhealthy ones.

In other words, a healthy person will react healthily—that is, to the best of his ability to effect the best possible solution to a given problem or set of problems.

So far, good enough. But what is the most effective way to deal with problems?

Here we're up against a fairly big question; and in the scope of the kind of story I'm trying to write here it can only be gone into rather superficially. I think it may be enough to say, though, that the most effective way is that which helps us to avoid pain. Not to avoid pain at *any* costs, but certainly to avoid it whenever pain in itself cannot help *to accomplish anything worthwhile* in terms of our own good or in terms of social good.

Anyone will agree that adult behavior is socially preferable to childish behavior. Well, what constitutes adult behavior in a given problem situation?

An adult meets a painful situation unlike a child, in that he examines it carefully, not only in terms of his past experiences with similar situations, but as a *new* experience demanding, possibly, new solutions. He then decides whether or not it is alterable, either in part or in totality. If it is, he proceeds to alter it to whatever degree he is capable. If it is *in*alterable, or at any rate inalterable in terms of the person confronted with it, he must learn how to skirt it or live with it in such a way as to derive the minimum amount of pain and guilt.

Now, I don't want to fall into the trap that all this can easily lead us into. I do *not* mean that the avoiding of pain should be used as a rationale to excuse a man from facing any painful situation at all. Too many of us are only too willing to find such convenient rationales, and I'm certain that this is at the bottom of ninety-nine hundredths of the misery and maladjustment we're surrounded by nowadays.

In other words, only after a situation is *clearly and honestly found to be inalterable* has an adult *the moral right to avoid it* or skirt it with the minimum of pain and guilt.

Now, there is little doubt that at fifteen I did *not* behave in an adult manner regarding my own attempt to deal with what had become for me a painful problem. But just in passing, and just in the event that you may be inclined to be overharsh in your judgments or evaluations of the way I behaved —let me make this one last statement before I go on with my story.

All this may sound easy. All I can tell you is that if you are an adult, and can do it, even most of the time, let alone all the time—well, you're a rare individual indeed. Personally, I'm just *beginning* to learn how to do it, and even at that I miss by a mile a good part of the time. However, I keep practicing, just as I once kept practicing on a saxophone, and I suppose if I keep on working at it long enough I'll eventually show some improvement in this matter of becoming an adult myself.

Anyway, let's see how this whole preamble applies to what I started to tell about.

Well, right here we come to a matter I've already discussed—the question of Jewishness and some of the problems a Jewish kid can run into on that score.

Earlier, I told how, at the age of seven, I was troubled by the painful situation of being relegated to the out-group. I also told how I felt when I realized that I could do nothing about it even after I grew up. At the age of fifteen, I was still unable to accept this situation; and I was completely and utterly unwilling to live with a kind of pain which was, after all, not of my choosing. So I decided to skirt it.

Not, however, without a good deal of guilt. In fact, I carried this guilt around inside of myself for a great many years, until it eventually began to permeate everything that happened to me, in such a way as to make it impossible for me to enjoy whatever success I was later to achieve.

At fifteen, though, I could have no idea of all these consequences. All I could do was to act on what I rationalized for myself as the necessities for getting ahead in the profession I had chosen.

The first thing that I told myself had to be corrected was my name. It was too long. It was unwieldy. Nobody could pronounce it. No one seemed to be able to remember it, even. Besides, what was the sense of going around with a monicker like that, when it would be so easy to change it to something easier to spell and pronounce? Why remain Arthur Arshawsky? Why not change it to a shorter name?

The one thing I never even allowed myself to think about at all was, of course, the really basic reason I wanted to change it.

That's right—I was ashamed of my name. Not only that, I was ashamed of being a Jew. There you have it. And it's only because I am no longer ashamed, no longer ashamed of being Jewish, *and no longer even ashamed of having been ashamed,* that I can speak about it now, after having buried it away for so many years.

I believe I can now be objective. But it took me a long time to arrive at the point where I could face this problem and deal with it realistically. And before I arrived at that point, I can only tell you that by then I had gone so far off the track that it's a wonder I was ever able to grope my way back again, and learn to deal with the pain of that one guilt so that it no longer exists as real pain but only as a sort of sense-memory of pain. In other words, as I said earlier, there is still a scar, and even an occasional twinge—but at least I have learned how to live with these souvenirs and try to make as valid a life for myself, in spite of them, as the disease which originally caused them will allow.

For the only thing a fellow can try to do when he has to live around a form of mental disease and be constantly exposed to it, is to try to maintain as much health as he can in himself. He's going to have a pretty rough time, and you might even say he would be more comfortable if he went a little off his rocker himself; but since he can't *will* himself insane he will eventually have to accept the situation and deal with it *as sanely as possible.*

That's pretty well where I stand today in respect to the whole matter of Jewishness and the manner in which this "category" is regarded by a great many of the insane people who exist outside of mental institutions and who—simply because they are outside—believe they are sane.

And so, having come at long last round Robin's barn—

Exit Arthur Arshawsky. Actually, as I was named by the rabbi who performed the minor operation all male Jewish babies are forced to undergo, my real first and middle names, translated directly from Hebrew into English, are Abraham Isaac—but for some reason my mother decided to give me the name Arthur. So perhaps it would be more correct to say, "Exit Abraham Isaac Arshawsky."

In any case, exit the Arshawsky boy.

Enter Art Shaw!

You see, of course, how simple this little transformation was. Presto, Change-o! A new name, a new personality. As simple as that.

What makes the new personality? Well, take a good look at both those names. On the one hand Arthur—or Abraham Isaac—Arshawsky; on the other, Art Shaw. Then ask yourself whether a fellow named Art Shaw could possibly grow up to be "the same" as another kid named Arthur Arshawsky, or Abraham Isaac Arshawsky. I think you'll see quite a difference in predictability. For the latter is obviously a Jewish kid, or at any rate some kind of a "foreigner," wouldn't you say?

As for this new kid we'll be dealing with from here on— let's see now. . . . Art Shaw. Doesn't *sound* very "foreign." Certainly doesn't sound much like a Jewish kid either, does it?

Well, what's he look like, maybe we can tell something that way? Dark hair, dark brown eyes, fairly regular features— could be almost anything, almost any nationality, Spanish, Italian, French, Russian, Greek, Armenian, damn near anything at all. Could be he's a mixture of a bit of every one of those. In short, an American kid—may as well let it go at that. Although Shaw *sounds* Irish, wouldn't you say? Or maybe English? Anyway, what difference does it make? At least he's not a Jew or a "foreigner," so that's all right.

Or is it?

Well, let's take a look and see. . . .

*". . . until their survival as a people is an assured fact, no person
of Jewish origin is spiritually free to disclaim his Jewishness.
He simply cannot make a free choice. For one thing, non-
Jewish elements will not permit him to do so; but, more important, his own conscience will not sanction such a choice."*

CAREY MC WILLIAMS

Chapter Thirteen

AT THE TIME WHEN I, or rather this Art Shaw kid who was
now beginning to masquerade as me, received my summary
discharge from Cavallaro's band, there were a bunch of fellows up in that vicinity who had banded together to try to
form an orchestra. Their idea was to work their way down to
Lexington, Kentucky, where there was supposed to be a job
waiting for them at a dance hall named—where in hell *do* they
get names for these joints?—the Joyland Casino. I had already
spotted some of these kids standing in front of the bandstand at the Bantam Lake dance hall and although I didn't
know any of them I was pretty sure, from the way they acted,
that they were either musicians themselves or fellows who
knew something about music.

In those days bands didn't as a rule have people crowding
around the bandstand as they did later on, especially during
the peak of the Swing Era. And mostly, when anyone *did* take
the trouble to stand for hours on end listening to a dance
band, the chances were, usually, that he had something to do
with music himself.

At any rate, the night after I was fired I went over to the dance hall and stood around rather disconsolately, listening to the band and making invidious comparisons between myself and the new saxophone player who had taken my place. About an hour after the band had started, I noticed some of these kids come in and go over to the bandstand as usual. Sometime later on, one of them spotted me and came over to ask me how come I wasn't playing that night.

I told him I'd been fired. He seemed quite excited to hear it. By the time intermission came around, he had brought the rest of them over, introduced them and himself, and asked me if I would be interested in joining their band. I was only too happy to hear more about it. By the end of the evening we were good friends. And since there was now nothing to hold me, I packed my clothes and instruments into the rear seat of their old jalopy, crowded in with the four of them who were there that night, and, bidding a none-too-sad farewell to the band cottage where I had been living for the last month or so, made a fast getaway.

That turned out to be the beginning of a frantic, but fortunately brief, interlude in my budding professional career. This outfit was almost as amateurish as the little Peter Pan group I described earlier, and couldn't begin to compare musically with Cavallaro's band. Nevertheless they had two distinct advantages over either of the other outfits. Unlike the Peter Pan group, these boys were at least sufficient in numbers to make up in sheer volume what they lacked in musical ability. And as compared with Cavallaro's band, where everybody else had been practically old enough to be my father, here was a band made up of kids somewhat older, but not actually enough to make any great difference. The oldest one, in fact, was around eighteen and, since I lied about my age and told them I was sixteen, that wasn't any difference to speak of.

However, before I got through with this bunch of kids, I had done more than lie about my age. I found, after a couple of days, that there were a number of them who had no great love for Jews. On learning that, I behaved automatically and compulsively: I said nothing about being Jewish myself. Not only that, but later on, when something turned the attention of some of my new companions to the question of what my own "nationality" was, I lied. I don't remember all the particulars, and perhaps that's because I don't specially like reliving this preposterous attempt to run away from myself, or that part of myself which I had been taught to believe was unacceptable to the world. Anyway, I got away with it. There was really no way for anybody to prove me a liar, so it was finally dropped.

For the rest of the time I stayed with them—which was right up to the bitter end—I was a gentile. I lived with them as one, my name was as Anglo-Saxon as any one of theirs, and in the end I almost came to believe I *was* one. Almost, I say, but never quite all the way. For there was always an underlying sense of guilt. There were periods when I could *almost* forget it—and there may even have been some periods when I momentarily did—but always, sooner or later, it came back to me in one way or another.

In fact, that guilt was the one thing that spoiled an otherwise almost perfect Utopia.

We called ourselves the Kentuckians, in anticipation of the locale where we expected to settle down and work and live happily ever after. During the first few weeks after I got together with them, we all lived together up in the woods near a little hamlet named Northfield, Connecticut. We slept on broken-down army cots and pallets, in an old barn near a little creek with a swimming hole, and subsisted for the most part on a diet of ham sandwiches and soda pop. None of us suffered any from this semi-pellagra diet, for we were all young and healthy and high-spirited. We rehearsed every afternoon, and after several days I had become more or less the unspoken leader of the band, by virtue of my professional experience, which, although still nothing much to brag about, was far more than any of the others had to offer.

We managed to pick up a few sporadic jobs at nearby summer resort dance halls. Finally we all set off in two old rattle-trap jalopies. After a series of minor mishaps, including endless tire-changes and filling of leaky radiators, we wound up in Lexington, Kentucky.

In order to get there at all, I had actually run away from home. I had not told my mother anything about leaving; and by the time she learned about my being fired by Cavallaro it was too late for her to do anything about it. No one knew where I was, certainly not Cavallaro. So now I was on my own for the first time.

But within one week after opening at the Joyland Casino, we found there was little joy connected with it for any of us. One night we showed up for work as usual and found the doors locked and the place deserted. That's all there was to it. The joint simply folded and to this day I don't know what happened (although the "music" we played in the few nights we were there *may* have had a good bit to do with the fact that practically nobody ever showed up except ourselves).

Now since I had run away from home without letting my mother know where I was going, for fear of her trying to stop me in some way, I was too proud to give up and admit I had been wrong to take matters into my own hands the way I had. I wouldn't write home for money, so I had no way to get back.

None of the other members of the band had any scruples about writing home. One at a time they drifted back to wherever they had originally come from. In the end the last one had gone.

I was stranded.

I soon ran out of what little money I had, and had to move out of the rooming house where I had stayed. For a week or so I slept in the open, wherever I could keep out of sight.

During the days I tried various dodges. But nothing seemed to work. Finally I had to hock my instruments so I could eat. Eventually that money gave out too, and after a couple of days I got pretty damn hungry.

By now I was beginning to look like a particularly haggard beachcomber. I had begun to take on a rather intense and sad-eyed look anyway. I have a couple of pictures of myself taken about that time, and the only description of my expression during those days that seems to sound right, is that I looked *driven.* Well, I *was* driven, by all those guilts and fears and compulsions I have already told about. On top of that, I hadn't had any clean laundry for over a week, my shirts had been turned inside-out to keep the dirty parts from showing, until finally *both* sides had become so dirty that it made no difference which side was out, and now, having been forced to go without eating for a couple of days—well, I must have been quite a sight.

What I finally did was to walk into a restaurant and order a meal. I still remember it with great vividness—breaded veal cutlet, mashed potatoes with brown gravy, rice pudding, and coffee. I gulped it down ravenously, and then calmly announced to the cashier that I had no money to pay for it.

The proprietor seemed curiously unenthusiastic about my particular type of patronage. He let out a howl of indignation, and promptly put me to work at the traditional job for this sort of petty larceny. For the rest of that afternoon and evening I washed dishes.

Before I was through I had managed to scrounge another meal out of it; but the next day when I went back to see if I could get my temporary job put on a more permanent basis, the proprietor took one look at me, hollered bloody murder, and told me to get out and stay out before he called the cops.

I then pulled the same gag, but with a slightly different

menu, in another restaurant. Same result. I continued this
for a few days in different eating places, but always wound
up with what appeared to be the same pile of dishes to
work my way through. Toward the end I began to get fairly
tired of this type of work.

However, my luck changed. About that time a band came
through Lexington for a one-night stand, and I managed
to get into the Hotel Lafayette Ballroom, where the dance
was being held. I have forgotten the name of the leader of
this little territory outfit. It wasn't much of a band. It was
made up of young kids who only played during the summer
and then went back to school or their regular jobs, but the
leader was a fellow who seemed to be able to get them
enough work to keep things together. I collared him during
an intermission, and somehow persuaded him to let me sit
in with the band for one set. I used one of the other men's
instruments, since mine were still in hock. Next day the
leader advanced me enough money to get my own horns
back and join his band.

We left town that afternoon. I worked my way down
through Kentucky and into Georgia with this outfit. The
whole episode is now rather blurred in my memory, but I
seem to remember one night when, during the dance, some
mountaineer lads decided to start a feud right then and there
in the middle of the dance floor. Along with several other
terrified members of the band, I took refuge behind the old
upright piano, where we cowered until the affair wound
itself up. This ought to give some idea of the type of engagements we played.

But the boys in that band were damn nice guys, as I
remember them, and I stayed with them for several weeks.
By that time I had scraped together enough money to pay
back what it had cost to get my instruments back. As soon
as I saved up enough more for fare to New Haven, I quit

the band in some little town in Florida, near Sarasota, and took a bus back home.

Once home in New Haven I made a Hail-the-Conquering-Hero entrance. As far as my mother could tell from the little I had written, I had been covering myself with glory. Of course, I had to do some plain and fancy lying to explain why, after all the wonderful things I had described in my letters, I was arriving home flat broke. I got away with it, though; at least, she let me think I did. So my status at home had not suffered because of my hinterland hegira.

I must have been pretty goddamn insufferable at that time. I had begun to consider myself not only a professional musician, and (in private only, of course) somewhat of a gentile, but also a grown-up man. By way of consolidating my position in the household as a grown-up, I one day broke out a pack of cigarettes and calmly lit one right in front of my horrified mother. For one of the few times in her life she was completely speechless; until I started inhaling deeply and nonchalantly blowing the smoke out through my nose—a little trick I had picked up during my trek through the Deep South—at which point she raised quite a fuss. In the end, though, she had to bow to the inevitable. No matter what anyone else might think about my being only fifteen years old, I was damn well convinced I was an adult, and furthermore, I was damn well going to act like one or drop dead trying. Frankly, it's a wonder I didn't. Also, maybe a shame. . . .

By now it was the end of summer. One day I got a phone call from Cavallaro, who by this time had cooled down sufficiently to let bygones be bygones. He was going down to Miami with his band for the winter season and offered me the job. I accepted, but there was one minor hitch connected with it. I didn't feel it worth mentioning at the time; for it might have meant losing the job. So I said nothing at all.

This was the trivial matter of my having to be able to play enough clarinet to double on it. Sooner or later, if a fellow wants to play saxophone professionally, this is a standard requirement. I had never owned a clarinet, and I hadn't the slightest idea of how to play one. By then, though, I was feeling my oats enough to consider this nothing more than a relatively unimportant matter, easily overcome. The thing to do, I felt, was to get the job first, and after that I could get hold of a clarinet and somehow learn to play it.

I finally did get hold of one of these complicated little wooden pipes. I bought it for thirty bucks from a guy who had apparently had his own difficulties with it and was understandably anxious to get rid of it once and for all. I took the thing home, and there, to my amazement, found that, although it had a mouthpiece and a reed not too unlike my soprano saxophone, and keys that pressed down in a somewhat similar way, there was no further resemblance between the two instruments. For the three or four days before I was due to leave town with Cavallaro's band, I fooled around with this new problem; but the results were practically nil.

We finally left town for New York in Cavallaro's old car. From there we took the boat to Jacksonville. On the way down, in between bouts of seasickness, I somehow managed to figure out a method of producing a few heart-rending squeaks and squeals on the baffling new addition to my growing arsenal of musical weapons (for by now I had also acquired still *another* saxophone, a baritone, this one almost as large as myself, but presenting no great new hurdles, since aside from its size it was the same as any 'other member of the saxophone family).

By the time we arrived at Jacksonville I had accomplished two things. The first was to drive everybody on board the luckless vessel absolutely out of his or her mind; and the second was that by dint of making these curious sounds on the clarinet over and over and over, I had got to the point where I was reasonably sure of being able to repeat them more or less at will, for whatever they might be worth— and as to that, I wasn't going to think about it until I had to. Once, Cavallaro overheard me and asked me if I was *sure* I could play clarinet. I told him I'd only been kidding around, of course I could. How he was ever able to swallow *that*, I'll never know, but he did.

At Jacksonville, we all set out in the car once more, and from then until we arrived in Miami, I had no further opportunity of establishing a more intimate relationship with my clarinet. So I philosophically resigned myself to meeting and dealing with whatever storms I might encounter at such time as they might burst on my confused head.

"Burst" is right. For if Cavallaro had been sore at me last summer, over the red bathing-suit *affaire*, this time his wrath reached majestic and downright Jovian proportions. He had always been, as I have already shown, a hot-tempered man. As a rule, his fits of anger blew themselves out after one quick violent explosion. Which was just as well for him, for no one could have endured a long-protracted spasm of the sort of rage he gave way to on occasion. Still, this one time, when I picked up my clarinet during our first rehearsal and he got a load of what I was now seriously trying to palm off as clarinet playing—well, there's no sense in trying to describe what he looked like.

However, I can give you a broad hint as to the general tone and character of his communiqué. Among all the other carefully chosen terminology he employed, one of the nicest things he called me was a "dirty little no-good son of a bitch" —if you want to call that "nice." Later on, when I got an opportunity to compare notes with the other members of the band, the general consensus seemed to be that this commentary on my cleanliness, size, general worth, and parentage, was practically a term of endearment, and, taken all in all, the single unimaginative low spot in one of the most inspired bursts of oratory it had ever been our privilege to overhear.

By keeping carefully out of his reach, I gave Cavallaro the rest of that day to consider the problem I had raised. This problem boiled down to these alternatives: one was to send me home immediately—the other was to let me stay and finish out the engagement, clarinet or no clarinet. The first of these was ultimately ruled out because it would have cost Cavallaro not only *my* fare back home (according to musicians' union rules) but the fare for some other musician to come down to Miami and take my place.

During the ensuing three months, he never quite managed to get over the shock of the first time he heard me poop out a few little squeaks and squawks on the clarinet. And every time I reached for it, he winced noticeably.

Nevertheless I managed to salvage something out of the wreckage. By the time we'd finished our stay in Miami and come back to New Haven again, I had learned to make out after a fashion on this innocuous-looking but dangerous little instrument I had acquired. Not that I was able to play the clarinet well—or even passably well, by all legitimate standards—but I was at least able to get through the kind of clarinet parts that were occasionally required in the orchestrations I was apt to run into in the average dance band of that period. So there was that one net gain, as far as I was concerned. As far as Cavallaro himself was concerned—fortunately that ceased to be a matter of interest to me shortly after we arrived home.

For at that point I got my first really professional job in the closest thing to a real orchestra I had yet had an opportunity to work in. Out of this new job, I learned my biggest musical lesson to date. That is, that just as there are all sorts of degrees and meanings in the term "amateur"—so there are many shades of meaning in the term "professional."

*"You've no idea what a poor opinion I have of myself, and
how little I deserve it."*

W. S. GILBERT

Chapter Fourteen

THERE IS AN ANECDOTE that illustrates one of the big differences between the professional and the amateur. In fact, it
makes the one big point, establishes the one real criterion,
by which an amateur can always be spotted, whether he
works professionally or not. This criterion is so basic and
so simple that it can be put in three words:

Ask another professional.

The anecdote has to do with a well-known and successful playwright. I had always heard it told in connection with
Moss Hart, but when I asked him about it he informed me
that it actually was about Sam Raphaelson.

Immediately following the first big Broadway success of
one of his plays, this playwright went out and bought himself a good-sized boat. Then he got himself outfitted in a
yachtsman's cap with the word "Captain" embroidered in
gold braid on it. When he presented himself all got up that
way to his old-fashioned Yiddishe Mama, she took one look
at him and asked him in some concern what this was all
about. "Don't you see, Mama?" the playwright told her, "—
I'm a Captain."

His mother smiled tenderly and wisely at him, and said,
"Look, my son. By you you're a Captain. By me you can
also be a Captain. But by *Captains*—you ain't no Captain."

That was more or less my situation at the time I got this new job. "By real professionals" I was still no professional, although "by me"—and even "by my mother"—I may have been considered pretty damn professional at that.

This job came into being around 1925, when the Publix Presentation Theatre policy was first inaugurated. The whole idea of this new policy was to present stage shows in large movie houses. A permanent stage orchestra, or "house band," was to play a new show each week, along with various acts sent out weekly by the Publix Presentation people in New York City.

Suddenly there began to be a lot of talk among the musicians around New Haven about the fact that the Olympia Theatre (since re-named the Paramount) was going to put in a large orchestra and that it would be conducted by some big shot conductor from New York and that it would be composed of New York musicians as well as local talent. Now to the average New Haven musician, the words "New York musician" meant almost as much as the words "Olympian deities" might have meant to a Greek of the pre-Christian era. The idea of having a band like that playing right there in New Haven where I could get to hear it whenever I wanted to, gave me quite a thrill.

A few weeks later, the bulletin board at the local union headquarters announced that there would be a series of auditions held for the Olympia Theatre job. The first thing I knew, I was up there making an audition; and the next thing I knew—and this damn near floored me altogether— I had been hired!

There was a little scuffle for a day or so over the question of who would play "first saxophone"—meaning the lead man in the section, the one who plays the melody part rather than the harmony parts. Heartbroken as I might have been if I hadn't been able to work in this orchestra, I had made up my mind that I would take the job only if I were hired to play "first alto"—and nothing could shake me from this position. In the end, I won my point.

That was actually the first time in my life that this question had been raised. Up to now there had never been any serious doubt about which chair I would occupy. For in most of the little bands I had thus far worked in there had only been one, or at times two, saxophones—an alto and a tenor—and since the alto saxophone, which is what my main instrument was, is always the "lead" saxophone in most orchestrations, there was never any problem. However, here I was going to play in an orchestra with a full complement —as it was considered in those days—of three brass, three saxophones, and a full rhythm section, as well as a small string section.

There were a number of other New Haven musicians in the band. But the important thing was that I was now working with a few real, honest-to-goodness New York musicians. One of these godlike figures sat right in "my" section. He played tenor saxophone and did a good bit of the arranging. There was also one New York man in the brass section—the trombone player. And these were the guys I hung around with. I used to trail after them like a puppy, eyeing them, watching carefully, listening to what they said, noticing everything they did, until I must have made a pest of myself.

However, they didn't seem to mind too much. Maybe they were a little flattered by the hero-worship. In any event, I became as friendly with them as the great difference between my age and theirs would allow.

The most important thing I learned from that whole job had less to do with music itself than with the way a professional musician was supposed to behave. All the kid-stuff I had been indulging in up to now, not necessarily in my playing but in my attitudes toward myself and the men I worked with—all that was out. I soon learned that these two men were perfectly willing to accept the fact that I was far younger than they were, but since I was on an equal plane with them in regard to work and pay, they treated me as an equal. Either I lived up to this treatment or they would have nothing to do with me at all. They made that clear right from the start, and although there were times when it seemed to me to be more of a disadvantage than an advantage, on the whole I had to accept the fairness of this attitude. In time I began to learn to conduct myself more in accordance with my status as a professional musician working with other professionals who took their means of livelihood fairly seriously.

There was little room for practical joking or gags in this new job. We had to play three or four stage shows daily, and between shows there were constant rehearsals for the following week's show. We reported for work at least a half hour before curtain time. This was an ironclad rule. And after having once violated it in my usual blithe manner, I soon learned that this kind of nonsense would not be tolerated. Either I behaved like a grown man and took my job seriously, or I would not continue to work with grown men. It was as simple and unarguable as that.

I had to take it or leave it. And I must say I took it pretty well, considering my rebellious attitude toward rules in general. All this was damn valuable for a kid of not quite sixteen who wanted to make something out of himself in a highly competitive field. In addition, there was also a good bit of stuff I was managing to learn about music.

"Music is a tough instrument," someone in the business once said. I now found there were a number of trade tricks you weren't apt to learn unless you got them from people who'd been around in the business for some time. I began to learn a new method of sight reading. The idea was to read three or four, or even more, bars ahead of where you were playing. I found out about new methods of tone production, and the various kinds of tones that could be used in different types of ensemble playing—dry tone, warm tone, the use of vibrato—wide and narrow—and when to avoid vibrato altogether. I was introduced to the whole matter of dynamics—which up until then had never even entered my mind. All I had ever known about dynamics was that a fellow either played loud or soft, depending on how many other musicians he had to be heard over—but I now learned that this is one of the most important things an orchestra player has to be aware of, and that he must modulate his own playing in accordance with it in almost every note he plays. In short, I had to learn so many technical and non-technical aspects of the seemingly simple procedure of blowing a horn in a dance band, that after a few weeks of it my head buzzed. I remember that I used to go home nights and have a terrible time getting to sleep at all. Round and round in my mind would go the "lessons" of each day.

But eventually the practical training began to show results; and I'll never forget the time when, after one of our shows during which I had played a short solo passage, the trombone player came over to me down in the dressing room and said, "That was damn good, Art. Sounded like a real pro."

I was so happy to hear that from him that I honestly believe I wouldn't have taken a thousand dollars instead. Not that I think anyone would have made the offer—but still. . . .

And speaking of money, I was now making more than I had ever made before in my life, or, for that matter, even thought of making. The scale on that job—union scale, that is—was eighty-odd dollars a week. And on top of that, there was scarcely a week when I didn't work some dance job at least once or twice, generally on Saturday and Sunday nights, after the last show at the Olympia Theatre. So I was averaging somewhere around a hundred and ten to as much as a hundred and twenty-five bucks every week.

Remember, I was still just a kid, this was New Haven, where that kind of money goes a long way further than it does in New York City, I was still living at home, and this was long before the dollar had dwindled down to half the size of a split pea.

So that was how things stood for several months; and it's hard to say how they might have wound up if I'd stayed on indefinitely. The leader of the band, a man named Alex Hyde (then billed, believe it or not, as "The Prince of Jazz"; when I last heard of him he was musical contractor at Metro-Goldwyn-Mayer in Hollywood), seemed genuinely pleased with my work and spoke about taking me with him when he left for New York City and some other job.

But that isn't how it worked out. Something happened through which I suddenly found myself going off to the mid-West for the following three years or more, then from there to California, after that to Chicago, and finally all the way back to New York, instead of going from New Haven to New York in the first place.

Of course, that's the music business for you—at least the part of the music business I've spent most of my life in.

The main trouble with it as a way of touring the country is that you usually wind up seeing the inside of a lot of dance halls, night clubs, assorted theatre dressing-rooms, and amusement parks; and after enough years of that sort of thing, a fellow's likely to end up with a rather distorted picture of the American Way of Life.

But none of this was of any concern to me at that time. There were too many other things on my mind. I knew where I was going, the whole wide world was my oyster, and I was on my way.

I was just turning sixteen when I left New Haven, Connecticut—as it turned out, for keeps.

"Endeavor, as much as you can, to keep company with people above you."

LORD CHESTERFIELD

Chapter Fifteen

TWO CIRCUMSTANCES COMBINED to make me leave my job at the Olympia Theatre in New Haven and set out for parts unknown. The first was that, because of a new shift in policy on the part of the Publix Theatre Presentation people, the Olympia Theatre orchestra had to take on a new job. This was still back in the silent motion picture days; and it was decided that in addition to playing four stage shows a day the orchestra had to play in the pit during the movie. Although this was a new and valuable experience for me, with a type of music I had never played before, nevertheless it also made for a pretty tough job, with very long hours indeed. Not only did we continue with our four stage shows daily, and our constant rehearsing for next week's show, but now there was additional rehearsing for the movie score, plus the hour and a half or so we had to put in playing the score four or five times a day during each showing of the picture.

At first, the novelty of this new kind of music was intriguing enough so that I didn't particularly mind; but after a couple of months the grind began to wear me down. After all, I was still a kid, and although intensely devoted to learning the mysteries of my craft, I was young enough to feel a restless urge to get out of there once in a while. On top of everything else, it was spring, and those were the days before air-conditioning—and the air backstage used to get pretty gamey after a while. After a couple of months of the new routine, I began to dread the idea of being cooped up in the theatre all day, from around ten in the morning to as late as eleven-thirty at night on Saturdays.

So I was about ready for a change anyway.

And just about that time, the other circumstances I referred to came along and offered me the change.

One early summer night, as I was going out the stage door of the Olympia Theatre, I ran almost head-on into a young fellow waiting on the sidewalk for me.

He turned out to be a musician I had met during the past winter, when I was in Miami. We had both sat in occasionally on little get-togethers with other musicians after regular working hours. The kind of thing musicians used to call "jam sessions"—but not at all like the present-day ones, where everything is cut and dried, and where there is even an audience which buys tickets. The kind of jam sessions I am referring to were strictly musicians' affairs. They usually took place in the back room of some joint where there was a piano, or in a regular dance hall or night club, after the customers were gone and the place was closed for the night. It was all pretty informal stuff. A few musicians would be out somewhere having a drink or something, and when one or two might get to feeling like "playing a little jazz," they'd round up a few others—any old instruments at all—and go off to hunt up some spot where they could have their session.

Mainly, these extemporaneous get-togethers are a sort of laboratory in which the musician can find stimulation, try out new ideas of his own and exchange ideas with others who are there for the same purpose. It was a good way to get to hear and play with guys who knew more than you did, and with whom you might not ordinarily get the chance to work. Many of these guys were pretty damn good and came to the sessions out of a strong need to play a kind of music they weren't getting much chance to play ordinarily. Except for an occasional "hot chorus"—as it was then called—their regular jobs didn't give them much chance to express themselves on their instruments.

I used to sit in on these sessions whenever I could. And it was during one of them that I met the young drummer who was now waiting for me outside the Olympia Theatre. His name was Chuck Cantor, he was from Cleveland, and—as he now told me—his brother was the leader of the band at the Far East, a Chinese restaurant on Euclid Avenue in Cleveland, Ohio. Chuck had remembered my playing from those few sessions in Miami, and now he and another member of his brother's band, a young trumpet player named Willis Kelly, had come to see if they could get me to go to Cleveland and join their band.

The job paid one hundred dollars a week, and they had a signed contract with them for me to sign. First, however, they wanted to hear me play; for it had been some time ago, after all, and they wanted to see whether my playing had progressed or "gone back."

This last, incidentally, can happen quite easily, due to the constantly changing and evolving styles in jazz. One day a man will be right up there with the best—a year later he'll be completely out of the picture. No one knows exactly why, but I suppose it is like any other skill of this sort. As the Red Queen said to Alice, "Now *here*, you see, it takes all the running *you* can do, to keep in the same place." And some musicians just can't manage to keep on running, I guess. The result is, they fall behind and the parade passes right on by.

So it was a perfectly normal thing for them to want to know about. The only problem was where to take them to let them hear how I was now playing. Finally, we got into their car, the three of us, and drove out to a spot on the edge of town, right behind the Yale Bowl, where I got out my horn and, with no other accompaniment than the night wind rustling the leaves of the trees, played for them.

In a little while the two of them were satisfied that I hadn't "gone back"—in fact, as they both said, I'd improved a whole lot even over what Cantor had heard and described to Kelly. It remained for me to decide whether I wanted to go to Cleveland or not. The contract was for the term of one year, which meant pulling up stakes in New Haven and relocating in a new part of the country. And although I had already been away for periods up to three months or thereabouts, this was a decision I wasn't sure I could make alone.

There was one more important element in my indecision. During that same week I had received an offer by telegram to join a band called the California Ramblers, a rather famous band at that time. They were a recording outfit, located in New York City, and I never did find out how they had heard about me to begin with. I suppose one of the New York musicians with whom I was working at the Olympia Theatre had told one of the men in the California Ramblers about my playing—that's how these things usually happen in the business. At any rate, I was trying to make up my mind about *that* offer when this new one came along. The only thing that had prevented me from immediately grabbing the California Ramblers job was that I wasn't sure I was good enough. I didn't want to try to bite off more than I could chew; for by that time I had already begun to acquire a healthy caution born of realistic experience. I was starting to lose some of my youthful brashness and was willing to concede that I had a lot to learn before I could consider myself ready to make a stab at the big time.

In the end I decided in favor of Cleveland. A year there, in the kind of band these two fellows told me they were in, would give me still more experience working with men who were more experienced than I and who knew a lot I still had to learn. After that I could go on and try my luck in New York if I felt ready.

For by that time I had formulated a rule for myself.

I'd made up my mind that any time I got to the point where I could not learn anything further from the band I happened to be working in, I would quit and join another band where I could go on learning.

That's all there was to the rule, but I stuck to it pretty faithfully for quite a while, whether the money was better or worse in the new bands into which I was constantly shifting.

On the basis of this rule, there was no reason for me to stay on at the Olympia Theatre any longer. Even my two New York colleagues had already advised me to get out and go on to something else as soon as I got the chance. They were quitting the Olympia Theatre job themselves.

So I handed in my two weeks' notice at the end of that week, packed a few belongings into the little car I had recently bought, and set out for Cleveland.

I went to work with Joe Cantor and his Far East Orchestra, and several weeks later I sent for my mother, who had insisted on joining me and "taking care of me." We got ourselves an apartment in Cleveland, and there I stayed for the next three years, going from one band to another, picking up a bit of musical experience here and there, learning what I could, managing to keep improving all the time, until finally I got to the point where there wasn't much more I could learn around Cleveland; at which time, as I had done in New Haven, I pulled up stakes once again and set out on another trek, this time all the way out to California.

But before going into that, there are a few things I ought to tell about what happened during those three years in Cleveland.

"Chance is a word void of sense; nothing can exist without a cause."

VOLTAIRE

Chapter Sixteen

ONE OF THE THINGS I LEARNED while I was in Cleveland was to arrange and orchestrate.

Actually I had long been interested in arranging, and curious as to how it was done. After all, the music we played—even those stock arrangements printed up by publishers, which as a rule sounded very much alike from the standpoint of orchestration—had been arranged by *somebody*. And now and then you'd get one that had something individual about it, something that made it sound different, more interesting than the usual run-of-the-mill stuff. So I used to wonder occasionally who the men were who arranged this music. But there was no way of learning much about it from any of the musicians I had played with up to then.

Once in a while I'd write out something for the saxophone section, a chorus to go along with the regular orchestration—but I had never even thought about trying my hand at a full-scale orchestration.

There's nothing esoteric about the job, actually. All it requires is a knowledge of the various instruments, and the ability to transpose what is written, in terms of these instruments. It is a technical matter, rather than anything else; but I knew very little about any other instruments except my own. I could transpose well enough to write for the other kinds of saxophones; and I might have been able to manage it for the trumpet, which is a B flat instrument just as the tenor saxophone is, or the soprano saxophone, or even the clarinet. But I'd have had to give up when it came to the trombone, which is mostly written in bass clef, or the bass, which is also scored in bass clef. And the piano seemed by far the most formidable of all, since it was written in both bass *and* treble. For by this time I had forgotten any last vestige of anything I might just possibly have managed to learn about it back there as a kid on York Street.

During my one week at the Joyland Casino in Lexington, Kentucky, I met an arranger-instrumentalist who worked with our band for two nights. I asked him so many questions that I'm sure he was delighted to be staying with us for only that short a time. I was a pretty intense kid, and terribly persistent when it came to learning anything I had any curiosity about. I clung to him like a leech and wouldn't let go until I had extracted a few bits of information from him about the different instruments in the band—their range, what was practical to write for them, and what would and wouldn't *sound* within their varying limitations.

Still, two nights is hardly long enough to pick up any more than a general smattering of technical information. It never even occurred to me to ask anything about the method of scoring itself. In fact, it never entered my mind that there might *be* a method. I had never heard the word "score" in my life except as applied to games like baseball or football.

My next little brush with the problems of orchestration had occurred at the Olympia Theatre. In that band we played mostly "special" arrangements which were written on manuscript paper, as against the printed stock arrangements which were all I had had any previous experience with. There I had an opportunity to observe an arranger at work—the one

New York musician I've already spoken of who played tenor saxophone in the band.

Somehow I must have missed the point when I watched him. Maybe it was because I happened to see him while he was copying out the separate parts rather than while he was working on the score itself; in any event I can't remember ever having heard anything about making a score at all, until a long time after I had already evolved my own crude method of scoring.

I had been working in Joe Cantor's band for about four months when it suddenly entered my head to try to make an arrangement—a whole, full-scale arrangement, with parts for every instrument, not just for the saxophone section.

Well, I wound up with quite a mess on my hands.

Let me explain.

I've already used the word "score" several times, so now, for the benefit of any musically uneducated person, I'll try to make clear just what a score is, and what its function is.

Before a group of musicians can play a piece of music concertedly, you have to have an "arrangement" of the piece. That is, you have to lay out a sequence of musical ideas, as well as the order in which each instrument, or combination or section of instruments, will play which parts. The arranger must also compose certain bits of music (introduction, modulations, interludes, and ending—or coda) to go with the piece of music as he conceives it.

After that, the arrangement is "orchestrated." Here, you write out the separate parts for each instrument in accordance with the over-all plan of the arrangement, making sure that each instrument will be playing the correct notes with (or against) the others, and fitting each part into the sequence of ideas as it has been worked out by the arranger.

Arranging, then, is a creative or interpretive job, involving a certain amount of actual composition; whereas orchestration involves nothing more than the technical skill involved in putting down on manuscript paper the individual parts for the various instruments used in the arrangement.

Finally, the parts themselves are written one below the other on a master sheet so that you can see which instrument is doing what, as it goes along; and this master sheet—from which all the individual parts are copied and which shows the entire piece of music as composed, arranged, and orchestrated —is called a score.

Some men work with a score immediately—that is, they arrange and orchestrate directly onto the score. Others make a rough draft of the arrangement or orchestration before making the score itself. This rough draft is nothing more or less than a sketch, an outline, a blueprint. But there are no rules; some arrangers make sketches, others do not. Anyway, there you have a rough general idea of the whole process.

Now, then—when it came to doing this rather intricate job myself—I had no idea where to begin, or how to go about it. I knew pretty much what I wanted the over-all effect to be, which instruments I wanted to play which parts of the music, and how they should play them. *But*—I didn't know about making a score, and I had no idea that there was even such a thing as a score to begin with. All I had to do, I thought, was to figure out in my head what I wanted the thing to sound like, and then go ahead and write down all the parts one at a time.

So that's the way I went at it.

But once I got into this job a little way, I found it was pretty difficult to remember what I had written for the various instruments. There were twelve men in Joe Cantor's band, and by the time I had written some fifteen or twenty bars of music for each of the twelve parts, I had to keep skipping back and forth from one thing to the other, in order to refresh my memory on what I had just written for some of them so that I'd know what to write for the *rest* of them.

With a score in front of me, I could have written one bar

at a time for all the instruments and known at a glance just what everybody would be playing at any given moment. Without a score, I had to try to remember all this. In the end I spread all the parts out on the floor of my living room, and got down on my hands and knees with a pencil (*and* an eraser!), jotting down a few notes on one part, and crawling around until I located the part I wanted to go with it, then the part to go with *that,* and so on until all twelve parts were more or less in accord. But of course I kept forgetting what I had done on the third or fourth part by the time I'd come to the tenth or twelfth one, and this went on back and forth among all the parts, until finally, twelve or fifteen hours later, I was completely pooped out, physically and mentally. I had been up all night long with this preposterous business, crawling around until I had almost worn grooves in the living room carpet; but at last I was finished.

Next day I collected all the parts, stacked them up neatly, and brought them down to rehearsal. I could hardly wait to hear the result of all my laborious planning, not to mention crawling.

Well, I announced with great pride that I'd made an arrangement of *Wabash Blues.* The rest of the band took this jubilant proclamation pretty much in their stride. I passed out all the parts, delivered a few anxious parental admonitions about the right tempo, and warned everybody to watch out for this or that little bit when they came to it. Then I let Joe Cantor start the band—and we were off to the races.

We hadn't played two bars before I realized something was fairly rotten. You never heard such a caterwauling in all your life!

The men tried heroically to go on with it, but after six or eight bars they had to give up the struggle. Everyone looked bewildered.

"Let's try it again," said one of them, with a baffled expression on his face.

"Wait a second, wait a second," said another, bending down to peer dubiously at the part in front of him. "Hey, Art—what's this supposed to be?"

I was so disappointed I couldn't say anything.

"Come on, come on, come on, come on," Joe Cantor himself was saying nervously. He was a mild, easy-going guy, and any disturbance used to affect him strongly. He would get jittery and upset whenever anything went wrong, and it was always difficult to calm him down again. This time he was about as jittery as I ever saw him get.

There was a lot of confused yelling back and forth among the various members of the band. I was doing what little I could to answer all requests for information.

"What the hell's this supposed to be, Art?"—"Hey, how'd you want this to sound?"—"Listen, how the hell can a trombone play anything like this?" And so on. That is, when you could hear anything at all above the noise of some of the other men who were trying to play their parts by themselves in order to figure out what the peculiar hieroglyphics I had written were supposed to sound like.

All the time this was going on, Joe Cantor kept trying to establish some sort of order. "Come on, come on, *come on,* COME ON!" he kept repeating, louder and louder and louder, until he was yelling at the top of his lungs.

Finally, little by little, things quieted down, and after a while we were able to establish communication once again. That accomplished, we even managed to get through the first few bars of my monstrosity.

Eventually we got the introduction straightened out and that wasn't too bad, so we went at the rest of it. But there was quite a bit of excavating and winnowing to be done before we could separate the meaning and intention of what I had written from the mass of errors in which I had evidently written them.

The trouble was, of course, that I had not only been ignorant of many things regarding the various instruments I had been trying to write for, but in addition, because of my confused method of substituting hands and knees for the relatively simple method of putting the whole thing down on a score in the first place, I had made plenty of mistakes—or "clinkers," as they are called in jazz bands. (When a man goes to play a note and misses he doesn't make a mistake—he "hits a clinker." Similarly, when a man attempts to write one thing and writes something wrong he has "written a clinker.")

That was my arrangement in one word. One big clinker from beginning to end.

Still, considering how little I knew about what I was doing at the time, the whole thing ultimately turned out a lot better than you might expect.

You see, there was nothing particularly bad about what I had had in mind for the men to play. I knew enough by then to understand what would and wouldn't *sound* good. The real difficulty came out of *their* having to find out what I had *meant* for them to play. As soon as they'd figured *that* out, each one of them put it down on his own part correctly. After that, it wasn't too bad; in fact, they thought it was pretty good. The only trouble with it was the kind of trouble that can be expected from any first attempt of this kind—I had been so determined to do something specially good that I had overloaded this one poor little arrangement; and instead of keeping it simple and confining myself to one musical idea at a time, I had thrown in everything but the chef of the Far East Restaurant himself.

By the time everyone had got through correcting and rewriting his own part, that rehearsal was over. Still, I had my first arrangement in the books, and although it had wound up being pretty much a collaboration between myself and the entire band, at least I could feel it hadn't been a complete waste of time.

That night, after work, I sneaked around and picked up all

the parts once again. I took them home with me, sat up all night, and studied them carefully to see what was wrong with what I had written, and how it had been rewritten. Most of the individual parts had the look of a well-used road map. There were so many scratched-out notes, substituted notes, and arrows pointing down to formerly blank pieces of manuscript where other phrases had been scrawled for the incorrectly written ones I had put down to begin with, that it took me most of the night to make out what had been done and how it differed from what I had tried to do.

However, in the end I managed to break down the cryptograms and see what had been wrong. I decided right then and there to make another arrangement immediately. But this time I decided to put all the parts down on one piece of manuscript paper first, so I could tell what I was doing as I went along.

That's how I "discovered" how to make a score!

It was several years before I also "discovered" that some guys named Vittoria, Orlandus Lassus, Palestrina, Bach, Haydn, Mozart, *et al,* had already figured out this trick some three or four centuries ago. And even if I *had* been told about it, I don't believe I'd have minded a great deal.

I have long since also "discovered" that there is no one who has a greater contempt for knowledge than the fellow to whom it is handed on a silver platter before he has come to the point where he has real use for it. Perhaps this has something to do with the vast difference between the self-educated man, who often retains his curiosity all his life, and the average college graduate, who can go around assuming that he is "educated" because he has a diploma to "prove" it; for what more does a guy need than a diploma to prove he is all through having to bother about such ridiculous matters as learning anything further?

Sure, it's easier when someone can show you how to do what

you want to do. But the big thing is to learn—some way—just so you *do* learn.

And at least one thing can be said about my method of learning. It may be a good' bit tougher—but once you *do* learn it my way, you don't easily forget what you've learned!

"The thousand strands of the web of fate are so wildly, so strangely entangled. . . ."

HENRIK IBSEN

Chapter Seventeen

So I WENT, stumbling along my own little rocky road to fame and fortune, making my haphazard way toward some unseen and incomprehensible goal that, far ahead as it might be, I was sure I would ultimately reach if I just followed my nose and kept going.

Meanwhile I finished out my contract with Joe Cantor. During that year I had become a pretty fair arranger. I knew enough about what I was doing to be able to turn out arrangements that sounded O.K. and at the same time were practicable, meaning playable by the musicians in the bands I was writing for. I was writing for other bands by then as well as the one I was in. And of course, the more arrangements I made, the more I learned from each succeeding one. Finally, I was offered a job with Cleveland's top band of that day— Austin Wylie's orchestra.

I took it, and with the exception of a few short periods when I left him to work with several other bands which couldn't pay as much money, I stayed with Wylie for the rest of the time I remained in Cleveland. These other bands, being basically musicians' bands, eventually fell apart from the simple cause of lack of work, but from each one I learned something more about music.

By the end of the two years I had been with Wylie, I had become more or less the leader of his band—not actually, of course, for he was the one who stood up there in front of the band and acted as leader. But in every important respect I was the musical director. I arranged most of what we played, conducted rehearsals, and had some part in the selection of the personnel whenever there was need for a change or replacement.

After a year or so, this became a pretty damn good band for its time and place. I was doing all right for myself financially as well as musically, for Wylie paid me well. In addition, we got along fine. He respected my ability, and I respected him as an employer. In all the remaining time I spent working in bands and radio and recording studios, up until the time I became a leader of a band myself, I never got along with any leader I ever worked for as well as I did with him. Even years later, some twenty years, when Wylie worked for me as road manager for a large orchestra I took out on tour around the country—even then, in that unpopular job, herding the whole band together and keeping them on the job, taking care of hotel reservations, bus schedules, and all the thousand-and-one irksome details connected with moving a group of musicians around the country and keeping things from going completely out of hand—I never heard any man in my band say a bad word against him. He was a damn nice guy, Wylie was, and I might have remained with his band in Cleveland a great deal longer than I did, if something completely unforeseen hadn't come along and once again changed the entire course and direction of my life.

During that period in Cleveland, the Chinese restaurants we worked in were the tony spots for most of the middle-class citizenry who wanted to spend an occasional evening in the nearest thing around town to a poor man's night spot. We played three sessions daily. The early session was a kind of luncheon dance affair, mostly attended by office girls who, between bites of chow mein, used to dance with one another, so that the floor was filled with nothing but women, young and old.

Our hours were from twelve noon to two-thirty for that session; from six-thirty to eight-thirty in the evening for the dinner session; and from nine-thirty to one A.M. (two A.M. on Saturdays) for the "supper dance" session. This went on seven days a week, except for Sundays, when the lunch session was omitted.

These hours were scarcely what you might call a pushover. Remember, playing a musical instrument, no matter what it may look like, can be hard work; and when you have to blow a horn that long every day in the week, it can be downright labor. In addition to all this, I had to take over two afternoon rehearsals each week, and on top of that I had all the actual arranging to do. I was a fairly busy kid.

Not that I minded. On the contrary. I wanted to learn anything and everything I could, and this was about as good a way to learn as anyone could possibly find. So I went on doing it and being glad of the chance to do it.

Still, now and then I couldn't help becoming a bit nervous and overtense.

One morning, after staying up most of the night to finish an arrangement I had to have ready for that afternoon, I found myself so jittery and overstimulated that I couldn't get to sleep. I finally decided to stay up and try to get through that day without any sleep at all. I had done this a number of times before and, probably because I was only seventeen years old and a highly energetic kid, it had never done me any particular harm, aside from making me even more preoccupied in manner than usual.

Since I still had several hours to go before it would be time to show up for the luncheon session at the Golden Pheasant Restaurant (where we were playing at that time), I picked up a newspaper that happened to be lying around the house, and started looking idly through it.

In those days I was no newspaper reader; there was very little time in which I could have become one. So, not being specially concerned with current events, I skimmed over most of the pages, did a crossword puzzle, looked over the comic strips, and so on, until I stumbled onto something that promised to help me kill the remainder of the time before going to work.

This was an announcement of a contest being held all over the United States in connection with the forthcoming National Air Races, which were about to be held for the first time, and in Cleveland at that. Each contestant was supposed to send in a title for a song to be written later to whichever title won first prize.

There was a further requirement, though, that presented a gamelike kind of challenge on which I decided to fill in the time before going to work that day. You were supposed to write a one-hundred-and-fifty-word essay on the subject of "How the National Air Races would benefit Cleveland." Or something like that—I can't remember exactly.

Well, I figured out a song title quickly enough. *Song of the Skies* seemed apt enough. (The title was supposed to have something to do with flying and airplanes. This is called a "tie-up"—as I understand these matters—in publicity circles. Very clever stuff.) After setting down this gem of a title I went to work on the essay itself.

But before I got through with that, I had learned a fairly basic thing about writing in general—which is that it is a hell of a sight easier to do a piece in a thousand or even two thousand words than to do one in a hundred and fifty words.

I once heard a story about Roosevelt which has bearing on this matter of brevity in writing, or speaking. As I heard it, someone asked F.D.R. to deliver a speech at some banquet being held in Washington, D.C. "How long do you want my speech to be?" Roosevelt asked. "Oh, it doesn't want to be very long," the fellow told him. "In fact, we'd just as soon have you keep it down to three or four minutes." "In that case, I won't be able to do it," Roosevelt is supposed to have replied. "I thought you wanted me to talk for an hour or so. If it's only supposed to last three or four minutes I wouldn't have time to get a speech ready."

That more or less illustrates what I learned the morning I tried to do a one-hundred-and-fifty-word essay.

I kept fooling around with the thing for quite a while, but somehow I simply couldn't seem to make it say anything. Of course, the fact that I hadn't the slightest notion of how these air races would actually benefit Cleveland may have had something to do with it.

Finally I got a very bright idea. I decided to ask myself the question that the title of the essay posed, and then see if I couldn't come up with some halfway sensible answer.

Once I had done that, the thing began to fall in line after a fashion. Actually, all I could figure out to say was that there would be a number of people coming to Cleveland to witness the event, so there was bound to be a certain upward spurt in local business affairs. There was also some reference to civic pride, etc., plus whatever else I could dream up along those lines.

In the end I had quite a bit of stuff written. Only trouble was, it all added up to about six or seven hundred words, instead of the required one hundred and fifty or less.

So I started cutting and pruning, a word or two here, a phrase there, and on reading it over I found that it had benefited rather than been damaged by being cut. So I went to work at it once more, until finally I got it down to about one hundred and thirty-five words. By then it was time to get dressed and go to work.

This game having served its purpose, I was about to throw

the whole essay away; but then I decided to send it in just for the hell of it. After that I forgot about the entire matter.

A few days later, when I came home from work, my mother told me that some man had called up and asked when he could come out to see Art Shaw. He wanted to bring along a photographer, she said, to take some pictures. It crossed my mind that it might just possibly have something to do with the contest. But I dismissed that almost immediately. More likely it was some publicity matter concerning Wylie's band. In any case, I wasn't interested enough to call back.

A day or so later, though, there was a letter for me, in an official-looking envelope marked Cleveland *News*. When I read it I almost did a tailspin right there in our living room.

The letter informed me that I had won first prize, and was entitled to an airplane trip to Hollywood as a guest of the Western Air Express, all expenses paid! That same day a reporter came out to the house with a photographer, and the following day there was a story about it in the paper, with a picture of me prominently displayed.

By the time I showed up at work that evening everyone in the band knew about it. I got quite a bit of kidding over it, but even so I could see they were all a little impressed.

A couple of weeks later, having arranged with Wylie for a leave of absence, I went off in glory as a "guest of the Western Air Express." After a fairly bumpy trip I arrived in Hollywood for the first time. I was met at the airport by a group of assorted publicity men, contest-officials, and—my father!

I find it difficult now to describe my true feelings on seeing him there. My first impression, I remember, was that he had grown much older. My second was that he was a far smaller man than I had pictured him. But as for my actual feelings or emotions—they were pretty much a blank. It had been too many years since he had had any real meaning for me as a parent, and there had been too many things going on in those years. His presence now, in the midst of all the excitement and hullabaloo, seemed—well, irrelevant.

And yet—underneath all the excitement and hullabaloo, and beyond the irrelevance of his being there (so that his unexpected presence constituted a problem, rather than anything else)—I was aware of a fleeting sense of pride. His having come out here could only mean one thing—he had heard about my winning the contest. In a curious way, this meeting was a sort of vindication for me, and I felt strangely glad to see him, in spite of the fact that I had so far forgotten him that it hadn't occurred to me until the moment I laid eyes on him that I might ever see him again.

We shook hands, quite formally, and managed to exchange a few words. He informed me that he had read an item in the Los Angeles papers about the contest and my having won first prize, and had decided to come out to the airport to greet me.

I mumbled something about being glad to see him after all this time; but it was embarrassing—for him, as well as for myself. I could tell by the way he acted. The reason was, I suppose, that there had scarcely ever been any real display of feeling between us, as far back as I could remember; and now, particularly under these circumstances, it was difficult to overcome the reticence we both felt with one another.

However, I found out where I would be staying and asked him if he would call me there sometime later that day. He agreed, and turned away. I watched him as he left, and felt a sense of regret. But for what, I wasn't sure. A short while later I went off with the officials on a Grand Tour of the town, with visits to some of the motion picture studios, where I was photographed with several movie stars. The only one I can remember now is Bessie Love, a blonde, blue-eyed woman who was no doubt as bored with the whole business as I was entranced by it.

Eventually I was deposited at the Roosevelt Hotel, and

given instructions to wait around for a call from someone who would let me know what the next part of the agenda would be. I went up to my room and sat around for a while in a daze; but I was too stirred up to stay up there by myself. So I told the telephone operator where I would be if a phone call came for me, and went downstairs.

I soon learned that there was a ballroom in the hotel—the Blossom Room—and that there was a famous band playing there, Irving Aaronson and his Commanders. They had made a number of recordings, played in several Broadway shows—among them a musical show called "Paris," written by Cole Porter and starring Irene Bordoni—and were known as one of the great "entertaining bands" in America.

Of course, it was not the type of band I'd have wanted to work in. An "entertaining band" meant, in those days, a group of musicians not necessarily skilled at playing their instruments but able to sing and do comedy bits, and even dance. The nearest thing to anything of that sort today would be an outfit like Spike Jones'. And as anyone who has ever seen Spike and his crew can testify, the word "band" is pretty much of a misnomer. I suppose "vaudeville act" covers it better.

Still, Aaronson's Commanders were a nationally famous organization at that time, and I made up my mind to hear them. But it was only around four o'clock in the afternoon and they didn't start playing till around eight-thirty in the evening, so I could do nothing but wait around.

About four-thirty I was paged by one of the bellboys and it turned out to be my father on the telephone. We arranged to meet the following day. Later, I got a call from the people who were supposed to be looking after me, and they told me there would be nothing more doing that day. So I roamed around town by myself for the rest of the afternoon, came back and had dinner at the hotel, and at eight-thirty found myself a spot on a small balcony overlooking the Blossom Room. From there I could see and hear the band, and look right down onto the dance floor.

I was pretty damn impressed with what I saw.

This was very big-time stuff to an eighteen-year-old kid, whose closest approach to this thing called Glamour had been the Golden Pheasant Chinese Restaurant in Cleveland, Ohio. For in those days—before rising taxes put a crimp into the goings-on in that corner of the world—Hollywood was quite a spot indeed. And this place I was looking down on happened to be, at that particular time, one of the hangouts for the various celebrities who made up this little world-within-a-world, this fantasy-factory, this Mecca of the show-business world, called Hollywood.

Perched on my little balcony, hidden behind some potted palms, I stared down glassy-eyed at such mythological folk as Jean Harlow, Joan Crawford, Charlie Chaplin, Richard Barthelmess, William Powell. Up to then, these stars had never seemed quite real to me. And now that I saw them for the first time in the flesh, they seemed if anything even more unreal.

I was too far away from the band to be able to distinguish any one of the members of it. I listened to one or two dance sets, however, and was not particularly impressed. Famous or not, this band played nothing that startled me; nothing I couldn't have arranged or played better myself. Why, even Wylie's band sounded better. After a short while I left and went back down into the lobby. A few minutes later, after finishing a dance set, some of the men in the band drifted out there. I looked at them with a certain amount of curiosity; for even though they didn't impress me as musicians especially, they *were* members of a famous organization.

Suddenly, I recognized one of them, a trumpet player some years older than myself who had worked in the same band I had worked in at the Olympia Theatre. He was a New Haven boy named Charlie Trotta.

I got up, ran over, and grabbed him by the arm.

He turned around, saw who it was, and said, "Hey, Art! What the hell are *you* doing here?"

"My God!—Charlie! I was just sitting up on the balcony listening to the band—but I didn't recognize you, it was too far away. I didn't know you were with Aaronson's band."

"Sure—I've been with him a couple of years now." He turned and looked over his shoulder. "Wait a second, let me see if I can find Tony and let him know you're here."

"Tony?" I asked. "Tony who?"

"Tony Pestritto," he said. "You remember him, don't you? He's a saxophone player, from Hartford, used to play with Cavallaro once in a while, before you went with Johnny."

"Tony! My God!" Of course I remembered Tony Pestritto. He had been playing saxophone that night I went up to audition for Cavallaro at the Cinderella Ballroom and made my sight-reading flop. Remember him? As if I could have forgotten anything connected with that night!

A short while later Tony came out. He recognized me immediately, and the three of us spent a few minutes chewing over where we'd been, what we'd done, and the bands we'd worked with since leaving New Haven. I told them how I had happened to come out to Hollywood. Then it was time for them to go back on the stand again.

I hung around until they were finished for the night. Meanwhile we kept getting together between sets, and they introduced me to several of the other men in the band. By the time the night was over Tony and Charlie had cooked up a little plan.

It seemed there was a spot in the band for a guy like me. Of course, this depended on a number of things—one of which was the same matter that had interested Chuck Cantor when he had come to see me in New Haven—"how I was playing now."

After we'd gone off to some after-hours spot where I could sit in and play a little, they were satisfied. The only question in my mind was whether I *wanted* to join this band.

I explained to them why I wasn't sure. But they both told me that Aaronson had recently decided to try to make a better musical organization out of his band. The trend in dance music was beginning to change toward slightly better and more involved arrangements, and, after considerable pressure from three or four of his better instrumentalists, Aaronson had begun to consider the possibility of adding one or two "key" men for each section in his band, in order to raise the musical level to a standard more in accordance with the sort of thing that was beginning to be expected of top dance bands of that day.

There was no need for me to make up my mind then and there. After leaving Hollywood, the band was going out on a road tour with a traveling company of the Irene Bordoni "Paris" show.

For one week, toward the end of the tour, the show was due in Cleveland. By then Charlie and Tony would have had time to work on Aaronson. Somehow they would manage to get him to come to wherever I might be playing in Cleveland and after that it would be a cinch to get me into the band.

By the end of the ten days or so that I remained in Hollywood, I had about decided to join the Aaronson band if I were offered the job. After all, it *was* a big-time outfit even if it wasn't the best musical band in the country. Most important of all, they were going back to New York City after next season's engagement at the Blossom Room, and once in New York—well, that was, after all, the center, the Big Apple, so why not make the break and get established there once for all?

◇◇◇◇

Meanwhile, during my stay in Hollywood, I was becoming reacquainted with my father.

The day after he had called me at the hotel, we got together and spent a couple of hours talking. And here, for the first time in my life, I was finally able to establish some sort of relationship with this man whom I had never really understood or known during all the years while I grew from childhood into adolescence. . . .

"The night my father got me
His mind was not on me;
He did not plague his fancy
To muse if I should be
The son you see."

A. E. HOUSMAN

Chapter Eighteen

TO THIS DAY I know very little about my father. I don't even
know the name of the city or town or place where he was
born. All I do know is that it was somewhere in Russia; but
strange as it may seem, my mother never learned his birth-
place.

My earliest memories are of a surly, disgruntled, and, on
the whole, miserable man. I must have begun to develop a
fear of him very early. And this fear, which eventually grew
into a kind of rebellious dislike, more or less set the tone of
our relationship until the day he left for California.

This is a tough thing for me to write about. Somehow I find
it difficult to go back all that time and dredge up all the painful memories and associations buried in that corner of my
mind. For another thing, the picture I have of him is dimmed
and blurred, partly by time, but even more because of the last
two times we saw one another. It isn't so difficult to adjust to
any one strong emotion toward another person—such as fear,
or even dislike. But it becomes difficult when the emotion gets

all mixed up and diluted by other elements such as sympathy and understanding; especially when the sympathy and understanding are arrived at years after the original fear or dislike has crystallized.

Actually, I have two distinct and separate attitudes toward my father. The first of these is almost entirely emotional. I formed it as a child, and it arose out of fear. The second is totally different. It was superimposed on the first and stems out of a more recent, and almost entirely intellectual re-evaluation of him, through which I have come to see him not just as my father but as a maladjusted, dislocated, and miserable man, who never managed to make a life for himself, to make anything out of his potentialities, who died alone, and, from all I have ever been able to find out, under wretched and poverty-stricken circumstances.

When I was very young, while we still lived in New York City, my feeling toward my father was a strange blend of curiosity, awe, sympathy, and love. He was a thick-set man who came and went in our house, treading heavily and speaking in a loud voice, which sounded harsh and frightening to me but fascinated me as well, so that I can even remember trying to imitate the sound of it, as a small child. On the few occasions when he spoke English at all—mostly he spoke in a guttural Yiddish—he always retained a thick Russian accent.

My mother and he worked together, all the time we lived on the Lower East Side of New York. And as I reconstruct it now, he must have bitterly resented the fact that she was the dominant one, that it was she who was the trained worker who knew the business of women's clothes, who understood changing styles and fashions, and who therefore set the pattern for their joint business dealings with the outside world.

There were a few times when he tried to break away from this domination. He struggled desperately, but always unsuccessfully, to establish himself in other lines of work. I remember once when he bought a photographic studio over on Avenue

C and, after a very short period, had to sell out at a loss. Each time one of these attempts turned out to be a failure, he would come back to the dress business—which my mother always managed to keep going. And each time, he would become more and more surly and miserable. Up to the very end, up to the day he finally pulled up stakes and left for good, he was still trying to get into something else, some line where he could run the show himself, where he wouldn't have to live with the nagging misery of what he must always have known—that his wife was better-equipped than he was to handle business affairs, to hack some sort of path through the economic jungle in which they both had to live and struggle.

I suppose, too—but this is a later knowledge—that I must have felt some childish resentment toward him because he was unable to make a living for us—as I could easily enough deduce from the endless bickering that went on between my mother and him. She was forced to work all day and sometimes a good part of the night, cutting cloth, sewing and stitching, copying patterns, and so on. It seemed to me, as a very young child, that his "weakness," his inability to make a living, was depriving me of my mother. The fathers of the other children I played with seemed able to get along all right—why couldn't mine? This was emphasized by something else that I hated—I was the only child in that neighborhood, or those various neighborhoods where we lived in New York, who had a nursemaid, a neighborhood girl who came in by the day to take care of me while my mother sat grimly at her sewing machine and my father surlily helped her.

I can't imagine how all this might have resolved itself if we hadn't had to move to New Haven. Here, the contrast between him and the fathers of other kids I knew became even greater. Not only was he unable to make a living, not only did he not "go to the office" as most other kids' fathers did, but now he became, by contrast with these other fathers, a "foreigner." He was "a Jew," he spoke with a heavy accent, which

—at the time I was first coping with the problem of Jewishness—seemed shameful and embarrassing.

There is no point now in making belated apologies for the way I behaved and felt as a kid of eight. I can only say once again that you can't expect logic or understanding from a kid that age—especially a kid who is filled with fear and guilt toward his father, who develops further fear and guilt because of the very fear and guilt he feels, and who is completely and hopelessly unable to talk out any of these feelings with the person toward whom he feels them.

In other words, my fear and shame of my father made me feel guilty, which made me fearful and hateful of myself. This being impossible for me to live with, I had to transform it, transfer it outside of myself, project it onto him. And that intensified the very fear and self-hatred which had caused me to do it in the first place. A vicious circle was formed, a pretty damn unhealthy kind of vicious circle; for a thing of this kind cannot go on without spilling over into all sorts of other exaggerated attitudes. Not only toward my father, but also toward the rest of the world. For example, out of my fear of him I developed an exaggerated feeling of love for my mother. And so on and so forth, until Lord knows where a thing like this can ultimately wind up, unless something is eventually done about it.

I realize how ugly all this sounds, but I can't do much about it now except tell it as it was. By the time I was ten or eleven, these attitudes had fairly well jelled, and they caused me to do some rather nasty things. I remember one time while I was playing in the street with some other kids, when I noticed my father coming toward us. I made some excuse to hide myself till he had gone by. I was so ashamed of his guttural accent that I didn't want these other kids to hear him talk to me, to have further reason to despise me for "being Jewish." For by that time I had already been conditioned to believe that there was only one possible attitude *any* gentile could have toward *any* Jew.

Poor man! If he had ever suspected how his son felt about him, I hate to think of how much worse his misery might have been. Fortunately, he was spared that much before he died. As it was, he had to go through enough in his comparatively short, unhappy, frustrated life. . . .

At any rate—here he was in Hollywood now. And here I was, at the age of eighteen, finding to my surprise and bewilderment that there was nothing about him to fear, and that he was actually a rather sad, unhappy failure of a man, who seemed to mean no great harm to anyone but had somehow lost his way in life. Most astounding of all, he seemed to be truly fond of me—and even proud of me, when I told him some of the things I had done since he had left home. Most of it he had had no idea about at all, for there had been almost no correspondence between him and my mother after he went away.

After a while, I began to see that, in his embarrassed and inarticulate way, he was hinting at something he wanted me to do for him, something I could never have dreamt of before that moment. He wanted me to persuade my mother to come out to California and join him.

I was flabbergasted. This was my first inkling that their separation had not been entirely a matter of his having "deserted" my mother and me. In the end, after he had explained the whole matter to me from his own point of view, I promised I would do what I could when I got back home. And it was then, I believe, that we came closer to understanding one another, to *feeling* some deep bond between us, than either of us ever had before in our lives. . . .

As it turned out, however, I was unable to do anything to help him. When I got back to Cleveland, I tried sincerely and to the best of my ability to convince my mother that it would be a good idea for her to go back to him. But by then she had built up such a resentment toward him that it was impossible to do anything with her. She reacted with such violence to my "disloyalty" in telling her that I had found myself liking my father, "in spite of everything," that I realized it would be better if I never mentioned it to her again. I have since come to understand that she was, of course, living with her own guilts and self-torturings. With my lack of awareness of what *her* real problems were, of her deep-seated need to keep them hidden from herself, it was impossible for me to help her.

So in the end I gave up my attempt to reconcile my mother and father, and went on with my struggles to get somewhere with my own life. And that in itself was problem enough to keep me occupied for a long, long time to come. . . .

"The world's misery lies in this, that a man hardly ever has a companion. Women, perhaps, and chance friendships. We are reckless in our use of the lovely word, friend."

ROMAIN ROLLAND

Chapter Nineteen

AFTER HOLLYWOOD, Cleveland seemed dull. I went back to work with Wylie's band, but now I found myself growing restless and bored with the daily three-session round, the everlasting rehearsals, the endless chain of arrangements I had to go on making day after day.

Even between dance sets, while the other men in the band went off to have a smoke or talk with their friends, I would remain in my seat in front of my music rack, putting down little black notes on sheets of score paper. I was beginning to feel as if I were lost in a jungle of musical phrases, introductions, modulations, melodic ideas, harmonizations, countermelodies. I was sick and tired of trying to make those trite tunes we played into halfway interesting-sounding music.

It got so the men in the band used to kid me about my constant scribbling. One of them—an older man, who had had some experience in "serious" music—took to calling me Littul Beethoven. The name didn't stick, though—maybe because most of the others had never heard of Beethoven and probably had no idea what this monicker meant. At the time, I don't believe I had ever heard of Beethoven myself.

After a while I felt I would blow my top if I didn't get out of the rut I was in. I began to feel trapped, doomed to spend my whole life in Chinese restaurants, working three sessions a day and making hundreds upon hundreds of arrangements between sessions for the rest of my days. I was beginning to dread the very idea of getting out of bed when I woke up in the morning.

During this time—perhaps out of some compensatory inner mechanism—I began to sleep so heavily that it became almost impossible for anyone to waken me. Occasionally I overslept and came to work late. Wylie was always nice about it. Maybe he understood what I was going through.

But my restlessness increased constantly, rising at times to a fever pitch. I remember one night, in the middle of a snow storm, I finished work and got into my car to drive home. But suddenly and impulsively, I decided that I *had* to get away from Cleveland, right then and there, if only for a few hours. I drove through a full-scale blizzard to Akron, thirty-odd miles away. By the time I got there, it was well after four-thirty in the morning. I drove to the Mayflower Hotel, got out of my car, went into the lobby, and sat there for over an hour. Just sat, doing nothing at all. Aside from two old charwomen who were mopping the floor, and a sleepy-eyed room clerk who watched me for a few moments and then dozed off again, I was alone. I knew how stupid it was to be losing all that sleep, I knew I would have to be back at work by noon again, right back at the same old three-session-a-day grind, but for some reason it felt good to me to be simply sitting there, in some place other than Cleveland.

That day, during the lunch session, I was queasy at the stomach; but after throwing up I was able to finish out the session. I took a nap that afternoon, and felt well enough to go back to work again. When the other men in the band heard about my "trip to Akron" the whole thing became quite a joke. But none of them seemed to understand me when I explained why I had done it.

Nevertheless, for a short while, I felt better. I had managed to get something out of my system.

And then a week later I was right back where I had been, still desperate for some sort of change.

There was no one I could talk to about whatever was eating at me. I had no real friends, only acquaintances. I was still not eighteen at the time, and the men I worked with were all older. There were a couple with whom I occasionally talked, mostly about music. But even our ideas about music were basically dissimilar.

Although I wasn't consciously aware of it, what I needed most of all in the world, was a friend—someone I could talk to, someone with whom I could share my ideas, not only about music but about all sorts of things which were beginning to interest me. I was sick with a very common disease, one of the most prevalent diseases in our particular kind of society, a disease that is by no means confined to the music business. We are all permeated by it, and the man who doesn't suffer from this sickness is either very, very lucky or else (what is more likely) has been sick with it for so long that he has come to take his sickness for granted as a "normal" part of life.

For there is nothing on land or sea, not death or taxes, not misfortune or calamity, not disaster or catastrophe, neither thirst, nor famine, nor even unrequited love as sung by all the poets taken one by one or all in a lump—not any of these, nor any other kind of human misery I can think of—that compares with this aimless, nerve-racking restlessness, this frightful, feverishly brooding lassitude shot through with pale gleams of sickly flickering energy, this pallid, shadowy visitor who makes his home in the lukewarm vacuum of lethargy, this gaunt and hollow-eyed monstrosity called—Loneliness.

Here is one of the deadly viruses, a true prime mover, one of the really special cankers of so-called civilized man—one isolated aspect of the fundamental disease of our particular time and place in history; and here indeed is a thing to fear when it reaches out to take you in its leechlike grasp.

It is the way you feel when you want something terribly but can't figure out what it is you want and there isn't one single thing that seems to make the slightest particle of difference. Nothing matters—but nothing. It is all one big fat blank and when you look for yourself all you can discover is a tiny cipher suspended in mid-air in the center of the whole inane emptiness. You have a dim feeling that this is where you came in, and you have a strong conviction that there is something wrong with the picture; but you can't seem to focus on the picture long enough to find out just what *is* wrong.

Melodramatic as it may sound, let me assure you that this is by no means an overstatement of the way I was feeling at that stage of my life. I can also assure you that after a couple of months of this kind of shenanigans the walls begin to close in on you till you're just about ripe for the nearest booby-hatch. And that is not a nice feeling for a guy to have, just in case you happen never to have had it.

"Without friends no one would choose to live, even if he had all other goods."

ARISTOTLE

Chapter Twenty

FRIENDSHIP, not love, is the thing that keeps our society from breaking down altogether. Out of the whole confused welter of fears, enmities, hidden aggressions and hostilities, out of all the curious (and for the most part unconscious) motivations of our day-to-day behavior, one thing seems to make sense—this strange relationship between people that goes by the name of Friendship. But it is as rare as it is strange.

I know this to be the truth; for at the time I've just been writing about I had the good fortune to find a friend.

One night, several guys from a traveling band which was playing a four-week engagement at a dance hall out on Euclid Avenue showed up at a place where I was working with Wylie. This was during the summer; the place was called Willy's Lake Shore Gardens and it was on the outskirts of Cleveland; and, for a welcome relief, there were no luncheon sessions, only dinner and late sessions, up to two A.M.

Some time during the evening I met these musicians who had come in to hear our band. One of them seemed like a particularly nice guy. He played the piano, he was about a year older than I was, and his name was Claude Thornhill. He seemed to be extremely interested in the band. When

he heard that I had made most of the arrangements he began to ask me all sorts of questions and listened to my answers with the most flattering attention. I was quite pleased.
I mentioned to him that we were going to run through one
of my latest efforts that night after work and try to "put
it in the books."

Just before we went up on the bandstand for our last
set, he asked me whether it would be all right for him to
stay and listen to the rehearsal. I assured him it would. I
knew Wylie would have no objection, and I myself was
pleased to have a new audience, even of only one listener.

However, there was the question of how he would get
back to his hotel, for the fellows he was with were leaving.
I told him not to worry about that. I had my own car and
would be glad to drop him off on my way home.

The arrangement we were to rehearse was one of my
more ambitious efforts, a rather elaborate, semi-concert
treatment of a tune called *Poor Butterfly,* which was then
several years old but still popular enough to have become
one of the "standards" that dance bands go on playing year
after year, long after their original popularity has died down.
I had made quite a point of it with my new acquaintance
and I was anxious to impress him, after all the interest and
attention he had shown.

Now, there is always this question with any arrangement
—how it will turn out, how it will *sound.* You have a certain
sound in mind when you write it, but no matter how much
experience you've had you can never actually be sure it
will come off as you expected it to—not until you actually
hear it. There is always a gap between what you hear in
your inner ear as you write something, and what comes out
of the band when they play the notes you've written. You
can eliminate a certain area of this gap after long experience, but in the end it's still there to some extent no matter
how much experience you've had—unless you want to play

it safe and write for effects you know will come off because you've already used them over and over before. But I hadn't done that with this particular arrangement. I had aimed at effects which were altogether new for me.

Well, as it happened, the rehearsal turned out fine. The arrangement came off even better than I had hoped. Best of all, I had lived up to my new acquaintance's flattering opinion of my arranging skill.

Anyone who has ever worked around bands will understand this. There is a good bit of exhibitionism involved in jazz music; for since the average patron of the kind of place where bands of this sort usually work hasn't the vaguest notion of what goes into the music he is dancing or listening to, what could be more natural than that the people who work seriously in this field should end up by playing or writing for themselves?

This is still true to a great extent nowadays—especially after the enormous evolution through which jazz music has come in the past decade or two. Even in those days there was already a great rift between what musicians thought was good (or "hep" as it was called in those days) and what they had to play for a living, the "commercial" dance music they had to grind out nightly in order to satisfy the paying customers, who were only interested, for the most part, in whether the music was soft or syrupy enough so they would have no difficulty in either talking over it during their eating or drinking, or recognizing the melody of the tune while they danced.

I could go on and on about this difference between the needs of the customer and the needs of the musician himself, especially when the musician happens to take his work seriously, as many jazz musicians do. Out of this serious need on the part of the jazz musician there has grown up —and is still growing—a rather impressive, if *sub rosa,* type of American music, an idiom which has become one of the few truly original contributions this country has ever made in any art form. But it's an involved subject, and could easily take up several volumes in itself—as it already has, for a number of writers and students in the field.

Anyway, we finally finished rehearsal that night, and the men in Wylie's band left. Thornhill and I were about to leave ourselves, when it suddenly occurred to me to ask him to play something. After all, I had no way of knowing how he rated as a musician himself, and, gratified as I was by his attention and interest, it still wouldn't mean much coming from someone who didn't know what it was all about.

He was a bit reluctant at first. At length, he went up onto the bandstand and played several pieces he had written himself, all as yet untitled. They were good. In fact, so good that I was astonished and more gratified than ever. He was not only a damn good musician but by far and away one of the best piano players I had heard. The only possible exception around Cleveland was a fellow named Chet Rykes, whose style was so different from Thornhill's that there couldn't have been any really meaningful comparison between them anyway.

We finally got out of there, and I drove him home. We parked on the street in front of his hotel; and there we sat until six A.M. During that time we talked and talked and *talked.* He must have been pretty bottled-up too, at the time, for he seemed to need all this talk as much as I did.

We parted at daylight. Although I had only known him for one night, I felt far closer to him than to anyone I had ever known in my life before.

Also, he was the first gentile I had ever known who some-how made it possible for me to speak easily and naturally about being Jewish. I can't explain how or why I felt this way; and it may be possible that I had met other guys who might also have had the same lack of prejudice regarding

what had come to constitute for me an enormous gulf between myself and all gentiles; in any event this may easily
have been one of the biggest factors in the development of our
friendship.

We used to get together quite often after that, although it
was tough going. He worked six nights a week on his job and
I worked seven on mine. Sometimes we met after work at
some place where we could drink a cup of coffee—neither
of us drank much of anything stronger than coffee at the
time. Other times I picked him up at his hotel when I drove
in from work. We used to take long rides out into the country or along the lake shore, gabbing our heads off about
everything and anything under the sun and/or moon—not
only about music but also about a little thing called Life.
Once in a while I brought my horn and we'd go somewhere
where there was a piano and stay up for hours on end playing any and all sorts of music, just by way of exchanging
further ideas or occasionally collaborating on an original piece.

There was only one possible resolution to the problem of
what would happen when it came time for him to leave
town with the band he was working in. I would have to
get to work on Wylie and persuade him to hire Claude. I
told Claude that if Wylie refused I would quit.

There was one big hurdle we had to get over. Although
I wanted Claude in the band almost more than anything,
I wasn't so ruthless as to want to have the present pianist
fired. In the end, what I did was to talk Wylie into having
two pianos in his band!

So that was settled. Some months later, when we went
back to work at the Golden Pheasant Restaurant, Wylie's
regular winter headquarters, Claude and I took a room together at the Winton Hotel right above where we were
working. From that time to the end of my stay in Cleveland,
a year or so later, we shared this little hotel room and ce-
mented our friendship. It's been a stormy friendship at times,

and there have been many occurrences that have threatened to rip it apart through all the years it has endured. For instance when, during the Second World War, Claude joined the Navy in order to work under me in a band made up of professional musicians I recruited to take to the Pacific. It was then that we both learned that no friendship, no matter how strong or lasting, can survive between the leader of a band and one of its members. So we arranged for Claude's transfer to another outfit before mine went off from Pearl Harbor to a series of island hops all over the South Pacific. And right to this moment—we are still friends.

We don't get to see much of each other these days. Claude has a band of his own now—a damn good band too, the last time I heard it. But whenever we do run into each other there is always that peculiar, strange, curious, whatever-you-want-to-call-it, feeling of *warmth* that still exists between us, and I'm sure it will continue as long as one or the other of us is alive.

I've gone into this at some length because friendship is to me an enormously important thing. In the kind of life I've led, a fellow almost never has the opportunity to stay in one place long enough to build up a continuity of relationship with people. You make acquaintances here and there as you go along on your road to wherever you're going, but mostly they come to nothing. The simple reason is that contacts of this sort—even when they are between people who might, if given sufficient time, find great community of interests—are usually far too brief. The life I've led has been largely a ships-passing-in-the-night kind of life. I know literally thousands of people, but I hardly *know* any of them.

Of course, a great many people *call* this sort of thing friendship. Mostly, I'm afraid, it is an excuse people use for not spending their time alone; yet, these same people are often more lonely when they are together than they might be otherwise. And relatively few people ever seem to learn that loneliness is not just a matter of being yourself. It can be even more acute when you are constantly surrounded by people with whom you have no real relationship. . . .

But I have to go back for a little while now, to explain about an obstacle that was beginning to obtrude itself between me and the road I was trying to travel. This obstacle was the growing conflict that was arising between my mother and me.

"A child may have too much of mother's blessing."

JOHN RAY

Chapter Twenty-One

ALTHOUGH I WAS AS YET only an adolescent I'm afraid I was hardly the kind of kid who could have been called an average adolescent. Most kids of seventeen or eighteen are still going through an adolescent phase; and I suppose I was no further developed along really adult lines than any other kid of my age. But since, at the age of fourteen or fifteen, I had started to make my living alongside of men much older, I now began to want to get off on my own. I felt perfectly able to take care of myself—at least economically; that much had already been demonstrated. For some time now, I had been paying my own way and supporting my mother as well. I felt I had as good a right as anyone to live the way I wanted to.

Several times I had tried to talk my mother into going back to New Haven, but each time, I had had to give it up. I could not face the unpleasantness that arose whenever I brought this up. Every time I tried to discuss it on what seemed to me a rational level, she would work herself up, weep bitterly, and carry on about how she had "given up her life to come and take care of me." I couldn't face the remorse she instilled in me because of these attempts. In the end I couldn't go through with it.

It is easy enough now to see how unhealthy the whole

situation was for both of us. At the time, though, I wasn't any too clear about it. I had neither the awareness to understand it objectively, nor the skill to make her see what was wrong with our whole relationship.

We had gradually drifted, without either of us knowing quite how or when it had happened, into something altogether different from the usual relationship that exists between a mother and a seventeen-year-old boy.

For one thing, the economics of the situation were all out of kilter; I was getting the kind of salary ordinarily earned by a far older man. In addition I was supporting her, automatically becoming the *de facto,* if not *de jure,* "head of the household"—so that it was already becoming impossible for her to assert her parental authority. And, since I had discovered that there are privileges as well as responsibilities attached to being a breadwinner, we had long since passed the stage where she attempted to curb me in any important way.

She had one weapon, and one only. She used it at all times; for there would otherwise have been no excuse whatsoever for her continuing to remain with me.

This weapon was the usual, conventional one—which, of course, had very little to do with the entirely unconventional and reversed nature of our separate roles in each other's lives. Nevertheless, she clung grimly, desperately, and at times even hysterically, to her point that I was still no more than a child who needed his mother to take care of him and keep him out of mischief. End of quote.

My answer was the obvious one—that my age had nothing to do with my status, that I came and went as I pleased, that there was nothing she could do about it, and that if I had wanted to get myself into "mischief" I'd have done so long before. For that matter, I could be doing so right at that moment without her being any the wiser if I didn't choose to enlighten her about my activities—"mischievous" or otherwise.

Inevitably, this produced the counterargument: since it was true that I had complete freedom to come and go as I pleased, when and if I pleased—then why on earth couldn't I be satisfied and drop this crazy idea of going off, "leaving my mother," and getting a place of my own to live in? Why wasn't it all right the way it was? Wasn't she "taking care" of me? Seeing to it that my clothes were taken care of? My food prepared the way I liked it, my home kept neatly and nicely and "respectably"? And, in Heaven's name, that being so—why on earth should I want to go off to live in some "dirty hotel room," eat "dirty restaurant food" and probably get sick the first week after I left home? Again, end of quote.

The simple, uncontestable, biological fact was that she was my mother. A mother was supposed to take care of her son; that was a mother's duty. A son was supposed to love and cherish and take care of his mother; that was the way it had been ordained, and that was the way it had to be—nothing else could be said or done about it. Still once again, end of quote.

"But of *course* I love you, Mom!" I would cry in baffled desperation. "But does that mean I have to go on living with my mother for the rest of my life? What's *wrong* with living like the other guys I'm working with? How does that *change* the way I feel toward you?"

No use. No use at all. Conventions were conventions, mothers were mothers, sons were sons, and nothing I could ever say or do would change these "facts" or the way in which they were supposed to work by fixed and inalterable decree.

So that whenever I attempted to make the break, I always had to give up. It was too painful to go on fighting.

Of course, the truth is that all the reasons I had ever been able to give her, for my wanting to move out and start living a life of my own, were false reasons. Even at the time I knew better, but I could not understand clearly myself, let alone make her understand, the real underlying compulsions I was feeling and trying to act on.

No matter how much freedom I had in coming and going when and as I pleased, and no matter how little parental authority my mother could or could not exercise over my life, still there was this real problem, which I couldn't bring myself to discuss with her, and which I could see no way of ever resolving as long as I went on living with her. So it went on that way, for quite a while; and, try as I might, I was unable to get her to give one inch in her bitter determination to retain at least a partial hold on me as my mother, no matter how little I went on behaving in actuality as a son.

My problem arose out of the fact that I was beginning to become interested in a little matter called sex.

"There my white stole of chastity I daff'd
Shook off my sober guards and civil fears."

Chapter Twenty-Two

I HAVEN'T TOUCHED ON THIS MATTER SO FAR. Before the time I'm now writing about there really had not been very much to touch on.

I have mentioned that during the time I worked in Cavallaro's band I became the butt for all sorts of joking and hazing. Among all the other gags, there was always one big one about my being a "virgin." Somehow, they never did tire of kidding me about that. I tried to deny this horrible charge—I even got so I began to believe my denials myself. But no matter how involved or lurid a tale of conquest I might dream up, I was never able to convince these colleagues of mine—probably because the very luridness and complication with which I used to clutter my fictions showed only too clearly that I had had no experience whatsoever. I had only the vaguest sort of information on the subject and even that was fairly well garbled. Most of it was stuff I had picked up as a kid hanging around the streets listening to the kind of sex lore a kid is apt to pick up that way. And most of that I had pretty much managed to forget anyway, since from all I could hear of it as a young kid, this whole sex business sounded like a rather unpleasant way for a guy to pass time.

After enough hazing, though, I began to regard this much-

[156]

discussed "virginity" of mine as just about the gravest possible shortcoming I could have been guilty of. To "lose my virginity," to "go out and get laid" (as they put it), became equated in my mind with "being a man." There was so much stuff of that sort going around in Cavallaro's band—having to do with not only the undesirability and preposterousness of the virgin state, but also the general thesis that "a guy ain't a man till he's had at least one dose of clap"—that for a while I believe I'd have been delighted if I had somehow been able to contract a nice little "dose" of gonorrhea, just to shut those guys up once and for all!

But during the time I remained with Cavallaro's band the opportunity didn't arise—neither to pick up a venereal disease nor to alter my status as "the band virgin."

Later on, though, after I was fired and joined the Kentuckians, I made a stab at altering my status; and even though no real change was effected by what happened, it enabled me to convince my new associates that there *had* been a change. That was all I'd really wanted anyway, and once that had been accomplished I think I'd have been capable of withstanding a fair amount of torture before I'd have confessed what really took place while I was supposedly in the process of "losing my cherry"—as they termed this de-virginizing process.

The following sordid incident illustrates the sort of idiotic sex indoctrination a kid can be exposed to in our society. Of all the taboos we live with daily, the so-called normal attitude toward sex is just about the most blundering stupidity we could possibly perpetrate on ourselves and still manage to survive as a species at all.

Anyway—this happened while I was still living up near Northfield, Connecticut, shortly before the band set out in its broken-down motor caravan for Lexington, Kentucky. There was another member of the outfit who was also a "virgin." The constant ragging we were both subjected to had resulted in a sort of loose bond between us. After a time we made a pact. We decided to take advantage of the first occasion that might arise to "do something" conclusive about our sexual ignorance —and in such a way as to be able to support each other's stories of our changed status.

Obviously, there was only one place where any such plan might work, and that was a brothel, or whore-house—or "cat-house," which was the term we actually used.

About two-thirty one morning, after playing a dance near Waterbury, Connecticut, this fellow-unfortunate and I took off for town with five or six dollars apiece in our pockets. Our chief difficulty, of course, was that neither of us had the slightest idea of how to go about locating a "cat-house." For my own part, I wasn't even sure there were such places. How could I be sure that the guys who had told me about them weren't simply pulling another of their gags on me?

However, my companion assured me that there were such places and that he had once even been in one, but had not had the necessary funds to avail himself of its delights.

Well, we kidded around for awhile thinking up possible methods of locating one of these joints. We even discussed the advisability of looking through the classified section of the telephone directory; and we went minutely into the question of whether they would be listed under W (for Whore-house) or C (for "Cat-house").

I can't quite remember how we actually managed to find what we finally did find. All I can remember is that after asking a cabdriver or two and obtaining no results whatsoever, we finally wound up following some Negro we had picked up somewhere in our wanderings. He led us into a disreputable-looking neighborhood, through a dark alley, and up to the door of a ramshackle building. Here he knocked confidently and in a short time the door was opened from inside and another colored man stuck his head out and wanted to know what gave.

"I got a couple of customers," our sponsor announced, and a moment later we found ourselves in a dingy, dimly-lighted kitchen.

And right then I came dangerously close to turning around and tearing hell-bent-for-election out of there, for over in one corner of the room sat a giant of a Negro gravely sharpening a large axe on a stone held between his knees!

My friend was whispering with the man who had let us in, while our sponsor stood to one side watching laconically. I was too scared to take any part in any of the complex financial arrangements.

Eventually we were given to understand that our guide was entitled to a small cut of the take. We "took care" of him, and he departed. Another whispering conference began, again between my friend and the "proprietor" of the joint, until they decided on a suitable fee for the commodity we had come there to purchase.

That detail finally having been worked out to the apparent satisfaction of everyone concerned (with the clear exception of myself, who would have been glad to get out of there immediately and never come back, virginity or no virginity), the only remaining question was: who would go first, my companion or I?

Up to this point, although I was completely disillusioned with the whole tawdry business, I had been prepared to go through with it anyway. But now, when I realized there was only one "girl," and that it was taken for granted that both my friend and I would "visit" her, I became a little sick at the stomach. I knew I couldn't go through with it—that's all there was to it.

So there was no difficulty about the question of who would be first. I urged my companion to go ahead. I was hoping against hope that by the time he was finished I might be able to figure out some way to get out.

He seemed to take an unbearably long time. There was nothing I could do but sit down and wait. And all the time I sat there, neither the "proprietor" nor the huge man (who kept right on sharpening his axe) said one word. When my buddy finally came into the kitchen again I learned that there was no way for me to get out of going "in there" myself. For it turned out that the price they had fixed for the transaction had been based on the fact that there were *two* customers. Apparently there had been a cut-rate deal made.

I went through the door like a man being led to the guillotine. I found myself in a pitch-dark room. For a moment I groped around, and then I heard a woman whispering to me: "Hurry up, boy, let's go, let's not stand here all night, for Chri'sake."

I was as panic-stricken as I have ever been in my life. Somehow I managed to get across to the owner of the voice that I would be only too happy to pay her, but only on one condition. She was to sit perfectly still and let me do exactly the same, until enough time had elapsed so that I could get out of there without arousing my buddy's suspicion.

Not having been able to see the woman during the entire time we sat there, I can't tell you anything about what she thought or felt about the novel arrangement I had proposed. With a few words of amazement she acceded to my request. And then she said nothing. And we sat there. I have no idea of what she looked like, whether she was young or old, dark or light, short or tall. And the only physical contact I ever did have with her was when we accidentally touched hands for a fleeting second as I handed her the money for my "visit."

At last I got out of there and rejoined my companion. And with no further mishap we were shown out, and found our way back into the streets of Waterbury. The streets in that neighborhood were dingy and the slum buildings were dilapidated, but nothing ever looked better to me in my life!

Of course I said nothing to my companion about what had actually gone on between me and the woman in that dark room; so there was no reason for him to doubt that I had done what we had gone there to do. He himself seemed quite happy, so I didn't doubt that he, at least, was no longer a "virgin." Later on, though, when I got to thinking about it, from his point of view I must have seemed quite satisfied myself, so there could hardly be any more reason for him to have suspected what I actually did in there, than for me to suspect him of doing exactly the same thing himself.

I've often wondered since. . . .

At any rate, that is the story of how I *officially* lost my virginity; and even though I remained an authentic "virgin" for quite some time to come, the incident served one real purpose at least: it put an end to the kidding I had had to take.

Later on, during the week we played at the Joyland Casino in Lexington, there was another episode.

"Gang shag" was a term I had heard before. But I had never quite managed to believe in the reality of it until I became an actual witness to such an affair.

There were six or seven guys involved—and one girl. What kind of girl, I can't even imagine, and I'm perfectly willing to be considered naive in this respect; to this day I can't conceive of any girl in her right mind allowing herself to be used as this one was. One at a time, off in a patch of scrubby woodland behind the dance hall where we worked, the six or seven boys took this one skinny little girl, right there on the ground. What there could possibly have been in it for this wretched little creature, I have never been able to figure out. There was no force used. There wasn't even the excuse of money, for no money was passed during the entire ugly business.

In fact, I'd just as soon skip this without going into much detail. I couldn't bring myself to participate in it, but I pretended to. It was a dark night, and there was a good bit of confusion about the whole affair, so there wasn't much difficulty in getting away with the deception. Even so, I was pretty well disgusted with my part in the affair; in fact, I'm disgusted with it right this minute. And the only reason I tell about it at all is that it seems to me just about as effective a way as any to bring home to anyone who has any last doubts about the necessity for healthy sex-education the proof for such a necessity.

Also, we may as well get my story right—just in case anyone has any remaining illusions about the way a fellow is apt to have to learn his way through life when he can't go to someone who can set him straight at the start. . . .

After I got back to New Haven again, and then went down to Miami with Cavallaro, it was taken for granted by my associates that I was no longer a "virgin."

Also, while we were down there in Miami I got myself a girl. This was my first girl, and our relationship was as innocent as anything of that kind can be. She was a chorus girl who worked in the floor show in the little gambling joint where Cavallaro's band played. She had been married and divorced, and had a baby daughter with whom I used to play occasionally when I went up to see her. She lived quite respectably and decorously with her mother. Now and then, in between dance sets, we would go outside, sit in someone's parked car behind the night club where we were both working—and neck.

I told myself I was wildly and ecstatically in love with her, and I suppose that if I had made a point of it I could have gone to bed with her; but somehow it never occurred to me. For she was what I would have called "a nice girl"—and going to bed with a nice girl was something you just didn't do. I can't remember just how or where I picked up this curious notion of morality, but I've since learned that there are plenty of men who feel the same way. So, although I still think it's curious, I suppose there's nothing unique about it.

Anyway, this girl friend of mine and I "went together" for

all the time I was in Miami, and after that we wrote each other sporadically for awhile. She lived somewhere in the Midwest and, like myself, had only been down South for the season. Eventually the whole thing wore itself out. My broken heart miraculously survived the strain and in a few months seemed to be functioning as well as ever. This astonished and disillusioned me. I was a pretty romantic kid, starry-eyed as all hell, and the very fact that I could not only forget this girl but actually begin to find it difficult to remember what she had looked like, and eventually even her name—that was a fairly tough thing to take in my stride. . . .

About that same time—it was while I was working at the Olympia Theatre—I finally did "lose my virginity," this time in reality.

What happened was that I met a girl at a dance hall in Savin Rock, an amusement park just outside of New Haven, where I had gone to listen to Barney Rapp's band, in those days one of the few organized big bands around town. Someone introduced us and, surprisingly enough—to me at any rate —she immediately made it quite evident that she liked me. We wound up parking in the woods, on the outskirts of town. Somewhere along the line I had heard about the old gag of taking the back seat out of the car and using it as a portable couch. I timidly proposed this scheme, and was amazed at the alacrity with which she accepted.

After it was all over I was unable to find that I had changed in even the slightest respect, let alone in any such essential manner as all the endless kidding I had taken about this terrifically important matter had led me to expect.

The sad truth, of course—disappointing as it was to me— was that I was still the same inexperienced, basically shy kid I had been before this miraculous event took place. Rather than having been anything particularly miraculous, the entire affair had been quite ordinary and not even especially exciting.

When it was over I took her home and never saw her again.

It had nothing to do with my liking or disliking her. She was a fairly pretty little thing, as I dimly remember her, although for the life of me I can't recall her name either. The whole trouble was that I was far too busy learning my business as an instrumentalist, and there just wasn't enough time left over for this sort of diversion.

Besides, I wasn't "in love" with her—and I took this qualification quite seriously. Perhaps I didn't really know what "being in love" meant. But still, I was pretty damn sure what it did *not* mean. So I decided to leave well enough alone and let the matter take care of itself, as I was vaguely sure it would sooner or later.

Which it sure as hell has. In fact, I'd have been astounded if anyone had tried to give me the tiniest hint of what I would ultimately have to go through, the devious paths I would have to travel through our twentieth century wilderness, in pursuit of this curious phenomenon called Love. As I've said, the big trouble with this Cinderella dame is that you can't know anything about her until you've caught up with her. And if I'd had the slightest idea what it would be like when I *did* catch up with her myself, I'd have turned and run like a thief while I still had the chance. . . .

However, since there wasn't any way for me to get a quick glimpse into the future, I kept right on dealing to the best of my limited ability with whatever the present had to offer as I went along. And, aside from several occasional, and on the whole fairly similar, experiences along the same lines as this first "back seat" incident, I went right on working at music and keeping myself pretty well uninvolved.

And then, about a year and a half after I came to Cleveland, I finally met a girl with whom I really did fall in love. This time it was a pretty real thing, as opposed to any of the other "real" ones I had got myself mixed up with up to that point— and this time I got so caught up that I can't see yet how I ever managed to "get over" it.

It happened more or less during the same time I was trying to find some way of making the final break away from my mother. Now I had two strong reasons for wanting this break. The first was that I wanted to share living-quarters with my new friend, Thornhill. The second was that I wanted to feel free to continue my "love affair" with this girl. But even with this double excuse for leaving my mother, it was still a painful problem. We had to go through a great deal of mutual bitterness before I could finally pry myself loose. Somehow, though, I managed to get through it; and after it was over I was at last free to go ahead with my life in the fumbling and confused way I thought I wanted to live it.

"The magic of first love is our ignorance that it can ever end."

DISRAELI

Chapter Twenty-Three

HER NAME WAS BETTY. The way I felt about her, it might just as well have been a combination of Eve, Lilith, Delilah, Salome, and Helen of Troy, for to me she was the embodiment of the most desirable qualities of every one of those legendary paragons of femininity, with none of their disadvantages—the greatest of these being, of course, that they had all been dead for quite a while. Betty was not only alive, and the most beautiful thing I had ever set eyes on, but best of all she was my girl.

She was sixteen and I was seventeen when we first met. By descent she was Scotch-Irish. By some genetic miracle her parents had contrived to construct one of the loveliest creatures it had ever been my good fortune to behold. Even after I got to know her very well, long after we had started "going together," there were times when I'd sit and stare at her with absolute wonder, for I found it difficult to believe that any mere human being could be so breath-takingly, magically, deliriously, ravishingly lovely. Even more incredible was the fact that for some reason I was never able to figure out she seemed as much in love with me as I with her; and I couldn't see how that could possibly be possible.

Language has certain definite drawbacks and this is one of the big ones; you can only do so much with words and after that you bog down. So I won't try to tell you what she looked like to me, except for the statistical information that her eyes were as blue as a cornflower—but with depths and shadings that no cornflower on earth has, or could ever have—and her hair was the color of new wheat, or, rather, the color a field of new wheat *might* have if it were powdered with pale gold-dust.

So. . . .

That was Betty.

We were with each other as often as possible, as a rule at least four or five nights a week. It wasn't easy, for I was working every night. The only way we could manage to spend much time with each other was to have dinner together between the evening and night sessions; then Betty would go up to the room I shared with Claude, and wait for me to come up between dance sets during the late session. I wasn't happy with this arrangement, but I could see no way of changing it and going on with my job. Betty constantly assured me that she didn't mind. Now and then we'd take a ride out by Lake Erie during the afternoon, and that was a little better, although even then we couldn't go far because I had to get back in time for the six-to-eight o'clock "shift" at that everlasting grind. Still, we made the best of a bad situation, went on meeting as often as we could, and fell more deeply in love every time we saw each other.

When I wasn't with her I used to talk about her—on and on and on—to Claude. He was a willing audience, for at that same time he was also in love, with a girl he later married, a girl he had met in my old stamping ground, Lexington, Kentucky. (Quite a while after he had come to work with Wylie's band, I learned that he had also played there some years earlier, with a pretty well-known band around those parts, called the Kentucky Colonels.) His being in love too constituted an even further bond between us, although we hardly needed it. Between sessions, when we weren't discussing music or practicing (which we both did, in spite of the hours we spent daily at our actual job), or giving each other "ear-training" exercises—each alternately hitting notes at random on the piano while the other sat at the far end of the deserted bandstand and called out the notes as they were struck—or when I wasn't with Betty, we'd sit around and compare notes (not musical ones at these times) as to the respective beauty, loveliness, and general desirability of our girls.

I've already spoken about my attitude toward "nice" girls. Just in case anyone has any false ideas based on some of the sordid aspects of what I've described as my sex "education," perhaps I should mention that during all the time I knew Betty, never, for one single moment, did it ever occur to me to try to have any sexual relationship with her, beyond kissing her and, now and then only, a certain amount of innocent-enough "necking." Even at that, it was always within certain undefined but nevertheless strict bounds.

By the time we'd known each other a year or so, although there was never any such thing as a formal "engagement," we'd both decided that sooner or later we were going to get married; so, despite a normal enough sexual desire for each other which we both felt, we also felt there was no real need to rush matters. That was all there was to it. We were both far too young to consider marriage as anything but a distant, future resolution to a love that would go on forever. But neither of us ever doubted that that was how it would wind up. I'm certain that ordinarily it *would* have wound up just exactly that way, too; and right now I'd be the last to say that I could have done much better. In fact, having gone a long way and done a good bit worse in the marital department (as far as *permanence* is concerned at any rate), perhaps it might have been the best thing that could have happened to me.

However, as the saying goes, it wasn't written that way.

For, a few months after I had come back from Hollywood,

Irving Aaronson's band came to Cleveland to play one week at a local theatre with that same Irene Bordoni show, "Paris." During their week in town, I learned that my two old New Haven musician friends, Charlie Trotta and Tony Pestritto, had apparently not forgotten our plan to get me into the Commanders. Now they went to work to put this plan into execution.

They worked on some of the more influential members of Aaronson's organization. They got some of them into the Golden Pheasant to hear me play, and pointed out that almost all the arrangements Wylie's band was playing had been written by me.

After a while this began to get results. The Aaronson band, as I've said, was not so good musically as to be able to turn up its collective nose at the kind of improvement I might be able to contribute. The fellow who realized this best was the one who did most of the arranging for *them*. He was a piano player named Chalmers (no one ever called him that, though, except as a sort of affectionate gag, and the nickname—by which he was known to many of the top jazz musicians of that day—was Chummy) MacGregor. After listening to a few of the arrangements I'd made, he went to work in earnest on Aaronson.

Before they left town, Aaronson himself came into the Golden Pheasant for one of our luncheon sessions, listened to me, and, after Charlie, Tony, and Chummy had bent his ear sufficiently, finally offered me a job with his band.

Because of Betty, I didn't immediately jump at the offer. If anything, that made more of an impression on Aaronson than anything else I could have done. He told me there was no necessity to make up my mind right then anyway, since the stuff they were playing in the Bordoni show was pretty much set and there would be no place for me in that. However, after they had finished the tour and gone back to their return engagement at the Blossom Room in Hollywood, he would send me an official offer by telegram, which I could confirm if by then I had decided to accept.

We let it go at that. But after he left, the other three guys hung around for a while and went to work on *me* now. Was I crazy? Did I want to spend the rest of my life working in Chinese joints, when I could get into a big-time outfit like Aaronson's and play the best spots in the United States? And so forth and so on.

But I was happy where I was, I told them. I had my girl here. I liked Wylie. He treated me well and, as far as that went, paid me as much as Aaronson had offered. And, although I didn't like saying it, still, as they themselves damn well knew, Wylie's band was better than Aaronson's anyway, certainly from a musical standpoint.

This last they ignored completely. As to whether I was happy here or not, they brushed that aside too. "Listen," said Charlie, "don't you know what it means to get with a band like Aaronson's? All right, so it isn't a great band. But it's one of the best-known bands in the country, and after you're in we can all go to work on the old man to get some more good men into the band. Meanwhile, you can learn a lot working with a guy like Chummy here, who's worked with the best guys in the business and knows the whole score from start to finish, and on top of that you'll be working in spots you won't get into with Wylie in ten million years! Why, after Hollywood we're going to Chicago, and from there to *New York!* What's the matter with you, Art—you nuts or something?"

The one thing in this verbal barrage that had any real effect was the statement that I "could learn a lot." However, for the time being there was nothing I could do either way, so I told them I'd decide if and when I got the wire from Aaronson.

"Don't worry, you'll get it," they assured me.

After they left Cleveland I talked it over with Claude and, of course, with Betty. During the time that elapsed between

Aaronson's leaving town and my getting the wire I did a lot of thinking about this proposed uprooting. There was a good bit to think about, a number of angles to consider.

When all the thinking and discussing was over, after every possible angle had been hashed and rehashed, I didn't know which way was up any more. I still hadn't made up my mind. I was still far too deeply in love to see anything straight, to make any decisions involving such a change as this. Although it would undoubtedly benefit my career, it had one decided drawback—it would also take me away from the girl with whom I was so desperately, ecstatically, and innocently in love.

I can't think how the whole thing would have ended if it had been left for me to decide; but, as things turned out, events decided it for me, and by the time the wire from Aaronson did come, the result was already inevitable.

"Leave thy home, O youth, and seek out alien shores; a larger range of life is ordained for thee."

Chapter Twenty-Four

BECAUSE OF THIS NEW-FOUND LOVE and friendship, and even in spite of my growing restlessness with the kind of work I was doing in the Chinese restaurants, I might still have decided to stay in Cleveland—had it not been for certain subtle changes that had begun to take place in my relations with Wylie.

As I said, Wylie and I had always got on extremely well. I respected him immensely—not necessarily as a musician (for he made no pretenses along those lines and was satisfied to leave that part of running his band to me), but almost in the way I might have respected a father. In a sense his manner toward me had a strong overlay of paternalism, a mixture of amusement and fatherly tolerance for my youthful foibles, and an evident pride in my overintense, almost fanatic, approach to the development of my skills as instrumentalist and arranger. He was well aware that his band had shown a decided improvement since I had taken over the musical end. The respect I had for him as an employer who gave me the opportunity for experimentation, was further heightened by my awareness of his pride in me, plus my unconscious gratitude to him for playing the role of father-substitute in my life dur-

[172]

ing a time when I needed someone to fill the vacuum left by my father's having gone away.

Wylie behaved toward me in an altogether different manner from that in which the average bandleader usually does toward the members of his band. As a rule, no matter how friendly a bandleader may feel toward one of his musicians, there is always the necessity for fairly rigid discipline on the bandstand, and this generally makes for a heightened awareness of the essential employer-employee relationship. There is a kind of curious formality underlying the seeming informality of this *milieu,* because it is next to impossible for a bandleader and one of the members of his band to bridge the gap off the bandstand and still maintain it *on* the bandstand; generally they retain only the sketchiest kind of friendliness in their over-all relations.

Basically, you see, the bandleader plays an altogether different role from that of any single member of his organization. He is the "front" man, the intermediator between his band and the public, providing, in a sense, the "personality" of the band, the focal point through which the public reacts to the entire band, whether favorably or otherwise. The musician, on the other hand—the "side man," as he is called—the member of the band who sits there as one individual *part* of the band is, for the most part, one relatively unimportant small cog in the machine—even when he is fairly well-known himself, as in the case of a singer, say, or a featured instrumentalist. In other words, the member of the band takes his identity from the band itself—he is a part of the band, and, while he is working in the band, gives up a certain portion of his individuality except for those times when the music allows him to step forward and assert himself; whereas the leader *gives* the band its identity, even when he is not the musical head of the band—and for that matter may scarcely know anything about music at all, as in the case of several nationally well-known "name" band leaders.

I will go into this in detail further on. For the moment it is necessary only to point out these few superficial aspects of the way it works, in order to explain what my relations had been with Wylie and how they now began to be altered.

I have already said that at that stage of my life I had begun to develop an inordinate need of sleep. I seemed to require a tremendous amount of it when I finally unwound at the end of a night's work and was able to get to sleep at all. I used to sink into what amounted to a deep trance, and after a time it became almost impossible for anyone to rouse me. I don't know whether this was simply my body rebelling against the hypertension under which I operated and the vast energy loads I expended every day of my life during that period, or some escape mechanism, some unconscious attempt on my part to alleviate the strain under which I was working, and which, being unable to find any real outlet, manifested itself in an increasing restlessness-lethargy seesaw.

Whatever it was, I remember that Claude, with whom I was by then sharing living quarters, used to have to resort to all sorts of weird expedients to get me up in time for the luncheon sessions at the Golden Pheasant. After a while even these expedients began to lose their effectiveness. At that point I asked him to try throwing a glass of cold water in my face when I wouldn't respond to anything else. That seemed to work for a few days. But it eventually got so I would wipe my face on the pillow and go right on sleeping (although he assured me that I didn't seem to take it any too pleasantly).

In fact, he was beginning to get a little nervous about this morning chore and at times he threatened to quit entirely and let me go on sleeping my head off. I finally came up with a rather special device, after just about everything else had failed. It was a pretty crazy idea; but it seemed to me it ought to work. I tied a piece of string around my little toe before going to bed and told Claude to give it a good hard yank in the morning. We both agreed it was pretty silly, but he was willing to give it a try; neither of us expected it to work out the way it did.

What happened was that when he gave the string the prescribed yank, it must have hurt. Instead of waking up, I jumped out of bed, still sound asleep, and leaped at his throat with the apparent intent of strangling him to death. He got out of my clutch somehow, barely escaping from this insane attack of mine, and promptly cleared out. He went to work, as he assured me later on, glad to escape with his life, leaving me to my seemingly uninterrupted slumbers. That day, after the first dance set, Wylie came up and finally managed to bring me back to some semblance of consciousness.

I was terribly apologetic, of course, but nothing would persuade Claude to lay a hand on me during my sleep for the rest of the time we roomed together. And since this curious somnambulistic tendency lasted for quite a while (in fact, even up to the time I had got to New York City and become established there)—since I continued to sleep like a dead man, it devolved upon Wylie himself to become my official waker-upper. Whether he had some special method of his own, or I had enough respect for him to be able, even subliminally, to sense who was trying to pull me out of the almost cataleptic state into which I used to sink when I fell asleep—whatever it was, for a while it worked. Still, even after I awoke sufficiently to get out of bed, leap into my clothes, tear downstairs to the bandstand, and grab up a horn and start blowing it after some fashion—nevertheless I remained in a state of semi-stupor for some time after I started to work. I don't believe I really became responsibly conscious until after several dance sets, between which I used to drink innumerable cups of black coffee.

It was inevitable under these circumstances that sooner or later my behavior began to get on Wylie's nerves. I can't blame him. After all, a man who is trying to run a band is harassed enough maintaining discipline. And my sitting on the bandstand practically sound asleep, day after day during the first three or four sets of those infernal luncheon sessions we had to play six days a week, was hardly a help. Musicians are not the easiest people in the world to keep in line anyway; and all this stuff of my either missing the first set every day, or else, after I finally did show up, sitting in my place in a coma for at least an hour or more, was beginning to affect the morale of the whole band. In one way it became a kind of running gag that provided us all with a certain amount of humor; which was O.K. as far as it went, for those hours we worked were pretty grim. But after a while it began to have other—and, from Wylie's point of view, non-humorous—ramifications. When other band members came late, as they were more or less bound to now and then on a job with hours like that, what could he say? After all, they could all see that I was getting away with it. Getting away with it? What the hell, there was the leader of the band, Wylie himself, going to my room and waking me up every morning!

So that without my meaning to take advantage of my special status as Wylie's musical lieutenant, it became fairly evident to the rest of the men that I was being treated in a rather special way. This never makes for good working relations, neither between the man who is receiving preferential treatment and the other men in the band, nor between the band and the bandleader himself. It wouldn't work very well in any kind of business, but particularly not in the sort of close-knit organization that a dance band essentially is.

Eventually Wylie began to feel that I was becoming a problem child. There was no way he could cope with this ridiculous situation without being made to look foolish, or, even worse, being forced to overlook obvious breaches of discipline on my part which he could not overlook on the part of the rest of the men unless he was ready to let his entire organization go to pieces.

Another difficulty arose at about that same time, this one a musical difficulty. I was getting stale. Not so much in my playing—for when I was awake that was all right—but in my arranging.

Wylie was paying me a weekly salary that averaged between one hundred and fifty and one hundred and seventy-five dollars, depending on the number of arrangements I brought in each week. Our agreement as to the number of arrangements I was to make was fairly loose, a sort of general understanding that I would do whatever work was necessary. Over the period of about a year and a half during which I had been in charge of this department, I had averaged at least three or four new arrangements every week. Now an occasional week would come along when I simply couldn't manage to make the quota. It got to where I would make two a week, then there would be an occasional week when I would bring in only one; and finally there came a time when I couldn't get myself to write one single note. The well had run absolutely stone dry.

After two or three such weeks in a row, things began to become strained. Wylie thought, naturally enough, that I was taking advantage of him. The truth was that I didn't mean to at all. I felt worse than he did, if anything. I respected and liked him so much that the last thing on earth I wanted to do was to give him any such impression. But I simply couldn't force myself to go on any longer at the pace I had set myself. Instead of going to him and trying to explain my predicament, I tried to get by without saying anything until—as I hoped—after I had managed to work my way through to whatever was at the bottom of the strange lethargy that had come over me. But as this state of affairs continued, I began to develop a guilty awareness of my failure to meet my obligations to him, and in turn this made it more difficult than ever for me to talk to him about my troubles.

He reacted in the way that might have been expected—at first he was embarrassed, then hurt, and in the end angry. He felt put upon, cheated, taken advantage of—and of course, from his point of view, he was entirely right.

The misunderstanding, which had originally come about because neither of us had been able to talk things out with the other, finally grew to such proportions that we began to feel a mutual hostility. Wylie, on the one hand, began to treat me as an ingrate, and, moreover, an ingrate who continues to accept money without doing what he is supposed to do in return for the money he is getting. I, on the other hand, out of growing embarrassment and guilt over the situation I had inadvertently created between us, began to dislike him and—illogically enough—blame *him* for what was going on.

Of course, there were other complicating factors, not the least of which was my constant worry about trying to decide whether I really wanted to join Aaronson's band. That, in turn, hung on the emotional problem of whether or not I was willing to leave my girl.

By the time Aaronson's wire finally did come, I was at a complete loss. I had arrived at a kind of psychic stalemate.

I was confronted with two broad choices. On one side, to stay on in Wylie's band, going along as I had been for the past few years, making a fairly comfortable living, and leaning back on the security I had established for myself in Cleveland. In spite of the present tension, this could have been worked out if I had had a serious talk with Wylie and explained what was eating me. The chief difficulty was that I wasn't at all sure what *was* eating me.

Which left only the one other choice, to take the job with Aaronson, pull up stakes and leave Cleveland once and for all, and go on about my main business of trying to get somewhere with music, to break into the higher echelons of the business.

When I discussed this with Claude, he told me that, given the chance, he would go with Aaronson himself. That had some influence in my decision.

What finally resolved it, though, was Betty. She not only advised me to go, but insisted on it. She went so far as to threaten to break off with me altogether if I didn't—on the grounds that she felt I was hesitating only on her account.

Actually that was partly true, but I denied it vehemently. She would have none of my denials. And when she presented me with her ultimatum—either join Aaronson's band or else make up my mind that she would not see me any more at all —I made up my mind to go.

I wired Aaronson that I would arrive in Hollywood some three weeks after my wire of acceptance, gave Wylie two weeks' notice at the end of that week, and, when that was up, packed my few belongings and set out all by myself, in my shiny red Auburn roadster, for the West Coast.

The night I left, I found it hard to accustom myself to the idea that I was leaving the place where I had lived for the past three years, put down a few tentative roots, worked steadily and made friends, found myself a girl, and in general started to make some sort of life. It was hard to believe that this part of my life was over.

Still, I kept telling myself, there was no doubt this was the best thing to do. After all, I also told myself, that was the music business, wasn't it? Here today, gone tomorrow—and after all was said and done, a guy couldn't stay in one place, especially a place like Cleveland, and expect to get anywhere in the racket. No sir, you had to go where you could better yourself, get to the top—and since the top was where I wanted to be, this was just part of getting there. At least I was on my way once more, and who knew what might lie ahead?

I knew I had plenty to learn; or rather, I thought I knew. If I had actually known just how much I had to learn, and if I'd had any realistic idea of how tough it was going to get at times, I might have turned my car around right then and there and headed back to Cleveland as fast as I could.

As to whether I'd have been better off if I *had*—well, who knows the answer to that one? Sooner or later, I'd no doubt have gone off anyway. I was wound up, even tighter than I myself realized; and since my generator was turning over at a pretty high rate of speed, it's a cinch I had to keep moving or else blow a fuse. I hadn't learned how to channel all that energy into any constructive, organized life plan.

All I knew was the little I had learned about my craft. And in order to learn more, I had to go to where there were people from whom I could learn, people who knew more about my craft than I did.

There were plenty of places to go, things to do, people to meet and learn from. And I was on one more leg of what would eventually turn out to be a long and devious journey— and a far more lonesome one than it would have been possible for me to believe. . . .

So I left Cleveland, left Wylie, left Claude, left Betty, left three years of my life behind me. I wouldn't have believed at the time that this would turn out to be the end of my first love. I told myself I would come back for her some day, after I had established myself and made a name in my profession. No one could have convinced me otherwise, any more than they could have convinced me of the misery I was heading for in my pursuit of that same old $ucce$$-Fame-Happiness-Cinderella constellation.

As things turned out, it is highly probable that my leaving this first love was about the nicest thing I could have done for her. I still had a good deal of poison in my system to get rid of, before I could have been of much benefit to her. And, although I have long since got over that first feeling of love—a feeling that, in the same intensity, I don't suppose it is ever possible for a man to recapture anyway—I have never forgotten her, or the life I might have had with her if I had only been healthy enough, or "normal" enough, to live it with her.

So, herewith my tribute to her and to one of the few lovely memories I can keep for the rest of my life. . . .

"It is easier to admit that which is criminal than that which is ridiculous and makes a man feel ashamed."

JEAN JACQUES ROUSSEAU

Chapter Twenty-Five

IT TOOK ME LESS THAN A WEEK to learn that joining Aaronson's band was a much bigger step than the mere geographic distance from Cleveland to Hollywood. I had worked on some pretty good jobs, played in some pretty good bands, earned pretty good money as a professional musician, but I now realized it had all been strictly bush league stuff. If Aaronson's band wasn't the major league, it was at least a fairly high-ranking minor league.

I'm not talking about music now. In that respect my apprenticeship had been sound enough. What I had learned at the Olympia Theatre, and later on during my three years in Cleveland, about playing and arranging, was all O.K. as far as it went. I discovered almost immediately that the only member of Aaronson's band from whom I could actually learn anything about music was Chummy MacGregor, the pianist-arranger who had helped persuade Aaronson to hire me back in Cleveland.

(Just in passing, Chummy was also the fellow I mentioned a while back, from whom I first heard about Dreiser. In fact, I remember to this day what he said to me when he told me to get hold of "The Genius"—"I envy you. I wish I'd never read it myself so I could read it again for the first time.")

Aside from Chummy, though, and to a lesser degree my friends Tony and Charlie, there were no musicians in this band of Aaronson's. These fellows played musical instruments after a fashion, but basically they were entertainers. They sang, they did comedy bits, and one of them was a pretty good dancer. Even Tony and Charlie were part of a singing trio, along with one other boy who played trumpet and sang. Art Quenzer, a fellow who worked alongside of me in the sax section, wrote special lyrics for the singing groups that came out of the band—all the way from trios and quartets to whole big choral groups. Phil Saxe, another fellow who also held a saxophone (but fortunately didn't actually try to play much), did all sorts of dialect comedy.

Everyone in the band did something besides playing an instrument. There was Red Stanley, the trombone player, who danced and sang, although he had a most peculiar, high, quavering voice; Charlie Trotta and the one other trumpet player, whose name I've forgotten, both of whom sang in the trio with Tony; a couple of fiddle players who both sang, one a baritone and the other an Irish tenor; the guitar player, Ralph Napoli, who sang ballads; and the drummer, Stan Johnson, who sang bass when he wasn't guzzling booze—which he seemed to be doing most of the time, so that his nose, a pretty good-sized feature to begin with, had gradually over the years taken on the rich color of a ripe tomato.

With such "entertaining talent" and "showmanship" on all sides of me, I began to develop a sense of utter worthlessness. The Aaronson band used to put on two, and sometimes three, shows a night, and everybody in the band had something to do in them, except Chummy MacGregor (who had to accompany the show anyway), the bass player, who also played for the show, and myself. The three of us sat on the bandstand while all those gilded birds-of-paradise paraded up and down in their gorgeous plumage, displaying their various "showmanlike" talents.

It was during this time that I conceived an absolute detestation for the word "showmanship." I used to hear the members of the band seriously discussing various aspects of the mysterious ritual of "selling" a song or a lyric. Sometimes I'd become outraged and furiously ask them, "What the hell are you guys supposed to be anyway? Actors or musicians?" I made no impression beyond convincing them that there was something faintly screwy about a guy who wanted to spend all his time learning to blow a horn.

The truth is, of course, that most of my fury came out of an overabundance of sour grapes.

During the first week I was in the band, I myself tried to make the grade as a singer. My method of getting into the limelight was simple—I made an arrangement of a tune called *Dinah* (good old Dinah, than whom there isn't anyone finer in the entire state of Caroliner) in which, by some curious coincidence, there was a vocal chorus sung by—guess? Those were the days before the microphone and loudspeaker had become standard equipment, so I had to hide behind a megaphone. To say that I never did set any of the places we worked in on fire with my singing ability, is one of the biggest understatements you've ever heard in your life. Still, for a while, I used to get up in the middle of my arrangement, pick up a megaphone, and regale the customers with my "rendition" of *Dinah*—and if they didn't come tearing up to the bandstand clamoring for more, at least they didn't go tearing out then and there to pick up a length of good stout rope.

However, I ultimately gave this up. It became increasingly clear to me that there was no great future in store for me as a singer. Not that I actually *sang* any worse than some of the other characters I was working with—if "sing" is the word —there were a few other members of the outfit who had plenty of dust in their throats. But there was the business of "showmanship"—the ability to "sell" a song. And in that department I was—to make another understatement—nowhere.

In fact, Aaronson himself, who once happened to be off at the other end of the Blossom Room when I stepped forth to deliver my nightly encomium to the manifold virtues and beauties of this Dinah dame, must have been considerably moved by what he heard—because the only times I ever got to sing at all after that was when he was off the bandstand and I could persuade Red Stanley, who took over in his absence, to let us play "my arrangement."

No, I never made the grade as a showman. Aaronson once made a comment on my "selling" ability which is worth quoting—his critique on my "performing personality" shows that he was an astute observer who didn't get to where he was at that time through sheer luck alone. What he said was, "Jesus Christ! That kid's got the personality of a dead *lox.*" (In case you happen never to have heard the word *"lox"* before, it is a kind of smoked salmon whose personality could at best be said to be only attractive to other salmon, and I don't suppose even to *them* it is always particularly attractive.)

In the meantime, I had "fallen in love" once again, although I still retained a strong and rather guilty memory of the girl I had left behind in Cleveland. The new object of my affections was a young stock-actress at one of the moving picture studios and, while I was nominally sharing an apartment with Tony Pestritto, I was actually doing most of my sleeping at the apartment of this new girl friend.

I was so pleased with these new living arrangements that I determined to remain in Hollywood. In the first place this was the first "nice" girl with whom I'd had such a relationship. It was amazing indeed to learn that a fellow could actually go to bed with a "nice" girl and still continue to like her. And in the second place—as you may gather, from my description of myself at that time—I had become pretty goddamn stage-struck.

So, a few weeks before Aaronson's band was to leave Hollywood, I devised a plan through which I could stay on and go on "living with" my new girl. I told no one about this new idea—not even Tony, with whom I had by now become quite friendly. For even then, young and idiotic as I was, I had a vaguely discomforting feeling that there might be something unusual in what I intended to do.

I had heard about a young banjo player, from some mediocre band around Hollywood, who had been picked up by a movie talent scout and given the lead in a picture called "All Quiet on the Western Front"—which I had seen. This banjo player's name was Lew Ayres. After seeing him in the picture I decided that I too might as well become an actor. O Youth, thy name is definitely not Humility! You see what was going on, don't you? Here was the good old Cinderella pattern again. I was simply repeating the same pattern I had acted out years back when, as a truant from an algebra class, I had sat in my seat in Poli's Palace, listened to a saxophone player play *Dreamy Melody*, and conceived the idea of becoming a saxophone player myself. Now I *was* a saxophone player sitting in a seat in the Carthay Circle Theatre, watching a young movie actor playing in a picture called "All Quiet on the Western Front," and conceiving the idea of becoming a movie actor myself. In both cases my reasons had just about nothing whatsoever to do with the realities of the life I was living. But since I had already come quite a ways toward the realistic accomplishment of my first fantasy aim, I couldn't see any good reason why I couldn't switch over now and go off in pursuit of a new one.

Of course, as I now know, this story was just one more in the endless series of publicity stories about the way movie stars are "discovered"—and I suppose the only reason Lew Ayres' "discovery" didn't occur in the classically approved manner, in the same ice cream parlor where all the other stars are first picked up by talent scouts, is that for one thing he was not a girl, and for another he wasn't going to Hollywood High and *had* actually been a banjo player before he got into the picture business.

In those days, though, I didn't know any of this. I hadn't yet learned that if a fellow wants to get into pictures, the best place to start from is as far away from Hollywood as he can get—preferably Timbuctoo or Tasmania. I decided to go at it the only way I knew—the most direct. After making a number of guarded inquiries, I heard the name of the agent who was reputed to have "discovered" Lew Ayres. I looked up the agent's name in the telephone book, and one afternoon, when no one was around the apartment, called up his office and asked to speak with him.

His secretary, or whoever it was that answered the phone, wanted to know who was calling.

"It's personal," I informed her.

"I'm sorry, sir," she replied, "but you'll have to give me your name."

"All right," I reluctantly said. "Tell him it's Art Shaw. I'm working with Irving Aaronson's band."

"What is it you wished to speak to Mr. Kahn about?"

"I—well, it's kind of personal."

"I'm sorry, but you'll have to give me some idea of the nature of your business with Mr. Kahn before I can put you through to him."

I was amazed to discover how involved my simple plan was becoming. What was the matter with this woman? Couldn't she understand that all I wanted was to discuss the possibility of an acting career with her employer? What was so peculiar about that? After all, it wasn't every day that a fellow like me decided he wanted to become a moving picture actor, was it?

But no matter how much I tried to tell her that my communication was meant for Mr. Kahn's ears and his alone, she grimly insisted on my telling her something more about it.

In the end I had to tell her. "You see," I said in the greatest confidence, "I just heard that the band I'm with is leaving town in a few weeks, so I decided that as long as I like it here in Hollywood I might as well stay on here. I called to see if Mr. Kahn might be interested in trying to get me into moving pictures—you know, like with Lew Ayres?"

There was a short—and no doubt, stunned—silence on the other end of the phone. Finally, "I see," said the woman, sounding as if she didn't at all. Then another silence.

"Well?" I said brightly. "Now can I talk to Mr. Kahn?"

"Mr. Kahn isn't in the office at the moment," she said. "However, if you care to leave your name and phone number, I'll give him your message when he comes in."

I gave her the information, and waited several days for the call. Nothing happened, so I called back once more.

This time, though, it must have penetrated even the thick layer of bone that surrounded what passed for my brain in those days, that perhaps this man into whose hands I had decided to entrust my career as a movie actor might not be as enthusiastic about my decision as I had expected. After several moments of crisp secretarial dialogue, the woman informed me that her employer had left town and would not be back for several weeks. But even at that I might still have gone on believing there was a possibility of achieving my aims by this method, except for what took place that very same night.

During the supper dance session at the Blossom Room that evening, Tony Pestritto, who now knew I had some peculiar interest in the man who had discovered Lew Ayres, turned to me in the middle of a tune and said, "Hey, look, Art—there's the guy, that's Kahn sitting with the girl over there. See? No, no—not there—over *there*, behind the big table—see?"

"You sure that's him, Tony?" I asked, once I had located the gentleman I had been told that day was "out of town."

"Sure it is," he said. "Ask Red Stanley. He's Red's girl's agent—ask him."

After we finished the set I did ask Red. He told me it was indeed Kahn, and in fact went over to the table and sat down with Kahn and the girl. For a while I pondered the question of whether to let Red in on my plan; then I decided I had better not. As the evening went on, I considered going over and introducing myself to Kahn and telling him I had been trying to reach him on the phone; but by the time I had almost made up my mind to try it, he and his companion got up and left. The next day, when I called his office once more and taxed his secretary with having lied to me, she told me sharply that I must be mistaken, and before I could say another word she hung up.

That was that. It began to dawn on me that maybe it wasn't so easy to become a movie actor after all. So I gave up this plan for the time being and went on concentrating on my original idea of becoming a musician instead. . . .

"There was a time when . . . the earth, and every common sight, to me did seem . . . the glory and the freshness of a dream."

WORDSWORTH

Chapter Twenty-Six

THIS IS GOING TO BE a chapter of odds and ends, disconnected fragments, scattered bits taken at random out of the memories of that one period of my life. In it, I want to try to give you some *feel* of the general atmosphere of that time, some sense of what was *in the air.*

The year was 1929, the season summer. The United States was still in the throes of one of the most preposterous attempts in our history to embody in concrete law the idiotic attitudes of a small minority of blue-nose crackpots. Prohibition was in effect—legally, if not actually.

It was the era of the speakeasy, of bathtub gin, homebrew, and "moonshine"; of "hooch," "pre-war stuff," "right off the boat" (the gag was, "Yeah, scraped right off the deck"). This was the period in United States history during which there was probably more plain and fancy boozing going on than at any other period before or since. It was the age of the "racket," and the philosophy of the times was embodied in such catch phrases as, "get-rich-quick," "don't be a sucker," "there's plenty of room at the top," "why work when you can play the market and become a millionaire overnight?"—and the official aim of the administration was "two chickens in every pot."

It was the time of The Big Boom and millions were out on The Big Spree. This was the culmination of the Twenties, the last frenetic bout of one of the greatest mass drunks in history; and the hangover had not yet begun.

America was the land of the free, the home of the brave, the gem of the ocean—and the particular facet of the gem that glittered brightest, that shot its tinseled gleam into every far corner of the land, was a small suburb of Los Angeles. Hollywood, U.S.A., had become a symbol, a magnet that drew young hopefuls from the prairies of the Midwest and the crowded slums of the East, the healthy farm-boys, the cynical-eyed poolroom hustlers, the hopeful beauty-contest winners, and the waitresses and manicurists who had their eyes fixed on stardom rather than on any particular star—the Wampus Baby Stars and the would-be "sheiks" from Iowa, Texas, Ohio, New York, and all points east, west, north, and south—all perfectly ready and willing to sell their souls for a mansion in Beverly Hills complete with butler, swimming pool, and oversized bed.

Jean Harlow, with her startlingly white hair, had just set the vogue for the "platinum blonde." She had exploded into overnight stardom in a movie called "Hell's Angels," produced and financed by a young multimillionaire playboy and amateur flyer named Howard Hughes. Clara Bow, a redhead, had come all the way from Brooklyn to electrify the nation with some mysterious sexual quality labeled "It." Still another of these darlings of fortune, a brunette, had danced her way into the erotic dreams of American youth and, as the typical Cinderella of the Jazz Age, parlayed the name Joan Crawford into a million-dollar career.

A bandleader named Gus Arnheim, whose orchestra played at a new Hollywood night spot called the Cocoanut Grove, had written a tune the title of which epitomized the American attitude toward sex and toward life itself—*Sweet and Lovely.* Another tune told the nation about *Looking at the World Through Rose-Colored Glasses*—which the nation dutifully did.

And in spite of the rose-colored glasses it saw *"Blue Skies, shining at me—nothing but Blue Skies do I see."*

Looking back at that era, I am startled to realize how many of the popular tunes had the same theme, the theme of ever-lasting hope and optimism and high spirits. There was *Singing in the Rain, Sitting on Top of the World,* and still another whose words ran, *"I've got the world on a string, sitting on a rainbow, got the string around my finger,"* etc., etc., etc.

Well, why not? *Wasn't* the market booming sky-high, magically converting nothing into something, pennies into dollars, hundreds into thousands and millions? *Wasn't* everybody getting rich overnight, except for the suckers who went around with long faces croaking doom and disaster and giving everybody a hearty laugh at their "sourpuss," "killjoy" pessimism? How could anything possibly be wrong in a world where there would never again be another war, never again be poverty and depression, never again be anything but joy unconfined and "unrefined"—as another gag went—never again be anything but Everlasting Prosperity and Happiness and Gaiety and Plenty, for anyone who wanted to avail himself of his innate, gilt-edged, absolutely guaranteed right as the citizen of the greatest nation on the face of the entire civilized globe to participate in all of these innate, guaranteed, and gilt-edged rights?

From where I sat on the bandstand of the Blossom Room of the Hotel Roosevelt right smack in my ringside seat, from which I could look out at the tinsel and the glamour, the joy and the glory, forever and ever, Amen—I certainly could see nothing wrong with it. And at the Saturday afternoon tea dances, I still could see nothing wrong with the sight of all these young Hollywood hopefuls, the high-breasted, long-stemmed American Beauties, the handsome lads who, when they hadn't enough money to bring in booze "on the hip," would order up a round of cokes and dissolve a few aspirins in them for a good-enough "kick" to take the place of "the real thing."

I too had my girl, my Hollywood starlet, my long-stemmed American Beauty. And not only that, I had my weekly salary, my big sleek shiny bright-red Auburn roadster, my brand-new tuxedo with the biggest padded shoulders that were ever put into a tuxedo even in Hollywood, Land of Dreams and Fantasies *and* Padded Shoulders. And with my music on top of all of this, I had everything and was on my way to getting even more.

That was what I kept telling myself, along with everyone else I knew who was also telling himself the same thing; and for a while, along with everyone else, I believed it was true.

There was a *feel*, a *smell*, an *atmosphere*, a golden, glamorous haze, that suffused everything during those days. My girl put it all into words one night when we were taking a long drive out through the orange grove countryside south of Los Angeles. The air was heavy with the scent of orange blossoms, and in the distance there was the sighing of a summer wind and the boom of the Pacific surf. And I was just nineteen, and my girl was the most magically, breath-takingly beautiful girl in the whole wide world, and she loved me, and everything was magic and loveliness and everlastingly right with everything I knew or cared to know. And as we drove through the summer night, she leaned back against the leather seat—the top was down and the wind blew through her hair—and the sky was crammed chockful of blue-white diamonds, and as she looked up at the star-studded velvet darkness she sighed deeply and murmured, "This whole place is made for love. . . ."

And of course I knew she was right. I felt in my bones how right she was—how could she be wrong? We were riding the crest of a huge wave. How could I know that the wave itself wasn't real, or, even if it was real, was about to break with a roar and a crash onto a harsh grating reality?

Meanwhile, there was The Dream, and there were we, and

we were far too busy living out The Dream to stop and worry about which was Dream and which Reality. At that moment, The Dream itself was the only everlasting and glorious Reality.

So we went on drinking our gin-and-Orange Mission, sipping our cokes-with-aspirin, living in our own magical, shimmering, glowing haze; and to those who croaked of the bitter reality our answer would have been, "If this isn't Reality—then the hell with Reality, and the hell with you!"

The magic glow, the tinseled haze, held me spellbound for over two months. It was the first time in my life I had allowed myself to relax. It was my first taste of adolescence, the first time I had given myself a chance to enjoy the bitter-sweet flavor of my youth, the first time I had let go for a moment— the first time I'd given myself a chance to stop pushing myself, to pause, live, breathe. And even if it made absolutely no sense at all to anyone else on earth, I—along with millions of others—was damn well going to have it while it was there to be had, and nobody had better try to stop me from taking what I could while the taking was good. . . .

But two months were soon over, and the time came for the Aaronson band to leave Hollywood. And all at once I saw that, although it had been a lovely vacation, life went on. I was not going to stay on in Hollywood and become a movie actor, I had to make a living and support my mother—who by this time had gone back to New York—and I had to go where my profession led me.

So I said goodbye to Magic, goodbye to The Dream, good-bye to my girl—and moved on.

During those magical two months I had seen my father once again. Only once, for we were both too occupied with our own lives.

Anyway, what was the use? There was nothing I could say to him that would help him. I told him I had tried to talk my mother into taking up her life with him again; and that she had refused even to discuss it. He seemed disappointed but nodded his head sadly as if he'd expected to be disappointed. I tried to comfort him with banalities. He shrugged and seemed to resign himself as philosophically as he could; and after that there wasn't a great deal more for either of us to say. I felt terribly sorry for him, I felt a bond of real sympathy with him—but it was too late for either of us to go back and undo the past. Our lives had taken their divergent roads, and we each had to go our own separate way. As it turned out, that was the last time I ever saw him.

My road led to Chicago—and after a few weeks in that bustling, bumbling beehive of a city I began to pick up the momentarily scattered threads of my musical life.

For, Dream or Reality, life was earnest, life was grim, and I had a long way to go, a long spell of apprenticeship to serve, before I could be ready to go where I had set out to go, to find out what I had to find out about what it was like farther up the road I was traveling. . . .

*"To write fully and adequately about jazz would be to write
the history of much of the generation."*

MARK SULLIVAN

Chapter Twenty-Seven

IRVING AARONSON and His Commanders spent no more
than six to eight weeks at the Granada Cafe at 68th and Cottage Grove on the South Side of Chicago. But in those few
weeks a serious student of jazz could learn as much as a serious student of a more traditional kind of music could learn
in a three- or four-year conservatory course.

In those days the South Side of Chicago was one of the
foremost jazz conservatories in the world. There was Earl
Hines' big band playing nightly at the Grand Terrace Cafe;
Louis Armstrong and his small combination playing at the
Sunset Cafe; Jimmy Noone playing clarinet in front of his own
little Apex Club outfit. And hanging around in these smoke-
filled, dimly lighted joints—some of them no more than
dingy cellars loosely converted into all-night speakeasies with
postage-stamp dance floors and dime-sized tables—were guys
like Bix Beiderbecke and Bud Freeman, Red Mackenzie and
Jimmy MacPartland; a black-haired, snap-eyed kid who
played drums and whose name was Gene Krupa; another
drummer, a sandy blonde boy named George Wettling; a thin,
dapper, sleek-blonde little Irish kid named Eddie Condon,
who talked out of the side of his mouth and looked and acted
like Studs Lonigan, but who could play up a storm on a

beatup little four-string guitar. Another Irish kid, this one
not tough at all but sort of pridefully shanty and gentle and
mild as only an Irishman can be, blew a short, sawed-off-
looking cornet and went by the name of Muggsy Spanier.
There was Fud Livingston, who made arrangements and
played tenor sax in a new band led by a fellow from the west
coast—a bandleader named Ben Pollack, who was supposed
to be one hell of a drummer himself, and whose band was
supposed to be a hell of a band. There was a young kid just
beginning to make a name for himself in the jazz world, a
kid named Benny Goodman, who played clarinet and was said
to have learned a lot from another young clarinet player
around Chicago named Frank Teschmaker. Teschmaker has
since died, and so have lots of other good boys who were
coming up around that same time, boys like Dick Mc-
Donough, Bunny Berigan, Don Murray, and so many others.
There they all were, listening and soaking up by osmosis this
new idiom in American music which could not then, and really still
cannot, be studied any other way.

That section of Chicago was a whole musical world in
microcosm; and while there were some musicians who did a
fair amount of boozing and whoring around and marijuana
smoking, there was also a hell of a lot of damn good honest
jazz being played around; and, although I was one of the
boys and went in for a certain amount of these extracurricular
activities myself during that period, the jazz was the thing I
was mainly interested in.

The Aaronson band worked till three A.M. every night at
the Granada Cafe. When we finished I would head for the
Negro district to sit in with one of the colored bands. Some
nights it would be the Grand Terrace, where I'd sit in with
Earl Hines' band, and go till daylight. Other times there
would be sessions with various guys like myself who were
making their living at some of the thousand and one cabarets
in "respectable" bands, but who had to get away once in a

while and "play some jazz." Meeting these musicians night after night, and playing with them either in someone else's band or at one of the sessions, I began to understand the curious musical category called Jazz. For these were the men who were setting the pattern, who were evolving a musical pattern from which the rest of the jazz musicians in the country were taking their lead and in turn passing it on, infusing with this particular flavor the entire body of popular music in America, and, later on, the whole world.

I remember one night—or morning, rather, for it started around four A.M.—when a bunch of us, who had decided to have ourselves a little session, wound up in some dance hall where they were holding one of the Marathon Dance contests that were always taking place in those days. Different musicians floated in and out, sat in for a while, played a few choruses, and then got up to let some other guy blow. There was a piano player named Jess Stacey, and another named Joe Sullivan. There was one trombone player, Floyd O'Brien, who had one of the most peculiar, lazy, deliberately mistaken-sounding styles I've ever heard. He would almost, but not quite, crack a note into little pieces, and each time you thought he was about to fall apart he'd recover and make something out of what started out to sound like a fluff—till after a while you began to get the idea that this guy not only wasn't making any mistakes at all, but had complete control over his horn. He would come so damn close to mistakes that you couldn't see how he was going to get away with it; but he always recovered somehow—and this trick of almost, but never quite, making the mistake, and each time recovering so that the things he played went off in altogether unexpected and sometimes quite humorous directions, was what made his style so peculiar to start with—although it's impossible to give the flavor of it in language.

Also on this same session was the clarinet player I mentioned a moment ago—Frank Teschmaker. I sat next to him

and watched him while he played. We were all slightly drunk
on bad bootleg gin, but it didn't seem to affect his playing
any. He too had this odd style of playing, but in an altogether
different way from O'Brien's. Even while he'd be reaching
out for something in his deliberately fumbling way, some
phrase you couldn't quite see the beginning or end of (or,
for that matter, the reason for in the first place), there was an
assurance about everything he did that made you see that he
himself *knew* where he was going all the time; and by the
time he got there you began to see it yourself, for in its own
grotesque way it made a kind of musical sense, but something
extremely personal and intimate to himself, something so
subtle that it could never possibly have had a lot of communicative
meaning to anyone but another musician and at that only to a jazz
musician who happened to be pretty "hep" to what was going on.

The bizarre thing about that particular session was that
while all this subtle and intricate musical stuff was going
on, while we were all playing and passing bottles of gin
around from one to another, out there on the dance floor were
all those pooped-out, broken-down Marathon Dance contes-
tants; and no matter what we played, no matter whether the
tempo was draggy or bright, there they shuffled like the walking dead, hanging grimly, wearily, on to each other, leaning
together like tired trees in a hurricane, clutching one another
for dear life, like punchdrunk fighters in a nerveless clinch
at the end of the last long round of a tough fight—and that was
what it was like all the time we were there, right up until we
finally quit around seven A.M. and packed our horns and left
the joint with these living corpses still clinging desperately to
each other, shuffling wearily two by two around the dance
floor in the damnedest caricature of dancing I have ever seen
in a lifetime of watching plenty of caricatures of that particular form of activity.

Then there was another night, while I was sitting in with

Earl Hines' band, when, right after I had finished playing a chorus of Earl's closing theme song, *All the World Is Waiting for the Sunrise,* I suddenly heard a trumpet coming from the other end of the long bandstand, and, looking over to see who was playing it (for it was nothing like any of the trumpet players in Earl's band), I saw for the first time that broad, large upper-lipped, grotesquely Irish kisser of Muggsy Spanier's.

A guy could go on and on remembering, reminiscing, dredging up all sorts of snatches of memory, but—well, it's all gone now. Yet in its own way, I suppose, it's still pretty much the same sort of thing nowadays, although the idiom is more involved, the harmonic element considerably advanced beyond the relatively primitive chord structures we were using in those days. The lingo is different today, the names are different, the personnel itself is different. Still, whether the word is "bop" or "swing" or just plain "jazz," the general underlying principle is the same. It's a bunch of guys playing music together, improvising, exchanging ideas, "digging" one another, picking up a "riff" here and a phrase there; so I guess it's still the same, no matter what the commercialized, publicized term for it may be in any particular period. It's a developing, living form of folk music, an idiom, a kind of music *in slang,* and although no one has ever come up with an over-all definition for it that will hold water, still, for all of that, it's one of the few truly American contributions to music itself, or, for that matter, maybe to whatever-this-thing-called-Art-is in general. . . .

So much, then, for what I was learning about jazz. At that same time, I made an important "discovery" about an entirely "different" kind of music.

I discovered the field of "serious" music, "pure" music, the broad field in which jazz itself occupies only one small area, the whole vast field in which the tradition stems all the way from the medieval troubadours up through the early church

composers, all the way from Vittoria, Orlandus Lassus, Palestrina, through Bach, Haydn, Mozart, Beethoven, Brahms,
Wagner, Debussy, *et al*, right up to the present day.

Of course I didn't discover this all at once. In fact, a fellow
doesn't finish such a voyage of discovery for the rest of his
life. But I did discover then that there *was* such a field; I say
"discover" because up to then I had known nothing whatsoever about it. For me, there had only been one kind of music
worth bothering about—the kind made by saxophones, clarinets, trumpets, trombones, and rhythm sections. Strings were
an occasional necessary evil, which as a rule only got in the
way of the rest of the band.

Naturally, I had been vaguely aware of another kind of
music called "classical," which was very dreary stuff indeed.
It was the kind of stuff the Hillhouse High School orchestra
used to play at assembly in the auditorium. It was dull, long-
winded stuff written by a lot of old geezers with long whis-
kers, whose names were spoken differently from the way they
were spelled, so that you could never be sure you were pro-
nouncing them right.

"Classical" music was also what I had been subjected to at
the age of eight when I was forced to take piano lessons. So,
as far as I was concerned, there was only one opinion anyone with any sense in his head could have about that kind of
so-called music.

It all stank . . . on ice.

That was that, until one day when I wandered into a little
record shop just off the Loop. Like any other jazz apprentice,
I used to listen to most of the new records being made by the
top men in the field. Not that I was cribbing stuff directly
any longer, as I had when I was a kid just beginning to learn
my trade. I used to listen to what was being done, the same
way any craftsman watches what is going on in his field—in
order to "keep up," to know where the field is going.

When I got into the record shop that day, I heard some

strange-sounding music coming out of one of the booths. I couldn't figure out what this stuff was. I listened for a few seconds, but then the door of the booth was shut, and I couldn't hear any more.

I was curious. I'd have been curious about any unfamiliar musical sound I might have heard in those days. So, when the clerk came over I asked him what it was.

He told me the name of it, but neither the name nor the composer made any impression; I had never heard of either.

"Would you like to hear it?" he asked.

"Might as well, I guess," and I took the album he handed me.

I went into another booth, and put on the first of this incomprehensibly long series of records. Six sides and all of them part of the same "suite"! Within a few minutes I was trying to recover from the greatest musical shock of my life. When I finished, I carefully replaced the records in their jackets, and, clutching the album tightly to make sure no one tried to get it away from me, went back to the clerk.

"Got anything else like this?"

"Do you mean something by the same composer?"

"Yeah—and any other guy who writes stuff like this."

He dug out three more albums, and then, as an afterthought, handed me one single twelve-inch record. I looked at them. None of the names of the pieces made any sense to me. Nor did the names of the two composers. One was this "guy" who'd written that first piece I had heard as I came in; the other was a different guy altogether, and I couldn't even pronounce the name of the piece, let alone his name.

I went home lugging all those records, the four albums and the one single record. All Stravinsky—including *The Fire Bird Suite,* which was what I'd heard in the booth, and *Le Sacre du Printemps.* The single record was Debussy's *L'Après-midi d'un Faune.*

That was my introduction to a whole new musical world.

And as the weeks went by and I began to accumulate a large but completely disconnected and scattered record collection of "serious" works by all sorts of "guys with screwy-sounding names," I understood that I had stumbled onto something "big" and that in my own way I might be able to learn something from all this stuff, something I couldn't learn even from such guys as the fellows I was playing around with on sessions. For, although I still had no idea of the real significance of all this "new stuff" I was listening to, I did have a pair of fairly well-trained ears by then, and it wouldn't have taken any great amount of perspicacity for me to recognize that this music I was now hearing was something altogether "different" from anything I had ever consciously heard or known about before.

". . . To die is different from what any one supposed, and luckier. Has any one supposed it lucky to be born? I hasten to inform him or her it is just as lucky to die, and I know it."

WALT WHITMAN

Chapter Twenty-Eight

DURING THIS STAY in Chicago my relations with the men in Aaronson's band—aside from the three who were musicians— became practically nonexistent. The rest of those "performers" and "showmen" couldn't figure out what was making me tick; and it would have been impossible for me to explain, even if I had wanted to. They would see me grab my horn and tear off to start playing at an hour when they were only too glad to be finished for the night. They began to regard me as "the band screwball." Which was O.K. with me, for by this time I had come to the conclusion that I had no future as a "show-man" or a "performer" anyway. Besides, I had all those new records to listen to and try to understand; and although most of my nonmusical colleagues pretended to scoff at my intense preoccupation with music, they had a certain grudging respect for it. In spite of their professed contempt for mere horn blowing, they were perfectly willing to concede that I knew my business in that department at least; so, screwball or not, I managed to retain some standing, despite the difference between my values and those of most of the other members of the band.

Meanwhile, Charlie, Tony, Chummy, and I were constantly

pressuring Aaronson to bring some other musicians into the band. He finally consented to hire another boy—a young saxophonist from Boston, named "Toots" Mondello, who joined us while we were still at the Granada. I became friendly with Toots almost from the very beginning. When it developed that he didn't like playing second chair to me in the sax section, I switched over to tenor saxophone. That was the first and only time I ever consented to stay on a job where I wasn't playing first chair. It was because I liked Toots, and respected his ability. Besides, at that time most of the jazz playing in the sax section was handled by the tenor saxophone, so this switch would give me something more to learn anyway.

But then something really important happened one night during work at the Granada Cafe.

The Granada was a typical large night club of the Prohibition era. Besides the usual sprinkling of pleasure-seekers, there were generally a number of gangsters and racketeers around the place, some of them small-time hangers-on, others pretty big-time operators. I had made the acquaintance of some of these kinds of citizens when I was still working around Cleveland, and had learned how to get along well enough with them to stay out of trouble. In fact, having become rather friendly with some of them, I had developed an attitude of cynical distrust toward The Law not too unlike theirs.

Of course, the occasional appearance of The Law was nothing unusual around these joints. And anyway, the various representatives of the police who did show up were usually regarded as "O.K." Mostly they knew their way around, so what difference did it make whether a cop was on the payroll of The Law, as long as he was "in" with the boys too?

Nevertheless, when I was told one night during work that there was a plain-clothes man in the joint looking for a guy named Art Shaw, I got a little worried. I could figure out nothing good about his wanting to see me.

After that dance set I went over to where he was waiting

for me. He reached into his pocket, pulled out a slip of yellow paper, and handed it to me without a word.

It turned out to be one of those intercity police messages, written in the jargon generally used in such communications. It had to do with my father. Apparently he had suddenly been taken ill and was in a hospital in Los Angeles. I couldn't tell from the message what was the matter with him. There was only a vague mention of "serious internal complications."

"What's this all about?" I asked the detective after reading the message over a couple of times.

"I don't know anything about it, Bud," he said, shrugging.

"How'd you know where to find me?"

He told me that the police in Los Angeles had been contacted by my father's brother—that same uncle, the house painter, who had brought me that barrel of books when I was a kid living on York Street in New Haven, and who was now living in Los Angeles himself. The Los Angeles police had then got in touch with the Chicago police and asked them to find me.

"What do you think I ought to do?" I asked.

"How the hell do I know what you ought to do?" he shrugged again. "I was told to get the message to you, so I did."

"How can I get in touch with anybody who can tell me what I. . . ."

"There's the name of the hospital where he's at," and he pointed out the part of the message which had that information.

"But. . . ." and I stopped, looking at him helplessly.

"I can't tell you any more'n that," he said. He took my address and went away a few seconds later.

What followed is all pretty blurred now. I have a confused memory of going to some police station that same night. Later on, I called the hospital in Los Angeles, but my uncle wasn't there and I was told I couldn't talk with my father, that he was unconscious. All I could think of was to leave a message, so that my uncle could let me know what was happening.

I thought of asking Aaronson if I could take a few days off and fly to Los Angeles. But that would cost more than I could afford. Also it meant getting a substitute to take my place while I was gone, and good substitutes weren't easy to find, for most of the good musicians were working steadily. Anyway, as several of the men in the band told me, maybe it wasn't too serious. I would no doubt hear from my uncle next day. Then I could decide better.

The following morning, while I was still sleeping, I felt someone shaking me.

It was Tony Pestritto, and over his shoulder I saw Charlie Trotta. Both of them were staring down at me with serious expressions. They looked funny. It took a few moments before I could remember what had happened the previous night.

Then I suddenly recalled the visit from the detective and all the rest of it.

"What's up," I said.

Neither of them said anything. They kept looking down at me with that funny look in their eyes and just then I saw that Tony was holding out a telegram.

I grabbed it and started to tear open the envelope.

"You up, Art?" Tony asked.

"I guess so—what time is it?" I was having trouble getting my fingers to work properly. For some reason my hands were shaking.

Tony took the telegram back and opened the envelope.

"It's a few minutes before twelve," Charlie told me.

Tony was holding the telegram in his hands now but not handing it to me, just standing there looking at me in that funny way.

"What goes on?" I demanded, now beginning to wake up.

"Listen, Art," Tony began and stopped.

I looked up at him and then at Charlie. "Come on, what's going on?" I asked. "What's it say, Tony?"

He showed the wire to Charlie. Both of them shook their heads in unison. It looked almost rehearsed. I felt like laughing out loud, but checked myself.

"What's it *say*, for Chri'sake?" I shouted.

"Go on, tell him," said Charlie.

I reached out to grab the telegram and tear it away from Tony. He pulled back and held it. "Listen, Art," he said. "It's a telegram about your old man—your father—and—now get yourself set, Art—it's bad news . . . You sure you're up?"

"Of course I'm up," I yelled impatiently. "Give it to me, will you, for Chri'sake?"

He handed it to me silently. I sat up in bed and read it. Both of them stood there quietly, watching me as I read.

It was from my uncle. It simply stated that my father had died in the middle of the night. It didn't say anything about what had been the matter with him. Just that he had died, and that he had left "some things" he had wanted me to have. That was all.

I stared at it for a while. I couldn't feel anything at all. I understood the information, I knew what it meant, and yet somehow I couldn't get the sense of it. I guess I must have stared at it for quite some time, trying to make it soak into my mind. Finally I looked back up at Tony and Charlie, who were still standing there looking down at me in that strangely solemn way.

There was something so utterly incongruous about the way they stared at me, that all at once I was unable to hold it back any longer. I snickered.

At this they seemed to draw back a little, and they looked more solemn than ever. Especially Tony, who also began to appear slightly offended. He was a chunky kid, with thick black hair that came way down almost to his eyebrows, so that he looked as if he were wearing some kind of fur cap all the time. We used to kid him about his low forehead. He was a Sicilian and had a ready temper, but he never stayed mad for long. He took all our kidding rather good-naturedly, and was always laughing and kidding around himself.

Still, he was terribly sentimental, with a strong sense of the bonds between children and parents, and he obviously couldn't understand my reaction at that moment.

I wanted to explain that I wasn't really laughing, that I certainly wasn't feeling mirthful about what I had just read in the telegram; but I couldn't say anything at all. The more I realized I couldn't explain it to him, the crazier it got. I began to laugh out loud. And as he grew more offended and drew back farther, I had to laugh even more.

I laughed at him, and laughed at Charlie. They stood and stared at me. The longer it went on the harder I laughed. I laughed and laughed, till the tears came out of my eyes.

Then suddenly Tony got mad. "What the hell kind of a son of a bitch are you anyway? Jesus Christ, I come in and wake the guy up and hand him a wire that his old man's—his father's dead and he starts in laughing like he's nuts or something."

That made me laugh even harder—I thought I'd split a gut if I didn't stop. But I couldn't stop. I gasped and shook and roared with laughter, and tried to wave to them to get out and leave me alone. I felt I could never stop as long as they both stood there staring at me with that ludicrously solemn expression on their faces.

At last Charlie put one hand on Tony's shoulder, and I heard him say, "Come on, Tony—let's get out of here. Don't get mad at him, he can't help it. Maybe he's hysterical or something."

They left. By then I was laughing so hard I began to ache with it. That last touch about being hysterical had been almost too much for me.

After they had been gone a few seconds, I stopped laughing. I lay there and tried to think. About my father. What it had been like those last couple of times I had seen him, and how it had always been before those times. I tried to visualize him. But it was hard. I couldn't bring up much of an image of him, not a very clear one at any rate. The old image that I had carried around inside my mind for so many years kept coming in between me and the one I had recently started to form. The old one had been with me too long, ever since he had left my mother and me, back there in that shabby little flat on Orange Street near Grove. It had been too long since I had tried to forget him, to forget that I had ever had a father at all. It had been too long since I had *had* a father for whom I could feel anything but fear and resentment. Now I lay there with conflicting feelings—the old and the new—and tried to realize that this man I had once so disliked and recently begun to like again, this man, my father, the man through whom my mother had conceived me, was dead.

But all that was only intellectual. I told myself all that— but I couldn't make myself *feel* anything clear. It was all mixed up and confused, something strange and far-off and entirely disconnected from the life I was now leading. And at the same time, underneath, there was a sense of something *lacking* in me, a feeling of guilt at not feeling more. I kept thinking to myself that I must be some sort of a monster, and that Tony was right for being mad, for after all it *was* my father who had died, and wasn't a fellow supposed to feel sad when his father died? But I couldn't get myself to feel sad, only strangely sorry, *for* him, rather than *about* him— or maybe for *him* rather than for *myself*, as I felt I ought to feel but simply couldn't. And all the while, underneath, I kept asking myself, *How can you feel sad about him when you never had much chance to get to feel love for him while he was alive?* And below that thought lay all sorts of other questions and vague emotions, until my mind began to feel like one of those Chinese boxes-within-boxes-within-boxes. After I had stayed there all alone on the bed opening up one after another of those boxes, after a long time of lying there wrestling with my inner self, trying to make myself feel one way or the other as I felt I ought to feel from one moment to the next, I finally had to give it up. My mind was unable to function any longer. I threw on some clothes, and went into the living room.

Charlie and Tony were sitting quietly, having their breakfast at a room-service table. I walked in and sat down over to one side. They went on eating for a little while, without saying anything. The sun was making big irregular splashes on the nondescript hotel carpet. There were bits of dust floating around in the sunlight. There was the occasional clink of a spoon against a coffee cup. You could hear the sound of traffic faintly from down below.

At last Charlie looked over and asked me how I was feeling.

"I'm O.K.," I told him. Tony didn't look up at all. "I'm sorry about laughing that way, Tony," I said. "I couldn't help it—I don't even know what I was laughing at. I just couldn't stop. I couldn't help it, that's all."

He said, "Ah, that's all right, Art—I guess it must've hit you all of a sudden. It's O.K. I just got a little mad. It's O.K. now." He looked at Charlie, who gave him a warning look. Then he started eating again. But I could tell it was all right again, that he was over being sore at me.

I decided I had better act out the role these two evidently thought fitting. So for the rest of the day and for the following three or four days I went around wearing as sad an expression as I could. It apparently satisfied them, for eventually they seemed to get over their original reaction to my irreverent laughter in the face of death.

As for myself, I eventually came to understand that there was no use condemning myself, or feeling guilty for not feeling a deep sense of deprivation over the death of a parent for whom I had never had enough practice in feeling love at a time when I would normally have if our lives had been different. . . .

For the real truth—although I could not bring myself to face this for many years afterwards—is that, given the life my father was leading, the obvious misery in which he had apparently spent most of his life, and the bitter hopelessness which he must have felt after learning that my mother would never, under any circumstances, come back to him again—given all this, plus the utter emptiness in which he'd no doubt have had to spend the rest of his days, he was probably far better off dead than having to go on. At least death is one kind of peace—and peace itself is not a bitter thing. . . .

"Man is born unto trouble, as the sparks fly upward."

OLD TESTAMENT

Chapter Twenty-Nine

ONE OF THE MOST DIFFICULT THINGS to accept about the circumstances surrounding the death of my father was that I could not learn anything further after that one wire from my uncle. I answered the wire immediately with a long telegram asking how I could help with the expenses for my father's funeral—and where he could reach me to send on those "things" my father had left me—but I never heard from him again.

It was a strange period altogether. This was toward the end of our Granada Cafe engagement and we were due to leave Chicago for New York within a few weeks. Meanwhile, I didn't know where to reach my mother in New York. I finally managed to track her down with the help of the long-distance operator who eventually located her and put through my person-to-person call.

I told her about my father's death. But of course she couldn't do much about it one way or the other; there she was in New York City, at one end of the country, there he was dead in Los Angeles, at the other end, and here I was in Chicago, somewhere near the middle of the fair-sized piece of real estate called the United States. So, having told her about my father, and that I would be in New York shortly myself, there wasn't much more I could do.

I waited anxiously to hear from my uncle. I was terribly curious to see what my father had left me. It didn't matter much what it was; I was eager to have something of his, particularly something he had said he wanted me to have. I waited a few days, assuming I was bound to hear from my uncle sooner or later, that he was no doubt too busy with the arrangements for my father's funeral, and so on. But after almost a full week had gone by and I had still heard nothing, I wired once more. I had tried to reach him by telephone, but there was no number listed under his name in the Los Angeles directory. My second wire remained unanswered and I wired a third time. No answer.

I have never heard another word from that day to this. To this moment I don't know where my father is buried, under what circumstances he died, or, for that matter, what the "things" were that he gave my uncle to give me.

So perhaps it is best to try to forget it. It may very well be that this sort of thing is better left alone. I can't bring myself to believe that my uncle deliberately appropriated whatever it was that my father had wanted me to have. Whatever it was, it couldn't have been very valuable, for my father was almost penniless when he died. I had offered him some money when I last saw him, but he had refused to take it, out of some sense of pride, even though he earned next to nothing as a tailor in some dingy little costume-making establishment. Also, my uncle had always been a jolly man who liked me when I was a kid, and who was always bringing me presents of some sort.

So I can't figure it out at all. . . .

In any event, I couldn't learn anything more at that time and a short time later we left Chicago and came to New York. And then, during the first couple of weeks, I ran head on into trouble. Big trouble. A kind of trouble that can happen to anyone, and does happen to a great many people all over the place, but is a damn tough thing when it happens to you.

I hit a man with my car.

It couldn't have been helped, for he stepped off a curb right in front of my car in such a way that it was utterly impossible to avoid hitting him. Anyone who happened to be driving in that place at that time would have hit him—it just happened to be me. And although all this happened many years ago, twenty-two years ago to be exact, I still can't write about it without a strong emotional involvement and a set of painful sense-memories. For I killed him. He died almost instantaneously.

However, if it is painful now, at the time it was absolute, unmitigated disaster. And through it, I was involved in an infinite series of legalities and litigations which stripped my mother and me of what little money we had and left us to flounder our way along as best we could. This went on for the next four years!

By that time I had come to the point where it seemed to me that the truest thing I had ever read in my life was a poem of Sandburg's containing the lines:

Why is there always a secret singing when a lawyer cashes in?
Why does a hearse horse snicker hauling a lawyer away?

I've since learned that this dreary affair that dragged on and on (until it was finally ended by my going into bankruptcy) could have been resolved almost immediately if I had had enough experience to get myself the proper representation right at the start.

Anyway, while it went on, it was one of the ugliest messes I've ever been in, not only for myself, but for my mother as well. I was under legal age at the time it happened, and in the resulting damage suit that was filed after the manslaughter charges were finally dropped, the plaintiffs sued not only me but my mother. The amount they were suing for was a mere eighty thousand dollars and they might just as well have asked us for the Hope diamond!

What the suit did, in practical terms, was to force me to remain in New York City after the Aaronson band had finished its engagement and left town. Being out on bail, I was unable to leave with them.

I had no money. I was out of work. Furthermore I knew no one around New York. And even if I had known someone who was willing to give me a job, I couldn't have taken it anyway.

Perhaps I had better explain that last statement.

The American Federation of Musicians is, like most unions, divided up into "locals"—meaning separate, and for the most part autonomous, local organizations which govern over the city or district in which they function. In order to discourage a sudden influx of musicians into any given locality where there happens to be a lot of work there is a ruling by which a musician must wait three to six months (depending on the locality) before he can get full membership in that local. In New York the amount of time was six months. As I recall, after three months the rule permitted prospective members some kinds of work—"club dates," as those little pick-up dance jobs are called—but since I knew no one who might hire me even for such work as that (for I had no "connections") it made no essential difference whether I waited three or six months.

Being practically dead broke, my mother and I rented a cubbyhole of a flat way out on the Grand Concourse, where she took in a little sewing to keep us in groceries. Somehow we managed to survive; but we couldn't possibly have managed without a few loans she was able to make among some of her relatives and friends who lived down on the Lower East Side.

It was a very rough period for me.

I was just nineteen, and this was the first time in my life, ever since I had started playing professionally, that I was unable to work. It was the first time I had actually been on my own—with no connection with any band at all—with the exception of the short time when I was stranded in Lexington, Kentucky; which hardly counted, for that had been more or less a lark as far as I was concerned. This was altogether different. This was New York City, the largest city on earth, and if anyone thinks it's tough to be alone, just let him try being alone in a city like New York for a while. And not only was I alone but there was a charge of manslaughter hanging over my head, which, after having listened to a couple of shysters, I believed was going to put me in jail for the next ten or fifteen years. No, this was no fun, even aside from the fact that I was unable to go on doing the only thing I knew much about at all. . . .

During the first couple of months, I used to take the subway downtown and walk aimlessly up and down Broadway. I would look into the faces of people on the crowded, brightly lit street, trying to find one I might miraculously recognize. That went on for some weeks but finally it became too discouraging and I gave it up. Later on I found out about Greenwich Village, and took to prowling around the streets down there. I would walk by one of the old brick buildings and now and then stop to gaze up at a window that was all lit up, through which I could hear sounds of merriment, men and women laughing and chattering, party sounds. At such times, I would imagine the pretty girls and handsome well-dressed men up there, together, drinking and having fun; and I'd walk on down the street so filled with a sense of my loneliness and misery and unhappiness and frustration that it was all I could do to keep from bursting into tears of bitterness and rage at what my life had suddenly become. Or else I might stand there on the sidewalk indulging in all sorts of fantasies and wishful daydreams, in which I pictured myself walking up the stairs into one of these parties and, through some pretext, being accepted and staying. I would fancy myself meeting some wonderful, sophisticated, beautiful girl with whom I would fall deeply in love and who would love me; and with her I would get to meet and know all sorts of bright, glib, assured New York people with whom we would embark on an endless round of gay parties. I would envision myself making a whole new beginning, starting a brand-new life here in this enormous city, a happy, carefree, glamorous, wonderful life, through which I could forget the misery and loneliness of the drab existence I was leading.

Now and then I would wander into one of those little clip joints that used to line the side streets of certain sections of Greenwich Village. I would sit at the bar and order a ginger ale or some other soft drink; I had no money to buy anything else, even in those dingy joints where it could be bought over the bar.

Strangely enough I never got into any trouble. I say "strangely enough" because these joints were operated on a basis designed to empty the customers' pockets in the least possible amount of time with the greatest possible efficiency. The girls who worked in these traps—who were actually the bait by which customers were lured in to begin with—were called B-girls (what the B stood for I've never been able to learn). Their job was to sit with the customer, the sucker, either at the bar or at a table, in between "floor shows," and consume large quantities of "champagne"—in reality nothing more than plain, or mildly spiked, ginger ale, for which the customer was charged champagne prices and on which the girl received a percentage of the take.

Possibly the reason I never got into any difficulties in these joints is that I was so broke there was no way I could be "clipped" of something I didn't have. Also I was quite honest about it. Whenever a B-girl came over to ply her trade I told her the truth immediately. As I later learned, from one of these girl with whom I struck up a random acquaintance, the mere idea of a guy telling the truth about a thing like that was in itself so novel that it made me some kind of interesting freak.

I remember this one girl telling me about the various lines

she was handed night after night, and how disgusted she got at times. "God!" she said, "I get so sick and tired of these big men, these big oil-well millionaires from way out West, these phoneys who tell me how much they appreciate a nice girl like poor li'l ole me who appreciates them and understands them—and first thing you know, they're going to buy me a mink coat and a big fancy car and set me up in my own penthouse on Park Avenue, and all I've got to do is be 'nice' to 'em and let 'em take me home after closing time. I don't know how I keep from busting out laughing right in their faces. What's the matter with these dopes—do they think I was born yesterday? Listen, I can spot one of those phoneys a mile off, I can even smell 'em by this time."

Most of these B-girls seemed to feel pretty much the same way, so I suppose my naive admission that I was dead broke must have been some sort of switch. In fact, there were any number of times when one or another of them wound up buying *me* drinks—and that, take my word for it, is quite a switch indeed.

I went on with this aimless wandering for weeks—haunting the dark streets of Greenwich Village like a pale and lonely ghost. I kept out of trouble and managed to kill time after a fashion, but despite occasional sporadic human contacts and the endless fantasies and daydreams I would spin out by the hour—underneath everything I was constantly obsessed, and at times almost overwhelmed, by a deep misery and loneliness that threatened to drive me over the edge of despair.

I was searching for something, something I couldn't have named, something that would have some meaning, that might occupy me and take the place of the only thing I had ever found to occupy myself and provide some outlet for my restlessness. Being unable to take a job playing music, I desperately needed to find something else to fill the vacancy—but I could find nothing.

I think now, as I look back into my memories of those few

weeks, or months, or years—for it seems forever that I went around hovering on the periphery of life but never managing to break through the wall that separated me from it—that throughout this whole period I must have been a little mad. I can't account for my weird state of mind at the time on any other basis. I used to feel like a man standing outside a house looking in through the window at a gathering of people dancing, laughing, talking among themselves; and I would get a sense of the warmth inside, but where I stood it would be cold and dark and I would shiver and shudder inside my skin; but no matter what I did I couldn't find a way to break through the sheet of glass that separated me from the life on the other side. So I would stand there, insane with jealousy and loneliness, like Tonio Kröger looking in at the dancers from his dark veranda, bitterly envious of the young lovers inside the warm, bright, music-filled room—but never able to break through and become a part of what he longed for so hungrily.

And then, when I got so tired and miserable that I couldn't walk the streets any longer, I would get into the subway and go home. But I remember time after time when I fell asleep in the subway, woke up at the uptown end of the line, got back in to go downtown again, fell asleep once more and this time woke up at the *other* end of the line, somewhere way the hell and gone out in Brooklyn—and this went on sometimes until broad daylight, so that by the time I finally got up to the Bronx, the sun would be shining, people would be going to work, the sidewalks would be filling up with screaming kids on their way to school and their mothers going out to shop for the day's groceries; and, stumbling into our flat, bleary-eyed and empty-sick with misery, I'd see my mother who could only stare at me helplessly and ask me what was the matter, but I'd be unable to tell her because I didn't even know myself, and all I could do was plead with her to stop worrying about me and let me alone. Then, realizing I had made her worry and stay up all night and was now making her even more unhappy, I would become filled with remorse and guilt and further misery out of my inability to explain what was gnawing away at me deep down inside my guts and intensifying my own misery with an even worse kind of loneliness—the kind that exists between people who feel love and sorrow for each other but are unable to help or reach across and touch each other and thereby alleviate the pain and loneliness with even the thinnest and barest illusion that they are not alone but alone together and therefore not altogether abysmally alone. . . .

I don't think I can ever really forget that phase of my life. For, aside from anything else that may have happened inside me as a result of it, and aside from anything else I learned from what I had to go through during this period —there was one thing it taught me, something quite valuable for a man to learn. Despite Donne's statement that no man is an island unto himself, I know that there are certain respects in which each man *is* an island, and that the possibility of bridging the terrible void that exists between these islands that we are and live on and within, is far slimmer than most human beings are ever given the time or opportunity to realize.

As to whether it is better or worse for a man to learn this particular lesson—that I can't say. I only know that to me, at the age of nineteen, it was a bitter lesson; and that ever since that time, ever since I first really learned it, I have never, or rarely, been able to escape the realization of it, not even at the peak of my career as a bandleader when, night after night, I stood up in front of my band surrounded by thousands of eager-eyed kids listening and watching and devouring with their eyes and ears this publicity-created symbol I represented and in a sense had become, and through which I acted as a kind of focal point for the daydreams and fantasies of thousands of other seventeen, eighteen, and nineteen-year-old kids not too unlike what I myself might have been like at their age, no matter how dissimilar our background and lives might appear on the surface.

And because I *had* learned this lesson, because I *had* become aware of the vast void between the islands of ourselves, I have never since been able to entirely dispel that original loneliness and lose myself in the crowds for whom I performed. If anything, the larger the crowds and the warmer the waves of admiration and love that I have felt pouring up from them, the more intense the loneliness and sense of isolation I have felt standing up there between the two separate worlds of my band on the one hand, and the audience on the other; with myself drifting, apart, between these two worlds, like a separate island, or some sort of lost planet, alone in dark, cold, outer space, wandering, like Shelley's moon, "companionless among the stars that have a different birth."

"If misery loves company, misery has company enough."

THOREAU

Chapter Thirty

THOSE FEW MONTHS I've been writing about were so filled with inner turbulence that it is hard for me now to disentangle fantasy from reality. There were all sorts of pointless little adventures I got myself into; furtive excursions into the twilight world of New York's dim, dark recesses, where I mixed with the debris of a vast city and brushed up against other night-wanderers like myself, castoffs from life, rejects, marred and imperfect products of the civilization factory—with some of whom I made brief and abortive contact before drifting on.

At length, through some accident I can't remember, I found my way to Harlem; and there I found temporary haven, a place to light for a while. Also, I found a friend.

This was a Negro piano player named Willie Smith, who was known all over Harlem as "The Lion." He worked every night from around midnight to six, seven, or even eight in the morning in a little cellar joint called the Catagonia Club—or, as it was more familiarly known to its patrons, Pod's and Jerry's.

After my first visit there, I felt that this tiny little joint, with its dim lighting, its small bar over at one end of the room, its sprinkling of red-and-white checkered tables, was what I had been looking for. It reminded me of the South Side Chicago hangouts I used to frequent. The clientele was more or less the same, but more important than the clientele was the whole atmosphere of the place. I felt at home here, for the first time since I had arrived in New York.

Mainly, it was the music that attracted me. And that was Willie Smith's department—for it was he, The Lion, who dominated this little joint with his piano playing. There were three other "entertainers" working in Pod's and Jerry's; but it was his piano playing that kept me coming back there night after night.

I had never heard any piano playing like that before in my life. He used to sit there at that battered old upright and make some of the damnedest music I've ever heard come out of any instrument. And all the time his dark fingers ran nimbly over the chipped yellow ivories at the keyboard, he would keep up a running accompaniment of short growls, intermittent but rhythmic—almost like little barks—going "huck, huck, huck, huck, huck, huck, huck," as if to himself, but actually creating a sort of syncopated, drumlike, contrapuntal undercurrent to what he was doing with his fingers and hands; and it was because of this odd half-growl, half-bark of his that, as I later learned, he was called The Lion.

His style of piano playing was something altogether new to me. It was full of old-time idioms; authentic old-fashioned ragtime; but scattered throughout the ragtime were occasional incongruously modern, modulatory passages—these last all his own, so far as I've ever been able to determine, for I have never heard anyone else play anything quite like them, with the exception of those who have since copied him and incorporated some of The Lion's little melodic tricks into their own styles. At that time he had achieved a certain celebrity in colored musicians' circles; but it wasn't until quite a while later that the white musicians got to know about him.

For the most part he accompanied the three entertainers I mentioned above. All three of these were singers—two girls and one man. One of the "girls" was a dark, chocolate-brown woman of about forty-five, with a typical "shouter" style; she

was by far the better of the two female singers. The other was
a lighter, younger, more graceful and rather pretty girl, who,
although she couldn't sing particularly well, managed to pick
up a fair amount of cash during working hours.

Those were the days, in that kind of little joint, when singers
worked mostly for whatever tips they could pick up from the
customers. The usual ritual was for the customer to fold a
dollar bill down the middle lengthwise, and hold it so it pro-
jected over the corner of the table. The singer would then half-
dance up to the bill, singing all the while, and, after hiking up
her skirt and flirting around the dollar bill with the lower portion of her anatomy for a short time, she'd eventually grasp the
end of the bill between the upper part of her thighs, draw
back, reach down with one hand, and carelessly take the bill
and tuck it into her bosom with a brisk "Thank you" interjected
between the words of the tune she was singing—all this without missing a beat. Or a bill! And so they would go, from table
to table, repeating endless choruses of the same tune, lingering
at some tables where the "picking" was especially good and de-
voting only a cursory few moments to others where it was evident there was going to be no picking at all, until having made
the complete round, they would "go out" at the end of whatever chorus they happened to be singing; at which the next
singer would get ready to go into her round.

The third entertainer, being a man, was obviously at a disadvantage when it came to collecting his tips. He was called
"Jazzbo"—just plain Jazzbo. I've seen him around now and
then, run into him any number of times since the old days in
Pod's and Jerry's. Only just before the war I spotted him in
some little colored night club in Atlantic City, but I never did
get to know him by any other name.

Jazzbo was a really fine little singer, and I used to get quite
a kick out of listening to him. But I also used to feel sorry for
the poor little guy. He was short, he reeked of some strong
perfume, he was hunchbacked and quite ugly, he had an al-

most jet-black skin and a mouthful of gleaming gold teeth. Still, he never seemed to go around being sorry for himself. He always grinned at you in a way that didn't seem forced, so, in spite of the fact that he was small, ugly, somewhat effeminate, hunchbacked *and* a colored man (all this in a world where it's hard enough for a man to be just colored and still make any kind of decent life for himself)—in spite of all this, about the only thing I could find to feel really sorry for him about was his difficulty in competing with those two gals who had that interesting trick of collecting their tips in such a way as to give the customers very little reason to tip poor little Jazzbo at all.

Still, as I've said, he could sing—and sing well enough to hold his own even when it came to tips—so that, in the end, he didn't even let you feel sorry for him in that respect. He was an extraordinary little guy, Jazzbo was, and by no means an Uncle Tom. I've often thought about him at times when things seemed tough. For here was a fellow who really had it tough, and nevertheless went on about his life (such as it was) asking nothing from anybody and managing somehow to bear up without imposing his problems on anyone, no matter what it may have been like for him under the façade he wore. . . .

To get back, though, to The Lion (for all this business of singing and entertaining was only window-dressing to me): all the while Jazzbo or one of the gals would be making their rounds, The Lion would sit there at that scarred old upright, chewing a ragged cigar stub, growling and barking and "hucking" away to himself, and creating endless and ingenious and complex variations on whatever tune was being sung, until these complications and variations made it seem some minor miracle that the singer was able to keep going without losing the beat altogether, let alone the thread of the tune itself, which — for a large part of the time — served only as a springboard from which The Lion would plunge off into those deep and murky musical waters in which he swam.

I soon struck up an acquaintance with him, and after that

plucked up enough courage to ask him if I might bring my horn down some night so I could sit in with him. He hesitated, then nodded. That was enough for me. The following night I was back with my horn.

From that night on I became a sort of unofficial part of the "entertaining" roster at Pod's and Jerry's—unofficial only in that I did not, of course, receive any pay. In every other sense I took my "work" as seriously as if I had been hired, and showed up every night regularly, by the clock.

Playing with The Lion was a brand new kind of musical experience. I had to try to adapt my playing to his odd style. It wasn't easy, and at first I couldn't manage at all without a good bit of fumbling. He would sit there, occasionally turning his head and playing something at me with a kind of arrogant look that turned the musical phrase he had just played into a challenge, as if to say, "There y'are, boy—le's see you get with that one," and I would do my best to get with it, until after a while I began to get the drift, to latch on to what he was doing to the point where I could have some general predictability of where we would end up whenever we slid into one of those complicated little modulatory phrases of his which always, somehow or other, managed to slither their way back into the tonality of whatever we had started out from.

All this was an enormously stimulating experience for me. In many ways The Lion was, as I now know, one of the very few "originals" I have ever encountered in jazz music. From a purely harmonic standpoint, he was far ahead of most of his contemporaries; for jazz in those days, however rhythmically complicated it may have been, was fairly primitive harmonically.

Aside from that, though, my nightly stint at Pod's and Jerry's gave me the one thing I needed to fill in the emptiness of my life at that time, a sense of *belonging*—a feeling of being *accepted*. Within a few nights I could see that The

Lion liked the way I played. I continued to come down and sit in every night; and since I had no money at all, he got into the habit of buying me a drink now and then, and some breakfast when we wound up at six, seven, or eight in the morning. Occasionally he might ask me along when he set out after work for some little musicians' hangout that stayed open till noon or even later, where he'd sit down at the piano and tell me to get out my horn in order to show me off to some of his colleagues. Whenever I played something they approved of, he would look arrogantly over at them and announce, "Tha's my boy—you hear that?"

After several weeks I began to make other friends around Harlem, mostly musicians I met through and with The Lion. No doubt because of his sponsorship, I was accepted among these Negroes and treated as one of them, and eventually came to feel more like a colored man myself than an "ofay" —Harlemese for "white man," derived, I believe, from a Pig-Latin corruption of the word "foe." (A good enough commentary, by the way, on the relationship that exists between the average Negro and the average white.) There is hardly anything strange about the way I felt. For the most part I was actually living the life of a Negro musician, adopting Negro values and attitudes, and accepting the Negro out-group point of view not only about music but life in general. In fact, on the few occasions when I was forced to realize I was a white man, I used to wish I could actually *be* a Negro.

Looking back at it now, it was a weird life, although at the time it seemed reasonable enough. I was keeping night watchman's hours—going to bed at one or two, or even as late as three or four, in the afternoon, getting up at nine or ten at night, going over to Pod's and Jerry's and "working" until early morning, then going off to some musicians' hangout and playing until noon or one o'clock in the afternoon; in between, grabbing a meal or a sandwich or a drink on the fly, and only going home when I needed a change of clothing.

At those times when I did show up at home, my mother would ask me reproachfully what I was doing to myself. She couldn't understand the kind of life I was leading; and even though I tried to explain, it couldn't possibly have made much sense to her. However, she had come to accept the peculiarities of this curious profession I had got myself into, and aside from a few remonstrances now and then, she let me alone.

As for me, I was content to continue as I was. Since I could find no way to break into the white world, I was willing to forget it and go on about the business of trying to make a place for myself in this colored world into which I had accidentally stumbled and in which I now felt I belonged in a way I had never felt in any other milieu I had ever been a part of. For with these people I felt a warmth and enthusiasm and friendliness, and a sense of life that had been completely lacking in most of the relationships I had ever had with members of my own race.

Some of the friends I made during that period remained friends of mine for years after I had gone my way into an entirely different kind of life. For example, there was Chick Webb, the miraculous little hunchbacked drummer, who was then beginning to make a name for himself as one of the great bandleaders of his race. Poor little Chick—he is dead now; but I'll never forget the time, many years after I first met him up in Harlem, when he was working with his band in a spot in Boston—a sort of combination eating and dancing place, called Lavaggi's, if I remember correctly—and I was playing one-nighters around New England and coming back to Boston to play two nights a week at the Roseland State Ballroom. By that time we were "rival" bandleaders, but there was never the slightest trace of rivalry between us. My band used to rehearse down in the cellar of this ballroom, and now and then Chick would drop in and watch the rehearsal, occasionally sitting in "just for kicks." I had a sincere admiration for Chick, and the best way of summing up what he felt about me is what he once said to me, right after one of those rehearsals of mine.

Throughout the rehearsal, Chick had sat silent and motionless off at one end of the dimly lighted cellar, where I could see him when I happened to glance over my shoulder. A dark little blob of a man with an almost sphinxlike expression on his chocolate-colored face, he sat quietly in the shadows, motionless except for the wagging of his lower jaw as he chewed his everlasting cud of Spearmint. When we were all finished, he came ambling over to me and said: "You know somethin', man? Some day I'm gonna be walkin' up the street one way and you gonna be comin' down the other way, and we gonna pass each other and I'm gonna say, 'Hello, best white band in the worl'' and you gonna say, 'Hello, best colored band in the worl''—you know that?" And he gravely shook hands with me on that statement, almost as if we were entering into a solemn pact—and in a way, I suppose we actually were.

There was also Billie Holiday, a young, healthy kid only about seventeen or so at the time I first met her, but already beginning to develop that distinctive style of hers which has been copied and imitated by so many singers of popular music that the average listener of today cannot even realize how original she actually is. For she has had so many imitators that even if you are hearing her for the first time it is as if you were listening to someone you've been hearing for a long, long time. And, although I couldn't have known it at that time, years later Billie was going to sing with my band and break a precedent of many years' standing, by being the first colored girl ever to have sung with any white band anywhere in this country. . . .

I could go on and on remembering all the friends I made during those few months among these people who took me in at a time when my own world had rejected me.

These friends were real, and true, and warm, each in his own way, and throughout the years, every time I have ever run into one of them, there has been that strange and subtle bond between us, that deep feeling of mutual understanding that exists between human beings who remember a long way back to a time when their life-paths crossed, back to a time when things were different from what they have since become, back to the days when there was time for kindness and laughter, understanding and sympathy, and the kind of friendship nobody can ever have too much of in this present world we all have to try to live in together.

"The business of life is to go forward."

SAMUEL JOHNSON

Chapter Thirty-One

BESIDES THE NEGRO MUSICIANS I had got to know through
The Lion and my association with him, it was inevitable
that I meet some white musicians. Through these occasional
white musicians who used to come up to Harlem from time
to time, I began to meet others who worked "downtown" in
the white world; and eventually I began to pick up a bit of
work here and there. I would be recommended for a job by
one, and then, meeting other musicians on that particular
job, there would be further recommendations and further
musical acquaintanceships, until, one thing leading to another (and my six-month waiting-period having elapsed, so
that I was now a full-fledged member of Local 802), I began to make a little money. Not much at first, but enough to
pay the rent again and ease the financial burden at home.
A short time later I moved out of my mother's flat and went
downtown to share a beatup apartment with one of the musicians I had recently met.

In the ensuing months, I became a part of the circle of
young jazz musicians who were then drifting around New
York. There was Artie Bernstein, the bass player, with whom
I roomed. Artie was at that time going to Columbia University and preparing to become a lawyer; but, although he
finally graduated and passed his bar exams, he never did go

into law but kept right on playing bass fiddle instead. The last time I ran into him he was working in one of the large Hollywood studio orchestras. There was Jack Teagarden, the phenomenal young trombonist who had just blown into town from the wild and woolly Southwest, and through whose completely new style the entire concept of what a jazz trombone could sound like was being changed; Jack's younger brother, Charlie, who played trumpet and sounded like a lazier, higher-pitched version of Jack himself; Joe Sullivan, Gene Krupa, Eddie Condon, Bud Freeman, Benny Goodman, Red Mackenzie, Davie Tough, Max Kaminsky, George Wettling, Jess Stacey, Wingy Manone, the whole "Chicago crowd," who had also come to New York at about that same time and were hanging on to try their luck at getting set somewhere in the Big Apple. There was Bix Beiderbecke, recently out of Paul Whiteman's large dance orchestra, where he had never belonged in the first place—now on the down-grade, a pitiable wreck of a guy, unable to control his drinking well enough to keep it from interfering with his trumpet playing. At that point Bix was on the last leg of his long bout with booze which killed him a few years later at the age of twenty-eight. He left behind little more than a few short scattered piano pieces, the memory of some of the freshest trumpet playing that had ever come out of the horn of any white musician, and a diffused and romantic legend that has since become the basis for a good bit of the general misunderstanding and romanticism that pervades the whole John O'Hara-Butterfield 8 era in American jazz. There was Jimmy Dorsey, a saxophone player with an astounding technical equipment, who had already established himself in the higher echelons of the radio and recording fields but who still came around now and then for one of our periodic "sessions"; Tommy Dorsey, Jimmy's brother, who was already beginning to make a name for himself as a "high-note artist" on the trombone; Bunny Berigan—also dead now, after an unsuccessful and frustrating battle with life and that Old Demon Rum—but at that time a young lad fresh out of Madison, Wisconsin, flat broke like most of the rest of us, also trying to find himself any little job so he could earn some kind of living with his trumpet, any old kind of job just so he could pick up a few bucks to keep going, pay for a hotel room, feed himself, and buy a drink now and then.

There was Dick McDonough, the guitar player, who is also dead, for much the same reasons as Bix and Bunny. Another guitar player, who had developed an entirely different style of jazz guitar from Dick's, but in its own way a whole new approach to the guitar as a jazz instrument, was a blonde, long-nosed, good-natured guy named Carl Kress. There was a crazy drunk of a trombonist named George Troop (now dead too), also a "high-note artist" but, unlike Tommy Dorsey, unable to stay sober long enough at any one time to keep any job he might start on; there was a very young, bright-eyed, intense young kid named Joey Bushkin who played piano and hung out with the Chicago crowd, who was then beginning to make a name for himself around New York. There were any number of others, almost without exception hard-drinking, fast-living, wild-eyed young guys living out their crazy, boozey, frantic lives, and without one single exception, every last one of them chockful of energy, facility, and enormous musical talent in a world that had not yet come to the point where it was interested in what they had to offer musically, aside from whatever commercial use the budding radio industry was occasionally about to make of their skills.

The musicians' hangout during that era was a tiny hole-in-the-wall of a speakeasy down under the Sixth Avenue El, where it crossed town on 53rd Street just west of Broadway—a joint run by a pale-faced, blonde-eyelashed young fellow named Jimmy Plunkett, stone-bald under the cap he always wore as he served up drinks from behind the initial-carved old bar. Jimmy was filled with an apparently boundless faith in these wild-eyed characters whose enormous thirst he was always ready to assuage, even when he had to carry them on the cuff for periods as long as a year or even more. Plunkett's served not only as a speakeasy but as a sort of unofficial musicians' club, where there was a bulletin board posted for the convenience of the habitués, so they could get messages to each other regarding club dates, recording sessions, and so on.

It was in Plunkett's that I first ran into a radio conductor named Freddy Rich, who was then conductor of the staff dance band at the Columbia Broadcasting Studios at 52nd Street and Madison Avenue. Someone—I think it may have been Tommy Dorsey, who had worked in this staff band before graduating into the free-lance field—gave Rich quite a build-up about my playing; with the result that, shortly after I had met him, when there was an opening in this band of his, he offered me the job.

I jumped at the chance to get this staff job. This kind of work was much sought after in the kind of business jazz music was then. For the most part, at that time, the only way a guy could make a halfway stable living blowing a horn was by traveling around with the few big commercial dance bands that toured the country in those pre-Swing days.

Rich told me I would have to make an audition, but that it was no more than a necessary formality. He assured me that the job was already as good as mine. A week or so later I showed up for this "formality," although the idea of an audition was something I wasn't particularly keen about. I had already begun to make a sufficient reputation around the business to feel that auditions were something you didn't do; either a leader knew enough about your playing to hire you, or he didn't. Still, as I say, I wanted to get into that kind of work, so I agreed to do the audition.

Although I had no way of knowing it at the time, there

was a lot of politics around the radio studios in those days, due to the simple fact that there were some hundred musicians ready, willing, able, and available, for every one such job as this one at CBS. And even if I had known, it wouldn't have made any great difference one way or the other; for I wouldn't have known what to do about it. I went through with the "formality"—only to learn, a week or so later, that there had already been some machination between one of the studio musical contractors and some friend of his who was also after the job. The contractor's friend had already been hired before I even made my audition.

The first I heard about it was when Rich called up on the telephone to tell me the bad news. At that point I got pretty damn bitter. I had built up my hopes to where I had counted on this job as an entrée into a type of work on which I might build some kind of halfway secure life. It was my first experience of this kind. Up until then, getting a job had always been a fairly clear-cut matter of ability. You were either good enough—in which case the job was yours; or you weren't good enough—in which case you had no legitimate beef and could understand it when you heard the guy who did get the job. But here, for the first time, I learned that ability had nothing to do with it; as Rich told me, the guy to whom I had lost the job was no damn good at all. In fact, Rich himself was pretty sore about it; but he was powerless to do anything in a situation which was more political than musical. All of which did me no good at all, and actually only made me madder than ever—especially when I once got to hear this guy play, this friend of the contractor's, this new type of political musician, who couldn't play *Come To Jesus* on a phonograph, let alone handle his own instrument in a way that might justify his having snatched the job right out from under my nose.

It was just a bit too much for me to take.

I was disgusted and full of rage, not only at this piece of

skulduggery through which I had lost a job I needed desperately (for I was still deeply involved in my legal difficulties over the manslaughter charge I was faced with)—but, illogically, rage at Freddy Rich, the Columbia Broadcasting System, and, in fact, the whole damn music business. It seemed to me, at the ripe old age of nineteen, that I had reaped nothing more from it than a crop of weariness, loneliness, insecurity.

I thought seriously of quitting the business altogether, for I could see no way out of the rut I was in. I was sick and tired of the endless struggle for a status, sick and tired of running around the country and batting from pillar to post in the feverish quest for some sort of stability. I couldn't see any sense, at that naive stage, in trying to get someplace in a racket where the ability to do your job well apparently meant nothing compared to the ability to suck up to the people who had power. I had had no experience in any other kind of competitive work, I hadn't yet learned that this same situation occurs almost every hour of every day in any line where there are more job seekers than jobs. All I knew anything about was how to play an instrument, and when that seemed to be getting me nowhere I became baffled, frustrated, confused, and angry. As I realize now, I was not only sick of all that, but just plain sick of myself and possibly a little world-sick as well.

This was also the time I became involved with Dreiser, O'Neill, Hemingway, *et al.* I had recently read "An American Tragedy" and couldn't help—out of my own personal involvements with the processes of legal justice—identifying myself with the boy in that book, Clyde Griffiths, whose story struck some responsive chord and caused me to feel a strong emphatic bond between him and me. I can still remember the sudden wave of helplessness that rushed over me when I first read the formal indictment under which I was being prosecuted. "The People of the State of New York vs. Arthur

Shaw"—and when the full import of those words struck me, I began to get some dim sense of the blind mechanism of legal justice, the machine quality of those huge unseen forces aligned against me and grinding ponderously and impersonally toward my destruction.

"They don't realize," I thought, "—can't they understand? What good is it going to do anybody to send me to jail? I didn't mean to kill that man. I couldn't help it. What good does it do anybody to put me in jail now? How can it help him? What good is it going to do a poor fellow who's already dead?"

And in between trials, first in one court and then in the higher courts, I used to walk up and down the streets and look at "The People of the State of New York" and feel sick to my stomach with the realization that none of them had anything to do with this blind force that was threatening to crush my life right then and there. What could I do? What good was it to try to do anything at all?

I felt trapped, helpless, bitter, desperate, enraged—like a wild animal trapped in a snare and ready to gnaw off its own leg to gain its freedom. Here I was, I told myself, just at the beginning of my life—and here was this juggernaut, this awful steam roller bearing down upon me and threatening to squash me out of existence before I had even had a chance to get started.

And on top of everything else, I was out of a job once more, with my mother to support, unable to get any work anywhere. The first effects of the 1929 Wall Street crash were just beginning to raise havoc in the music business as well as all other businesses.

The only thing that stopped me from throwing in the sponge and quitting was that I had no idea what else I could do. I thought of various possibilities but none of them added up, nothing seemed to hold out any promise of making me a living. I was doing a lot of reading, as a way of keeping my mind off my problems—and at one point it occurred to me that if I applied myself I might possibly manage some way of making a livelihood in that field. In fact, I tried, in my fumbling way; I did a lot of tentative scribbling. But of course it came to nothing at all. I knew nothing about writing, outside of the scattered reading I had done; and I knew no way of going about it, I had no real point of view from which to write. I was simply a miserably confused kid, with no idea of the realities of either my misery or my confusion; so whenever I tried to write something it turned out just about as miserable and confused as I myself was, and not only that but awkward and amateurish as well.

I finally had to give it up, out of a recognition of my complete inability to deal with written language in any organized way. Nevertheless, I was intrigued. Partially, I suppose, because it seemed to me a wonderful way to earn a living. A fellow could sit down and go to work whenever he had something to say, and not, as in my own business, have to wait for the phone to ring and somebody to hire him. But even beyond that naive notion, I should add, in all justice to myself, that I also was beginning to develop an honest (even though confused) *interest* in reading, writing, and the whole world of books and literature in general.

But before I could arrive at a more realistic understanding about all that, I was suddenly offered a job in one of the famous jazz bands of that day, Red Nichols' band. I went to work at the Park Central Roof; and as a result of the working-hours and the fact that I was once again doing something I knew about, I had to abandon my abortive attempts at formulating some status for myself in The Life of Letters, and go on with the more pressing pursuit of my day-to-day livelihood.

Then one night there came what for me amounted to a sort of vindication. There was a telephone call for me—from Freddy Rich, that same studio conductor who had offered me the job at CBS.

This time, he stated, the job was definitely mine. But by
now I was bitter enough to make it tough. My first stipulation
was, "No auditions." He agreed. Then I announced that he
would have to pay me twenty-five dollars a week more than the
union minimum scale for the job. This almost threw Rich for a
loop. Such a demand was practically unheard of for a job of
that sort; but I didn't care about that. I was determined to
have this small satisfaction or else the hell with CBS.

After a lot of haggling back and forth, it was finally settled
—my way. A few weeks later I started in at my new job; playing first saxophone in the Columbia Broadcasting System staff
orchestra. . . .

It was during the following year, while I worked at CBS,
that I met Guy D'Isere and, because of my encounter with
him, set off on that reading jag I've already described.

So I can now pick up that thread again where I dropped it,
and trace the steps that led to my first real break with music,
how I started on my search for some of the answers to the
questions I was beginning to ask myself—a search for self-
orientation, an attempt to organize my self-understanding,
a pressing desire to find out who I was, what I wanted,
what my real values were, and what, in short, might constitute
for me a meaningful life.

The process through which I finally arrived at a set of temporary answers; the premature and blundering efforts I had to
make before I could finally learn the important lesson that
there are never any answers *but* temporary ones; the way in
which I arrived at my present state—all this is the subject of
what now follows. For from this point on I am going to deal
with the basic theme I'm concerned with—the real-life Jekyll-
and-Hyde dichotomy, the struggle between true and false
needs, the battle with the Outer and Inner Enemies, and the

resolution of which *is* Enemy and which is Friend *in our own natures,* that must be engaged in, fought out, and arrived at before anyone can go on to the complex business of living any kind of meaningful life in what T. S. Eliot once called "a world of lunacy, violence, stupidity, greed . . ."

At a Red Cross Concert in Wellington, New Zealand, 1943

With Admirals Halsey and Fitch in Noumea, New Caledonia, 1943

At a U.S. Navy Field Hospital on Guadalcanal, 1943

A recording session in Hollywood

At the Strand Theatre, New York

The Author in 1945

In the control room listening to record play-back

A recording session in Hollywood

With Jerome Kern and Steven Shaw to whom this book is dedicated

In London editing *Cinderella* at the Savoy Hotel

At the Strand Theatre, New York

An impromptu session at the Decca administration office. Duke Ellington on piano, Chick Webb on drums.

Part III

The Trouble With Cinderella
(an outline of identity)

Part III

"A father sees a son nearing manhood.
What shall he tell that son?

A tough will counts. So does desire.
So does a rich soft wanting.
Without rich wanting nothing arrives.
Tell him too much money has killed men
    and left them dead years before burial:
    the quest of lucre beyond a few easy needs
    has twisted good enough men
    sometimes into dry thwarted worms.
Tell him time as a stuff can be wasted.
Tell him to be a fool every so often
    and to have no shame over having been a fool
    yet learning something out of every folly
    hoping to repeat none of the cheap follies
    thus arriving at intimate understanding
    of a world numbering many fools.
Tell him to be alone often and get at himself
    and above all tell himself no lies about himself
    whatever the white lies and protective fronts
    he may use amongst other people.
Tell him solitude is creative if he is strong
    and the final decisions are made in silent rooms.
Tell him to be different from other people
    if it comes natural and easy being different.
Let him have lazy days seeking his deeper motives.

The Trouble with Cinderella

Let him seek deep for where he is a born natural.
Then he may understand Shakespeare
and the Wright brothers, Pasteur, Pavlov,
Michael Faraday and free imaginations
bringing changes into a world resenting change.
He will be lonely enough
to have time for the work
he knows as his own."

CARL SANDBURG
The People, Yes

"If only we could say that comprehension establishes a link be-tween men. Except, however, for a small elite who speak the same language, this is not the case, because, according to their culture and their intelligence, men give different meanings to the word 'comprehend.' An explanation that will satisfy one man will seem quite inadequate to another."

LECOMTE DU NOUY

Chapter Thirty-Two

WHEN A MAN SETS OUT to tell the story of how he arrived at a given state of mind, he must sooner or later realize that there is never going to be any way for him to know whether he has succeeded in communicating any true idea of the effect of his experiences on his own subjective development. In the first place, there is the matter of selection—of trying to figure out what might be significant for someone else. In the second place, since the connotations of any single experience are quite different for every human being, there is always the possibility that the other fellow is translating anything you say in terms of his own experience. In other words, there are no guarantees when it comes to anything of this sort. All I can do is go on flying blind and keeping my fingers crossed. And all the time I go on I have to bear in mind that any real communication of the kind I am trying to make here may be as yet impossible for us as creatures, at least at our present stage of evolutionary development.

True, we've come a long way since the Tower of Babel. To-day we have no linguistic problems when it comes to building a tower—or even a skyscraper. We have no difficulty in com-municating on practical, mechanical levels; and as a result we are able to construct instruments so powerful and ingenious that the touch of a child's finger on a pushbutton can move a mountain. But that does not mean that we can communicate to the child (or even to the average grownup) *any real under-standing of the means* by which the power is obtained, har-nessed, and released. So far, we haven't even learned to com-municate with one another well enough to work out a method of living in peace with either ourselves or our fellow creatures on any sustained basis.

So that there comes a time when, if you're at all concerned with such matters, the near-impossibility of real communica-tion on any such level of abstraction as the emotional, subjec-tive forces that go to make up a single human being looms up as a crushing, overwhelming fact. And when you once come to this point, you are forced to realize that you have only—by and large—two broad alternatives.

Number one—you can try to override the sense of futility and isolation by releasing a spate of words, either written (as I'm doing here) or oral (as most of us do for a large part of the time), one little set of syllables at a time; and if you can man-age to avoid boring your listener (or reader) and somehow contrive to keep him entertained, stimulated, or even amused long enough for him to go along with you until you've finished, you can hold his attention and maybe convince yourself that you've devised a way of poking your head through a tiny chink in the thick wall that separates each of us from everyone else.

Choice number two is even easier—and certainly it is by far the more common choice. This is simply a matter of saying nothing at all outside of those everyday banalities we all ex-change with one another on what we call social occasions and by which means we delude ourselves into the fond belief that we are conversing.

Well, perhaps we are. The whole point is that conversation is not necessarily communication; and there are a number of times when I've wondered whether the kind of conversation most of us indulge in isn't actually a negation of communication. The average conversation seems to be, mainly, only one more way for us to huddle together in a seemingly-gregarious companionship and thus delude ourselves into believing we are no longer alone, while at the same time we maintain and even build up and further strengthen, the wall that exists between us.

In any event, there isn't a great deal of choice between the two alternatives I've just presented. And as far as that goes, even in these, the one a fellow is apt to make has already been at least partially determined by an infinite number of factors (and those in turn determined by an infinity of other factors, and so on, *ad infinitum*—until no one can ever be sure whether any choice is "of his own making," or only another result of the interaction of (say) the state of his endocrines with the total effect of our entire cosmic history as a peculiar species of evolving organisms inhabiting one relatively microscopic speck of planetary dust whirling through intergalactic space on its way to nowhere at all that anyone has yet been able to conceive.

Perhaps the simple truth is that, although most of us *think* we want to reach out and touch some other human being, we are actually scared to death of ourselves and one another and only pretend to be gregarious in order to hide our fears both from ourselves and others. Most of us live with hidden fear, each of us imprisoned within his own individual cellophane wrapper, peering timidly and cautiously out at the world, smiling with our faces and cowering inside our skins, paying lip-service to a kind of social ideal we are unable to live up to in reality, and deeply suspicious of our only-too-recent and only-too-well-recognized animal heritage.

But—as a result of these fears and suspicions, and because of our deep-lying awareness of these innately hostile, predatory, anti-societal, dog-eat-dog impulses that lie buried away deep down in the make-up of every last one of us—we are sometimes inclined to overlook certain other qualities that run through the very grain of the *particular kind of animal we are,* precisely because of which qualities we can regard ourselves as human beings, as well as animals.

The point is, one does not exist without the other—and we can never be truly human without honestly facing, understanding, and coping with, the greedy animal that is also there . . . crouching . . . waiting . . . ever watchful. . . .

Getting back now to the kind of animal I was at the time I first began to seek some orientation for myself in a hostile and competitive world, perhaps the following incident will be illuminating. This took place while I was working in the staff band at the Columbia Broadcasting System. I was then about twenty years old. One evening I took a walk through Central Park with a friend. It was summer, I remember, and along toward sunset. Lights were just beginning to wink on here and there in the thousands of windows in the huge sprawling architectural masses that make up the Central Park South part of the New York skyline. Without saying a word, my friend and I stopped and stared at this man-made fairyland, each of us occupied with his own thoughts and gazing silently up at the gray buildings bathed in the reddish glow of fading sunlight.

My friend said, "What does it make you think of, Art?"

I didn't even have to stop to consider. I spoke up immediately, right out of what had been going through my mind at that moment.

"See all those windows up there with all those lights going

on in them?" I said. "Well, back of every one of those there's
somebody. And one of these days everyone of those people up
there behind every one of those windows—is going to know
my name."

Straight enough to the point, wouldn't you say? Certainly it's
honest enough, if that's what a fellow is after; and you may be
sure that was exactly what I was after—and what I was damn
well going to have or bust. Also, it ought to give you a pretty
good idea of what was driving me and what I must have been
like at that age, how cocksure I was of where I was heading
and what I wanted out of life.

Well, as far as it goes, it's an accurate enough picture at
that—the only trouble being that it's only a picture, and therefore only two-dimensional. There's another dimension you
have to bear in mind, without which the picture isn't complete—a dimension that sets up a conflict, an incompatibility
between two sets of needs. This conflict wasn't resolved for a
long time.

But before I go into the nature of the conflict itself, let alone
the manner in which I finally resolved it, let's go a little further into this picture and examine what it tells about how I
was ticking.

For one thing, it seems to indicate quite clearly that I was
wound up tight and on my way somewhere. But where? What,
exactly, did I think I was after?

Money? Well, yes—money was part of it.

Fame? I suppose that was part of it too.

Success, in other words? Or rather, $ucce$$?

Of course—all that stuff. Cinderella, in fact—doesn't that
about sum it all up?

O.K., fine. But then what about all that other stuff that was
also going on at the same time?

For there was that other side of me—which was driving me
into a search for "education," a feverish need to *know* about
things. It was this need that had already caused me to approach

D'Isere and ask him for a list of "foreign authors" and afterwards plunge headlong into a whole sea of books in order to vindicate myself for my stupidity in his eyes. It was as a result of this need that I was already at that time waist-deep in extension courses at Columbia University; busying myself with all sorts of matters entirely unrelated to the practical aspects of pushing myself onward to satisfy my insatiable and basically greedy Cinderella-drives.

How could these two altogether different (if they *were* different) sets of goals exist side by side? How could I work out some course of action, some behavior-pattern in accord with these two conflicting (if they *were* conflicting) kinds of needs and drives. All I can tell you is that I was seething with feverish energy, and it took me a long, long time to work out any kind of sane answer to what I now recognize was a practically schizoid need—on the one hand for power, success, public recognition and acclaim on a mass scale, and on the other hand for some kind of stability, self-knowledge, personal orientation, and inner peace.

But, you may ask, what's wrong with ambition? What's wrong with a desire for success and public acclaim? Why should it be impossible to achieve a worthwhile objective, and *still* attain success and public recognition? Or, even failing to achieve all these on any ideal level—why, then, isn't it possible to work out some sort of sensible compromise?

A fair enough question.

I see nothing wrong with ambition and drives toward success in themselves. These are perfectly healthy, normal components, and as such are worthy enough. But—ambition and success-drives *to what ends?* What, in other words, is the ambition directed at—what constitutes "success" for the particular person who is driving, or being driven, toward it?

Now let's see where that leads.

Will this do? That success as an aim must be considered in social terms rather than in individual and self-seeking power-drives? That the man who is ambitious and aims at making a success in any given field is behaving socially—hence healthily (if we accept socially acceptable behavior as the only kind of healthy behavior)—*only as long as* he wants success merely as it makes for *acceptance* of himself by the world, makes for love and warmth between himself and the world—in other words, by implication, entails an acceptance on his part *of his responsibility to the world, and the necessity of earning love, acceptance, warmth,* or, in short, Success in these terms? And that the moment a success-drive becomes warped into a vindictive desire to *get even,* to make up for past suffering, to punish the world for fancied—or even realistic—injury; the moment a success-drive, or power-drive, if you will, is acted on only out of such motivations as these, you are dealing with someone who is very sick and hence a potential menace, large or small, depending purely on his capabilities and the circumstances in which he acts?

As to what I was trying to act on—well, the truth is that there was some of both—sickness as well as health, a desire for love and acceptance as well as a desire to "get even." And if you were to ask which side was pushing the harder, I'm afraid I couldn't possibly give you any accurate "one-hundred-per-cent-correct" answer. All I can say is they were both there, both working together, acting on each other and interacting, so that as time went on they began to merge, one into the other, to the extent that by the time I got down to trying to disentangle them and understand them for the purpose of being able to deal with them sanely and functionally—they gave me one hell of a time before I could ferret them out.

To come back to the question of why the two kinds of drives are incompatible and whether it is or is not possible for a man to arrive at some kind of inner peace and self-understanding in order to do something truly worthwhile (in other words, attain some worthwhile objective in terms of social good and achieve stability for himself) and still have great public recognition and acclaim—my answer to all this is a definite No. But before anyone jumps on my neck for that, perhaps I should qualify that to say that while it may be *possible* it is nevertheless one of the most extremely rare things that can ever happen to any man *in his time*. This in spite of the occasional exceptions, the Picassos and Bernard Shaws and those few others who come along once in a blue moon and through some series of freakish circumstances manage to achieve both artistic and financial success. For these are the exceptions, and as everybody knows, exceptions prove nothing at all. Almost anything *can* happen, of course, and according to the laws of probability, even the most unlikely eventuality may take place occasionally; but it's hardly something to gamble a lifetime on. While it is true that a man may occasionally do something very worthwhile indeed and still earn a lot of money for it, even in his lifetime—nevertheless, it's safe enough to state categorically that the man *who deliberately sets out* to make money, or achieve success, or power, or what-have-you along these lines, is far more apt to turn out junk (even skilfully contrived and highly polished junk, but junk nonetheless) than anything that might come under the heading of "worthwhile."

There was also the question of the possibility of compromise-solutions to conflicting needs. And here I believe we can come up with a quite simple answer. It depends on *the given individual's capacity for compromise*. That's all. Or to put it differently—it depends on whether the compromise itself becomes so painful that it overshadows the rewards. . . .

But the only aspects of all this that need concern us for the moment are those that apply to any man's attempts to find solutions to his own set of conflicting ambitions and desires. Those aspects are what I am going to deal with in the following pages of this saga of my own personal and subjective Odyssey. And since it has finally led me to where I now sit pecking away at a typewriter in the attempt to communicate some idea of How and Why I got here, and What it's like where I am—suppose we take it as it comes, one chunk at a time, and for a beginning at any rate, let me tell you about some of the decisions I had to make as I went along on my road to finding a few answers to all these questions.

"The life of every man is a diary in which he means to write one story, and writes another, and his humblest hour is when he compares the volume as it is with what he vowed to make it."

J. M. BARRIE

Chapter Thirty-Three

WITHIN A YEAR AND A HALF after I had started on my job at the Columbia Broadcasting System I evolved A Plan; for at that point I thought I had a pretty good idea of how I wanted to spend the rest of my life. However, I still had to finance my plan. So, having built up a sufficient professional reputation by then, I quit my staff job and went off into free-lance work, where there was more money to be made.

Besides earning more, I also had more time. And during this period my life began to enter a whole new phase.

Before getting into this type of work, while I was still a dance band musician, I had always worked nights and slept a good part of the day. Now, for the first time in my life, I was earning quite a bit of money, some weeks as much as three or four hundred dollars, and mostly I was through by nine or ten in the evening. Just having my evenings free was quite a big change in itself. Aside from anything else, it gave me a new point of view. I began to regard music as a way of earning a living, as a *business* as well as a craft.

The truth is, it was far more business than anything else. The work I was now doing had a lot more to do with selling soap than with music. On most of the programs I did, there was little or no room for any sort of individual musical expression. Radio music is run by a stop watch. Musical phrases are metered out in terms of minutes and seconds, rather than in terms of musical feeling or anything connected with musicality.

I remember, for instance, one program I worked on in those days, on which, God knows why, we were playing something of Wagner's. It just so happened that the music had in it a "Grand Pause"—which simply means a pause between two phrases. Naturally, when we came to that part of the music, the conductor paused. The whole thing couldn't have lasted more than a couple of seconds at the very most—for this was, after all, a radio pause, and, with all due respects to Mr. Wagner, radio time costs so much a second and the conductor knew enough not to throw away too many seconds merely to humor some dead composer.

As we started in again, we were interrupted by the raucous sound of the loudspeaker. "Hey—what was that long silence?" came the booming voice of the production man inside the sound-control booth.

The conductor stopped the orchestra. "It's a Grand Pause," he yelled into the microphone.

There was a short lull. The production man conferred busily with the agency man and the sponsor's representative. Then— "Cut it," he spoke up into his microphone.

Some of the men in the orchestra snickered. The conductor glared them down. He made one more attempt to maintain the musical proprieties. "It's Wagner," he shouted. "The music is marked 'G.P.' We have to pause. I'll cut it as short as I can, but we've got to pause or it won't make sense."

"Hold it," came the Voice of God from the control booth. More conferring. Finally the voice came booming out again. "No pause."

The conductor looked harassed. He appeared to be about to make one last protest, but he must have thought better of it, for he turned back to the orchestra. "O.K., boys, you heard that. Cut the pause."

The orchestra men got out pencils and gravely crossed out the two letters "G.P."—and that was that. The sponsor won, Wagner lost. Period. . . .

There was another incident, which occurred during the rehearsal of one of the big cigarette programs—a program which is on the air to this day, with exactly the same formula as at that time, some eighteen or nineteen years ago.

One of the arrangements called for a sixteen-bar *ad lib* clarinet solo. When we got to it I went into a cautious, radio-ized kind of improvisation—almost straight melody, except for a little twist here and there to give the illusion of jazz phrasing.

Suddenly we were interrupted by that same Voice of God roaring from the control booth. (It's remarkable, by the way, how similar people's voices can sound when they are distorted by these loudspeakers.)

"What's the idea?"

"What idea?" the conductor asked, after stopping the orchestra.

"How many men are playing in that spot?"

"Just solo clarinet and rhythm section—five men altogether. Just for that sixteen-bar spot," said the conductor.

Silence. Conference in the control room. Then—"No good," the loudspeaker rasped. "The sponsor's paying for thirty-five men, and thirty-five men are what he wants to hear."

"But you can't play ensemble all the time," said the bewildered conductor.

"The sponsor doesn't care about that—he's paying for a full orchestra and he doesn't want to hear five men. Fill it in."

"But—" and the conductor subsided.

By the time we went on the air that night, it had been "filled in" and this time the whole orchestra was playing ensemble throughout. I assume the sponsor was happy.

As a result of this sort of thing, the musicians working in

radio in those days were some of the most cynical people I have ever known anywhere. Most of them were—as indeed they had to be in order to get into this kind of work to begin with— fine musicians. Among them were some of the best instrumentalists in the world—men like Johnny Corigliano (now concert-master with the New York Philharmonic); Freddy Fradkin (erstwhile concert-master of the Boston Symphony); Saul Caston, now conductor of the Denver Symphony (then playing first trumpet in the Philadelphia Orchestra under Stokowski); Harry Glantz, at that time first trumpet with the New York Philharmonic under Toscanini. As for the jazz players—well, there were Tommy Dorsey, Jimmy Dorsey, Benny Goodman, Bunny Berigan, Manny Klein, Chauncey Morehouse, Dick McDonough, Carl Kress, and I don't know who-all else—the pick of the white jazz musicians in the country. Every one of them was well-enough "routined" to be able to read almost anything at sight and play almost anything put up in front of him—whether jazz or anything else.

And I never knew one of them who didn't feel exactly the same as I did about what we were doing. Which could be put into the following words: "Sure it stinks, but it pays good dough, so the hell with it."

The miraculous part of it is that they still did their jobs and did them extremely well, and never betrayed their enormous cynicism during working hours. Except perhaps for the look of delight and gratification on their faces whenever anything went haywire on any of these programs.

I was no exception. I was doing it purely for the money; and as soon as I could get together enough money, I intended to quit the business and never come back.

As for what I wanted to do with my life once I did quit, in his "Experiment in Autobiography," H. G. Wells says: "What was once the whole of life, has become to an increasing extent, merely the background of life. People can ask now what would have been an extraordinary question five hundred years ago.

They can say, 'Yes, you earn a living, you support a family, you love and hate, but—*what do you do?*'"

That was it, exactly. I was earning a living, supporting myself and my mother, doing a certain amount of loving and hating, but—*what was I doing?*

Well, I've already answered part of that where I described some of my preoccupation with reading, studying, learning about writing, etc. I was still seeing D'Isere from time to time, and with his help I went on studying what I was interested in learning. I studied French so I could read men like Flaubert, Proust, Mallarmé, Baudelaire. I was taking courses at Columbia and learning something about the various literary forms— short story, novel, essay, drama, etc.

I had made up my mind to save enough to buy a small house someplace out of New York, where I could live inexpensively and give myself enough time to learn to support myself as a writer. I was thoroughly disillusioned with music; but since I had come that far with it, I decided to use it to finance myself into a new field.

I don't mean that I disliked music itself. All I am saying is that what I was doing musically had nothing whatsoever to do with music.

Elbert Hubbard once said, "Music is the only one of the arts that cannot be prostituted to a base use." But Elbert Hubbard never had anything to do with commercial radio, so he couldn't have had a very good idea of what can be done with music.

But I have—I have a good idea.

And if there is anyone who has any remaining doubts, I wish there were some way to make him listen to just one so-called musical program I used to have to do once a week—Manhattan Merrygoround. For all I know, it may still be on the air to this day, although how it ever got on the air to begin with is more than I'll ever be able to figure out.

As for this present-day monstrosity, commercial television— well, the usual argument, of course, is that TV is still only an infant industry. After all, say the people who are unlucky enough to be trapped in that racket, radio too was pretty bad when it first got started, wasn't it?

The only answer I can make to this is that as far as I'm concerned radio is still pretty goddamn bad—but of course that is a whole big long discussion in itself, and what's the point in kicking a sick dog?

"To be conscious that you are ignorant is a great step to knowledge."

DISRAELI

Chapter Thirty-Four

ONE FINE DAY, after I had saved up a few thousand dollars out of all the musical *mishmash* I was engaged in, I picked up my horns and took off from the environs of Radio City. I bought a small "farm" of about twenty-five weedy acres, with a dilapidated old house on it, the whole thing costing three thousand dollars, and moved out to Erwinna, Pennsylvania, in the now-quite-fashionable county of Bucks.

After settling down, and accustoming myself to such rural delights as an outdoor privy on a cold winter night, or having to travel some hundred yards to a spring whenever I needed water for bathing, drinking, or cooking—I ultimately managed to establish a routine for myself. At which point I began to write.

However, I soon learned a most peculiar thing.

I found that the ability to write grammatically, the ability to make sentences that sound good, or even the ability to use words skilfully—all these do not make a fellow a writer.

There was one thing missing.

I couldn't figure out what I was going to write.

That's all. Not period, but exclamation mark.

Now you'd think that would be something any fool could have learned before going off and getting himself all involved in a whole new kind of life, wouldn't you? Well, perhaps you'd be right, but I don't think so.

You see, what I learned out there on that little "farm" of mine is something quite important for a guy to know—especially if the guy happens to have the idea that he would like to be a writer and is only being prevented from becoming one because of lack of time. What I learned out there is something altogether different.

Time alone won't do it.

The ability to make sentences won't do it.

Even a headful of ideas won't do it.

What will, then?

Well—ruling out that mysterious thing called "talent," which I've already said I don't know anything about—let's just see what else we have left.

It seems to me that one of the most important things—and certainly one of the most obvious—is the simple matter of *having something to say,* something a fellow is so full of that he *has to say it or bust.* And not only something to say—but something so strongly *felt* that the saying of it is necessary enough to sustain the labor involved in saying it.

I think that when it's all said and done, the fundamental requirement in order to write is a clear and urgent desire to say something. Given that one thing—plus, of course, a certain minimum amount of articulateness—anyone can do it. As to whether it will be good writing or not—ah, that is an altogether different matter. . . .

By the time I'd been at it for a year or so, I'd learned that there was a great deal more I had to know about what I wanted to say, before any writing I might do would satisfy me any more than what I had been doing musically for the past couple of years in commercial radio.

I had a whole lot more to learn—not only about writing, but about myself.

This became more and more apparent as time passed. I was

doing a lot of reading, in between the times I was chopping wood, drawing water, taking care of all the other details involved in the life I was living out there on that "farm" of mine.

Then one day about a year after I'd gone out there to live, the whole thing came to a head.

I had been reading a book called "The Modern Temper," by Joseph Wood Krutch, in which there was a reference to the speed of light as "the cross-grain of the universe." I remembered hearing about the speed of light, back in my high school days, and I knew it was somewhere in the neighborhood of 186,000 something-or-other per second, but I couldn't quite recall whether it was 186,000 feet or miles—I was pretty sure it wasn't inches.

I got out the volume of the Encyclopaedia Britannica (14th Edition) marked Libi to Mary, turned to the word "Light"— and started to read.

Well-sir—as soon as I'd gone into this little dissertation a short way I was doing some extremely fancy floundering. Here's one sentence—And I Quote:

"The most accurate measure of the velocity of light (*see* VELOCITY OF LIGHT) assign it the value of $2.99796 + 4 \times 10^{10}$ cm. per sec." There's quite a bit more; the whole article runs to some twenty-five or more pages. But there was no sense in my trying to go any further, since there was no way I could kid myself that I understood it even up to there.

As I sat staring blankly at the words on the page, I suddenly got a mental picture of myself sitting there like a chimpanzee with a book in his hand. As far as actual meaning was concerned, the letters on the page might just as well have been so many little black bugs.

I put the volume down and began to get angry. And the more I thought about it the angrier I got. Then and there, that very same day, I made up my mind as to what I was going to do about it. The hell with the "farm" and the hell with any further attempts to write—I was going back to school again.

Which is just exactly what I did.

Because the way I figured it, I had no business trying to write anything until I was at least able to read and understand what some other fellow had already written. After all, wasn't writing a way of telling people something you wanted to tell them? And who the hell did I think I was to tell anyone anything, when I couldn't even understand what I was reading?

That took care of my "literary" endeavors for the time being —the "time being" (as it turned out) being the next fifteen or twenty years.

Of course I had no idea it was going to be anywhere near as long as that. Or how far afield I might go before getting back to my original intention. Or how different that intention was going to become by the time I finally did get back to it. Or, for that matter, how much change would have taken place in me by that time.

All I knew was that I didn't know anything. I was obsessed with a sense of my own total, abysmal ignorance. In short, I was just plain disgusted with myself; and out of this disgust came a brand new concept—brand new for me, at any rate.

Up to that point in my life I had always been driven by an overpowering desire to prove myself, to vindicate myself, to assert myself, in my dealings with people. I'll leave it to you to figure out, from what I've already told you about myself, exactly how, when, and why all this arose. However, up to that point, no matter what the circumstances, it had always functioned as a *competitive* drive. Vindication had always seemed to me a thing arrived at through competition. Life had always seemed to me a kind of race, between me and the rest of the world; and I had accepted it as that, hence geared myself up, tensed myself, given myself a charge, so to speak, in order to get up enough speed to compete in the race against anyone in my immediate environment who might have been lucky enough to start with certain advantages I hadn't had. In other words, I had always functioned out of some dim feeling of having to make up for lacks in myself. Or, to put it another way, whereas most people I knew were starting more or less from scratch, I—as it seemed to me—was starting from way behind scratch; so, naturally, in order to be in the running at all, I had to run twice or three times as fast as the next fellow—not too unlike a fellow named Sammy Glick.

That's pretty much the picture, and I can't help it if it seems fairly odious; at least it may give you a little better idea about the way I had always behaved up to this point, and why.

As to this new concept I mentioned—and what I mean when I say it was for me a brand new one—here's what it came to.

For the first time in my life I was beginning to realize that the most important person in whose eyes I had to vindicate myself was—my own self.

Of course, at the time, all this was entirely unarticulated and unformed. I wouldn't have been able to put it into clear language; and if anyone had asked me what I thought I was going to get out of going back to school, my answer would have run to something along these lines:

"I feel ignorant. I feel there's a lot I've got to learn. I'm sick of going around not knowing anything. I'm sick of feeling inferior to everyone I meet, everyone I have the slightest respect for. I want to *know* about things. I want to know about the world I live in. I want to know about books. I already know a little about them—but I want to know a lot. Not only about books, but about writers and writing too. I want to know about this whole business of what makes a man try to express himself, whether it's writing or painting or even music. Sure, I've played music myself—but I want to know about those guys who composed the stuff, the real stuff of music—those fellows like Bach, Mozart, Haydn, Beethoven, Brahms, Wagner, Franck, Debussy, Ravel, and all the rest of them. And those fellows like Cézanne and Van Gogh and Manet and Degas and Daumier and Goya and Renoir and Greco—all those. I want to know more about the guys who wrote the books out of which I've learned what little I've already learned. What made a fellow like Veblen tick? Or Dostoievsky? Or even Dreiser, for that matter? O.K., I know a little tiny bit about all these things—but now look where I am. Here's this whole new business, this thing of science and that whole complicated language of science, a whole branch of knowledge, a whole language of mathematics, and I know absolutely nothing at all about any of it. I'm going to school and start learning these things, and I'm going to keep right on learning until I feel I know all the things I have to know. Then, maybe, I'll be able to feel I know enough to start trying to write again."

I suppose all this sounds terribly half-baked. Or it may even sound pretentious. I can't judge. The only thing I can do is to tell you the actual truth, as closely as I can recall it now.

A week or so later I moved back to New York City and started figuring out ways and means of going about the business of filling in the large gaps in my small store of formal education—which, as you may remember, had been abruptly curtailed during my second year at Hillhouse High, back there in New Haven, at the time I was blithely embarking on a brand-new career as a professional saxophonist with Johnny Cavallaro's Cinderella Ballroom Orchestra. . . .

"Sciences may be learned by rote, but wisdom not."

LAURENCE STERNE

Chapter Thirty-Five

DURING THE YEAR I had spent in the bucolic life, I had learned a little bit about chopping wood, and a good bit about my own ignorance. Those were the two net gains. On the other hand, since I had not touched a saxophone or clarinet during the entire year, I now had quite a time getting back to being able to produce musical sounds on either of them again.

These were the only tools by which I could expect to support myself while I embarked on this next lap of my quest for knowledge.

My idea was to get myself a couple of radio programs, just enough to support myself; the rest of my time was for attending classes, studying, and reading, reading, and still more reading.

So before anything else, I put in a few weeks practicing, getting my playing muscles back in shape again. By way of explanation for anyone who has never got himself tangled up with a wind instrument, perhaps I ought to tell something about what is involved in the playing of one of these gadgets.

I used the word *embouchure* earlier, when I spoke about my very first attempts to play the saxophone. Let me see if I can't define that word a little more clearly now.

Every wind instrument requires the use of certain muscles —in the chin, the cheeks, around the mouth, and even in the lips. The *set* of these muscles, the actual grip of them developed through constant use in one specific manner—that is what an *embouchure* is. That's all there is to it.

But it takes quite a while to build one up. And once an *embouchure* is built up it must be maintained by a certain amount of day-to-day practice; much as any athlete must keep himself in condition by using his muscles constantly in order to maintain their "tone" for his particular kind of activity.

There's a great deal more to all this, but it is largely technical and could be of no great use to the average reader.

Anyway, I eventually got back to where I could handle my instruments again. Then I renewed some of my old studio contacts and within several weeks was able to get myself set on a couple of radio programs. That took care of such items as rent, food, etc. Then I started investigating ways and means of getting on with what I had come back to New York to do.

I soon discovered that, in this matter of getting myself some sort of education in the sciences—just as, some years earlier, when I had started learning to play my first saxophone—I would have to learn to walk before I could begin running. Before I could start taking the courses I wanted to take, before I could begin learning the things I wanted to learn—there were certain elementary things I would have to know first.

I had several conferences with various people on the advisory staffs of the faculties of both N.Y.U. and Columbia University. The upshot was that I had to face the fact that there was no way I could get any benefit out of the courses I proposed to take unless I could also get permission to do the laboratory work connected with the courses. I could attend whatever classes I desired—as long as I didn't intend to work toward a degree. But lab work was out of the question, without the requisite amount of "credits"; which actually meant I could not go ahead until I had had at least a high school education, "or the equivalent."

Since there was no way I could prevail upon the authorities

to waive this ruling, or even relax it in my case, there was nothing to do but go about getting caught up. So I went about that. I enrolled in a little tutoring school and started earnestly trying to make up for lost time.

But apparently I was still in too much of a hurry. I ran up against a number of snags quite soon. In the first place, because of the reading I had already done, as well as the Columbia University extension courses I had taken, I found myself impatient with a lot of the stuff I now had to study. A great deal of it I already knew, and a lot more was stuff I wasn't the least bit interested in knowing. I soon began to see that most of the instructors themselves were apathetic and indifferent to what they were teaching. To say nothing of most of the students, who were apparently only there for the purpose of getting a diploma so they could get themselves the kind of job they couldn't get otherwise.

One of my instructors tried to enlighten me one evening after we'd finished his class. He was a flabby, middle-aged, frustrated, and bitterly cynical man, whose name I can't recall; and when he took me aside after class that one evening we had what seemed to me a quite distasteful conversation.

"What are you doing here?" he asked.

"Trying to get through with this so I can get on to something else as fast as I can," I told him.

"I'm told you're a musician, is that right?"

"That's right."

"You play in radio?"

"Yes."

"I understand there's a lot of money to be made in that kind of work."

"I suppose so."

"Well, what do you want to fool around with this for?"

"I told you—I want to finish my high school education so I can go on to something else."

"*What* something else?"

I told him.

"You mean to tell me," he said, smiling rather patroniz-ingly, as if he were talking to an idiot child, "you want to spend your life fooling around with all that, when you've already got yourself a good trade and can earn the kind of money you can?"

I began to get a little sore. "What's wrong with it?" I de-manded.

He shrugged. "Nothing *wrong* with it. I just don't get it, that's all. My God! If I could make the kind of money you fellows make, I wouldn't be here five seconds from now. What do you think you're going to do if you finally do finish all this education you're after? Eh?" The way he said the word "edu-cation" made it sound like a sneer.

"I'm not too sure," I said. "I thought maybe I might try to get a Ph.D. and eventually get myself a job as an instructor at some school or other where I could work out some kind of quiet life and be able to do what I'm really interested in do-ing—" For some reason I didn't want to be more explicit with this man.

All he did was shake his head and stare at me pityingly.

By the time we got through talking I was so mad I had to turn around and walk away from him before I might say some-thing I'd be sorry I'd said. Later on, when I got over being mad, I realized there was actually no reason why I should have been mad at him at all. He was rather pathetic himself, regardless of what I may have seemed like to him.

Still, there it was. That was the general level I encountered, when it came to the instructors; and, as I've already indicated, the students themselves were, if anything, even more cynical than that.

So what I did was to ignore all that and go on with what I had to do. Altogether I stayed on for a year or so at that school. From there I went to another such school, where I went on working at what I had by then decided was to be the main body of my interests for the next several years. For by that time I had narrowed the whole thing down to one basic subject—mathematics.

This all took place almost twenty years ago, so it won't sound strange if I say I have now forgotten just about everything I spent so much time learning in those days. But while I don't actually now remember much more about mathematics than I then remembered of what I had once so laboriously had to learn about piano playing some fifteen years previously, I did get something out of all this study, which remains to this day.

Perhaps these words of Bertrand Russell's will explain what I'm now trying to say:

"Mathematics, rightly viewed, possesses not only truth but supreme beauty—a beauty cold and austere, like that of sculpture, without appeal to any part of our weaker nature, without the gorgeous trappings of painting or music, yet sublimely pure, and capable of a stern perfection such as only the greatest art can show."

As a further example of what I am trying to point out—and also as an indication of the relevancy of all this interest in mathematics to my continued interest in literature and writing—let me cite one more statement of Russell's.

"Literature," writes Russell, "embodies what is general in particular circumstances whose universal significance shines through their individual dress; but mathematics endeavors to present whatever is most general in its purity, without any irrelevant trappings."

During the couple of years I fooled around with this branch of investigation, I began to get some idea of the actual aesthetic beauty of pure, cold logic. I remember that by the time I got through with the Euclidean treatise, I was at times so moved and overwhelmed by the sheer loveliness of the logical structure of what this man had created over two thousand years ago, that I felt as if I were entering into an entirely new dimension of thought, different from anything I had ever heard of or known before.

All the time I was studying mathematics, I had an amazing feeling of *certainty*, a sense of logical *absoluteness*, so that, while I worked at the various branches of it, I seemed to be living in an atmosphere of complete and utter security. When it came to taking examinations, for instance, I can remember the absolute confidence with which I approached them. There was never any doubt in my mind as to the results. And the results themselves bore me out. There was never any question of passing or not passing—for you either knew the subject (in which case there was no doubt about it at all and you got a perfect score of 100%), or you didn't (in which case you had no business taking the exam until you had finished learning what you had to in order to know it); and because these mathematical studies were giving me, in some curious way, the only sense of actual security (on any level) I had ever known, I was about as happy, intellectually, as I had ever been in my entire life up to that point.

So much for that, though. There were plenty of other things going on. Life was still fairly grim and earnest for me, and I was still aware that I had a long way to travel on my own particular road.

Though I was certainly learning some valuable lessons in logic, aesthetics, science, and the inter-relationships between science and art (with or without the capital letters)—there were a number of things I still had to learn, a number of practical problems I had to solve. And in solving those, I eventually got to the point where most people seem to get.

It is a point of no return for most of us, for once it is reached the average man finds himself so swamped in the means he has chosen, that he must resign himself to foregoing the ends. It can even happen that he finally forgets the ends entirely, and I've known a few who don't even remember that there ever *were* any ends.

I speak about this with a good deal of personal knowledge and conviction, since I came dangerously close to all this myself before I was through my thirties. But I didn't get altogether lost.

However, let me first tell you the manner in which I got lost. It is a quite important part of my story; for the way in which a fellow gets lost in the first place can have a strong qualitative effect on how he finds his way back again—*if* he ever does.

"The world in which a man lives shapes itself chiefly by the way in which he looks at it."

Chapter Thirty-Six

THROUGHOUT THE TIME I was engaged in my lofty pursuit of The Absolute, I was occasionally forced down to earth by such practical matters as the necessity of earning a buck. I tried to keep these interruptions down to the minimum; but there was no way of eliminating them altogether. For instance, from time to time I'd learn that one of my two radio programs was going off the air; at which point I'd have to hustle around and see if I couldn't find another one so I could continue to earn what I needed to pay expenses.

This meant that I'd occasionally find myself having to do three programs in order to be sure of doing the two I actually needed for the small amount I was living on. Also, these programs varied, not only in the amount of money paid but in the amount of time required for rehearsals. So that there were sporadic periods when my academic pursuits had to give way to economic reality.

On the whole, though, things worked out fairly well and it began to look as if I had a chance of achieving my objective.

I've often speculated on what my life might have turned out like, if I *had* continued in the direction I was then headed. One thing is certain: it would have been an altogether different kind of life from the one I have led. My objective was realistic enough. Had I continued as I was, I could probably have eventually managed to get myself a Ph.D. That done, there was no real reason why I couldn't have got myself some kind of instructorship at some small school or other—where, I suppose, I might have finally attained an assistant, or even a full, professorship and lived out my normal life span in a more or less normal manner. As to how all that might have worked out—well, looking at it from where I now stand, it seems fantastic enough (in view of where my life finally did lead me), but from where I stood at that time, there was nothing particularly bizarre about the idea.

Right here, however, we come up against another example of the old Free Will vs. Determinism problem. For our old friend Determinism suddenly showed up and took over, and by the time the taking-over was finished I found myself completely turned around, heading in the opposite direction from the one I'd been going in.

Determinism took the form of a new friend I made, who taught me something realistic about the goal toward which I was heading.

He was then assistant professor of biology at one of the nation's large universities, an excellent mathematician, and in the early stages of a research job in biophysics which has been occupying him from that time to this (1951). Some of his findings have already resulted in his becoming recognized as one of the greatest living authorities on the physical, inorganic properties of organic matter.

It is on the whole better for me not to mention his real name. Embarrassment might result for him in my now repeating some of the things he told me about the kind of life to which I was then aspiring.

For one thing, he pointed out, in an academic career such as I had in mind, instead of achieving any real freedom from preoccupation with petty details, I would only bog down in more petty details. "You'll find yourself, some twenty years from now, worrying about money, worrying about trying to meet your annual expenses on a salary no self-respecting plumber would be willing to work for. On top of that you'll be all snarled up with campus and faculty politics, disillusioned with teaching, because for every one student who wants to learn anything you'll run up against five thousand who are only there for the sake of a degree by which they hope to better themselves financially, and in general you'll wind up a tired, cynical, disgusted old man, wondering why the devil you ever got yourself into such a *cul-de-sac* to begin with."

At first I tried to argue with him. "But it *is* a secure life, isn't it?" I insisted. "And in it a fellow *can* find time to write and think and work toward some constructive end, can't he?"

"Oh, sure—I suppose it's *secure* enough, as far as lives go," he told me. "But it's a kind of living death, too. And as far as constructive ends are concerned, you're better off trying to earn some money in your own profession, where you've got a good chance of doing that, and *then* figuring out what you want to do about constructive ends. At least you'll have some freedom of choice that way, whereas once you get yourself involved in the life you'll have to live as a teacher, you'll soon find yourself so disillusioned you'll be glad to get away from anything connected with what you do for a living."

I still wasn't convinced, however. I went to his laboratory with him several times, and when he showed me some of the fascinating work he was doing I was more unconvinced than ever. Finally, though, he managed to show me graphically what he meant.

What he did was to take me along to a faculty "tea." After that, I began to see the light.

One other thing occurred at about this same time, which had its effect on my ultimate decision.

I was taking a course in American History. I had originally enrolled for this course only because it would give me some credits "required" before I could take a certain chemistry course I wanted to take. I understand there are now a few schools where this sort of nonsense is almost entirely eliminated; but at that time (in the schools *I* was attending, at any rate) it went on all the time.

Anyway, idiotic or not, I had to go through with it. Somehow, though, right from the start, I managed to tangle with my instructor. There was never any room for discussion in his class. All questions, all matters of interpretation, were solved "by the book." No matter what anyone ever said or asked, "the book" was always the final and absolutely indisputable answer. Altogether, this instructor was one of the most narrow-minded, dull-witted, unimaginative, uninspired, insensitive, and downright stupid hacks I have ever run into in my entire life—not only in "his" field but in any field I have ever even brushed up against.

The blow-off came after I had taken my examination for this "course." He flunked me. It all resolved itself down to one question in the exam. I asked him what my mistake had been. The exam had asked for "three causes of the War Between the States." Although the answers I had given were all correct enough according to several historical sources I referred to, they were not the ones "in the book"—meaning the particular textbook used for that particular course. And there the matter rested, as far as he was concerned.

"But aren't there *any* other books you're willing to recognize as having any authority?" I demanded.

"I don't believe," he said primly, "it is the place of a student to inform his instructor as to which are or are not proper sources."

"That wasn't what I was trying to do," I said. "I'm only saying that there ought to be some room for further or even other causes than those given in that one text we've been studying."

"I'm sorry," he replied, more primly than ever. "I'm afraid my decision must stand. Your answer may be correct according to other sources than the ones *I* accept. In that case, I can only suggest your taking this course with some other instructor."

I walked out of there, and out of the entire Academic Life as well. . . .

Now, that one silly affair by itself would not have been enough to cause such a decision. I knew enough not to blame all instructors for my misfortune in getting tangled up with this one cretin. The point is, this came as the culmination of my gradually increasing discontent with a great many such people I had met during the past couple of years.

So that took care of that.

And all at once I found myself right back where I had started when I had come back to New York City from Bucks County. My whole world had suddenly collapsed. All my aspirations had exploded in my face. I couldn't figure out where I was or what to do. The only thing that seemed to make any sense at all was to go on back to music again, try to save up some more money, and see what might turn up. . . .

A few months later, I was once more working my head off in the radio and recording studios, making several hundred dollars a week playing on soap and cereal programs. Now and then there would be a recording session, where there was a chance to play something a little less sickening than the music required by the advertisers and sponsors for whom I did most of my work—but even that was not enough.

Now I had no goal at all; and I had to try to accustom myself to working in a vacuum. There seemed to be no road ahead from where I stood. As far as I could see, looking into whatever future lay ahead of me, I would have to go on playing an infinite succession of radio programs in which the dull mediocrity of the music was enough to kill anyone's taste for music of any kind whatsoever. In spite of my most determined resolutions to ignore music altogether and concentrate on the only reason that made any sense for playing this kind of music to begin with—the amount of money to be made at it—nevertheless it could hardly have been called a pleasant prospect.

Before a year was over, I was again just about ready for anything that might come along that could promise some way out; in other words, right back to where I'd been as a kid in New Haven trying to find a way out of *that*.

I tried going back to arranging again. But here, too, the amount of money to be made was in almost direct inverse ratio to the quality of the music to be arranged; and after a short while I couldn't take it. As I've pointed out, arranging is a semi-creative job, and in order to do it well a fellow has to be able to maintain at least a vestigial remnant of respect for the music he has to deal with, and try to make it sound like something at least halfway worthy of being called music at all. On the whole, bad as it was, it was easier to *play* the stuff than to have to try to dream up ways of putting it down on paper in new and interesting forms.

The only other choice would have been to go with some dance band and start traveling around the country again. I considered this seriously. In fact, after quitting my job at CBS some years earlier, just before going off into free-lance work, I had done just that, taken a job with Roger Wolfe Kahn's band and gone down to New Orleans, where we worked for six weeks or so. But although you got a chance to play some decent jazz with an outfit like that (which was at least stimulating from a musical standpoint), it was plain to see you weren't getting anywhere. Traveling around that way, from one place to another, never staying in any one place for any length of time, was something I was all through with by then. I was still trying to find time for reading and learning to write —and this business of living out of a suitcase was hardly conducive to that.

At least there were compensations in living in New York. It was full of all sorts of things by which you could manage to forget what you had to do when you were working. And if a fellow really wanted to, I kept telling myself, he could at least work out some halfway regular life and still manage to retain part of himself.

So I went on with what I had to do—until finally something happened that precipitated me into a whole new life.

At the time it happened, I was, as I've said, just about ready for anything. Otherwise I don't believe it could have turned out the way it did. For as I look back at what I was like at the time, and compare that with the way I had to behave in order for me to wind up where I finally did, I can find only one possible state of mind out of which I could have driven myself to the place I finally arrived at—and into a life I couldn't have dreamt of at the time I started.

I was obviously desperate.

And the longer I went on, the more desperate I became— so that I eventually got to the point where I simply *had* to "succeed," since I couldn't have brought myself to accept "failure." I don't know what I might have done if I hadn't achieved the $ucce$$ I had by then set myself as a goal.

But before I get all involved in telling you how I found my way out of radio and became a bandleader, let me explain several things I haven't gone into up to now. I think a certain amount of summing up is in order right at this point. For I still had a considerable distance to travel before I would have to worry my head about the *problems* connected with $ucce$$ —aside from the one big problem of how to arrive at it. . . .

"Life is a progress from want to want, not from enjoyment to enjoyment."

SAMUEL JOHNSON

Chapter Thirty-Seven

WE STARTED OUT WITH A THEME, something to do with what I called Cinderella-solutions. Let's have a little closer look now and see how this theme applies to my own story, not necessarily in the order in which I've told it, but as it actually happened. And let's also take a look at how it applies to anyone else. For the only thing about my life that can possibly have any real meaning to anyone outside myself is the story of what happens to a guy who sets out to achieve a fantasy-goal—and finally achieves it.

In the first place, we begin with a child born of first-generation immigrant parents. This child is raised on the Lower East Side of New York City, and has no great difficulty in making at least an ordinary surface adjustment. However, after a sudden shift to an entirely new environment, he is confronted by certain definite and, to him, at the age of seven or eight, hostile aspects of this new environment. Because of these, he begins to feel alien, "different," undesirable. On some basis he can neither understand nor cope with, out of any previous experience, he finds himself in a despised out-group minority. All of which, plus various other conditioning influences (such as his relationship to his parents, etc.), combines to turn him in upon himself, causes him to develop into a shy, generally introspective, and oversensitive boy.

He seeks ways to escape from these painful problems. He takes to reading as one form of diversion and escape. Later on, as he starts high school, he begins to seek a status. He becomes fascinated by show business, and fixes on music as a way to get himself out of an environment he has by now come to hate, and into a new environment where he hopes to find acceptance.

Now, up to this point we have the story of any average boy growing up *under more or less similar conditioning circumstances.* But from this point on we have a slight divergence; for, whereas it is quite normal for the average boy to indulge in fantasy and daydreams as a way of escape from painful problems which he cannot cope with—here we have a boy who determines *to act out his daydreams, to live out his fantasy and translate it into reality.*

Right here we come to a rather interesting question. It might well be asked what's wrong with trying to turn fantasy into reality? Isn't that, in one sense, what any artist, or any creatively inclined person, is always trying to do? In other words, isn't this ability to translate fantasy into some sort of reality precisely the ability of the artist—and even of the scientist, once you deal with science on a creative level? Doesn't success *as* an artist (or a creative scientist) depend on exactly this ability and the degree to which a man perfects it?

Obviously, the answer to all this must be Yes. But—and it's a very big "but" indeed—there are a few qualifications.

It is really a matter of ideals. In a sense at least, all fantasies and daydreams are nothing more than that—the wishful expression of ideals. Well, then, you may ask, what's wrong with ideals in themselves? Don't we all have them, don't we all try to live up to some ideal or other? And aren't we, after all, better off trying to live up to an ideal than just going along taking things as they come?

Again the answer must be Yes—but this brings up important

further questions. What kind of ideals? And what are our individual capacities for achieving the ideals we set up for ourselves? At what point should a man begin to examine his ideals
in terms of his own abilities and capacities? Is it not advisable
for any man who is going to start out after any given ideal to
take stock of himself first, to arrive at some awareness of his
own limitations, so he can avoid what may easily turn out to
be nothing but a wild goose chase?

In other words, what good are ideals unless they operate
within some reference frame, some self-understanding, some
clear awareness of the nature of reality? Reality, that is, not
in any absolute sense (for who has ever been able to tell what
reality really is?) but in relation to ourselves as individuals?

All I'm saying, then, is that in order for any ideal to serve
as a constructive, rather than a destructive, force—in order for
an ideal to serve as a motivating drive toward some sort of
healthy life—it is a very good idea for the fellow carrying it
inside his head to examine it in terms of whether it is "an intelligent ideal" for himself to aim at. For if it isn't, the chances
are it will only serve to make him miserable.

What I mean is, it's O.K. to hitch your wagon to a star—but
don't go around feeling sorry for yourself if you never get any
higher than the rooftops. For no sane person could possibly
delude himself into believing he is ever going to reach the star
he has hitched his wagon to. If hitching your wagon to a star
gives you a goal to aim at, an incentive to work toward—good
enough. If, however, you actually set yourself the task of trying to *reach* the star, all you'll ever do is knock yourself out in
a futile attempt to do something that can't be done.

Now then—taking all this back to that kid daydreaming and
trying to live out his fantasy—we'll have to concede that his
ideals are at least fairly intelligent, insofar as they evidently
are within his capabilities. He *does* finally manage to achieve
his original ideal of getting into show business.

But let's have a little closer look at these ideals he's setting up for himself, and let's see what could be predicted in terms of how he's going to feel if and when he ever does manage to achieve them.

For one thing, what does he *want* out of them? That's as good a place as any to start from. If what he wants is something more or less in keeping with his real inner needs as a human being, then the chances are that his ideals are O.K. for him and that he will feel gratified if he ever catches up with them. If, on the other hand, all he's trying to do is to run away from himself—well, you know the old gag about that. Wherever you go, you've pretty much got to take yourself along. And not only that, but this too: that self of yours isn't going to remain the same as you go along.

From what I've already told you about this kid, it ought to be pretty clear that what he thinks he's after is hardly the thing that's going to satisfy him once he gets it.

For he isn't so much looking for something concrete as he is searching for some sort of self-vindication, some feeling of validity, some method of dealing with a basic self-contempt, a sense of worthlessness he's extracted from the life he's led.

In fact—and here's the most curious thing about it—this belief that he is indeed unworthy, contemptible and undesirable as a person *is what he is really trying to prove.*

For when it comes to almost any single neurotic belief, the dynamics of the person who has the neurosis are quite the opposite of what you might imagine. Instead of trying to work out a life for himself which will prove his neurosis is not real, the neurotic goes around unconsciously seeking *those things in his environment which will corroborate his neurotic conditions.* Or, as someone once said, "The neurotic seeks in the universe the parable of his neurosis." Which is as good a way of stating the case as any.

The truth is, in the case of this kid we're examining, that show business, or any other kind of public life, is exactly what a boy with his conditioning should do everything in his power

to keep away from. Haven't we already seen that he has none
of the personality qualifications for this kind of exhibitionistic
business? He's shy, he's introspective, he's withdrawn. What
the hell does a kid like that want with a business where the
very opposite qualifications are demanded?

But it is precisely *because* of these factors that he is almost
bound to pick out something of this sort to get himself into—
for the very reason that show business is one of the best ways
he can find to prove to himself that he *is* what he *believes* he
is: unworthy, undesirable, unacceptable.

And of course there are many other aspects of show business, surface qualifications which would *seem* to point to it
as the best way by which he can prove himself to be *just the
opposite* of what he believes he is. For aren't there also all
those quick and easy gratifications in show business? Doesn't
the successful performer work in an aura of warmth and love
and immediate acceptance? To be sure, he does—but don't
ever forget that the audience which roars its approval of
the successful performer at one moment can at the very next
moment turn on the same performer and practically rend him
limb from limb. For an audience is in many respects no more
than a mob under loose control. And in my time as a performer I've seen moments when the control slips. And at
those times—brother, it ain't a nice thing to look at, take my
word for it. . . .

But of course this kid won't find out about any of this for
a long, long time. By the time he has gone through the next
few years and somehow elbowed and jostled his way into the
top ranks of his profession, he has already begun to realize
(if only vaguely) that there is something wrong somewhere.
The only difficulty is that he keeps searching for more and
more, rather than examining what might be wrong with himself for not being able to relax with what he already has. He
is like a man who keeps compulsively traveling from place to
place, who every time he arrives at a new place finds some-

thing wrong with it so that he has to keep on traveling. What is he looking for? What does he expect to find? He can't tell you that. All he can do is go on acting out his compulsion; he is certain that sooner or later he will find the perfect place and there make a place for himself to rest in.

The one thing he doesn't seem to understand—not as long as he goes on acting out of a compulsion—is this:

There *is* no perfect place, and there isn't even any rest, until a fellow learns that by and large most places are pretty much the same as most other places.

And once he learns that, he can start making a place for himself where he already is. . . .

"In all things, success depends upon previous preparation, and without such preparation there is sure to be failure."

CONFUCIUS

Chapter Thirty-Eight

IN SHOW BUSINESS you're apt to hear a good deal about "getting the breaks," but whenever I hear this phrase I wonder whether people have the slightest idea of what they're overlooking when they talk in these terms.

Of course, I understand what they *think* they are saying. I've even heard another and far more colorful expression that covers the same thing. The first time I ever heard it was when a certain agent was speaking of one of his bandleader clients —a fellow named Artie Shaw, that fellow I've already told you a few things about, but definitely *not* the fellow I've been talking about throughout most of this.

What the agent said—and I quote it verbatim—was this: "You're the kind of guy who can fall into a pile of shit and come up with a diamond."

Well, I don't know. My own experience with the only such pile I've ever fallen into—namely, the band business—is that a fellow is far more apt to come up with shit than diamonds; although I suppose there *may* also be some diamonds down there somewhere.

In any case, what I'm getting at is this whole concept of "breaks"—and how inaccurate it is. There is almost no one on earth who could truthfully say that his luck has been so extraordinarily bad, over the entire period of his lifetime, that he has never been presented with an opportunity to prove himself. And as for the old saw about opportunity knocking but once—well, as in the case of most old saws, this one too should be taken with the proverbial grain of salt. Most of us are often presented with opportunities; the difficulty is that most of us are unwilling to take on the actual labor involved in *making* something of these opportunities. Either we are too inertia-ridden, or else we are not conditioned to take on the challenge. For that is essentially what most opportunities—or "breaks"— entail: Challenge.

Then too, there are those times when a man is presented with a chance to do something he wants to do and is furthermore willing to take on as a job—but finds he is not yet *able* to do it. This is nothing unusual, and scarcely the tragedy lots of people try to make it out to be. The chances are the man will sooner or later have another chance—if not for the same thing, at least for something nearly as good; possibly even better. Here, though, the way it works out many times, the trouble is that the average guy who once actually was willing to accept a healthy challenge, may, by the time he gets another chance, have slowed down, become tired, discouraged, or what-have-you; so that instead of accepting a new challenge he has now become inclined to look backward and bewail the "bad breaks" involved in his having once had a good opportunity at a time when he was unprepared; thus indulging an essential defeatism which is the real reason for his not being able to conceive of anyone else being able to get on except through what he calls "getting the breaks."

Now I am not intimating that I don't believe there is such a thing as "a good break"—that would be pretty silly. But the fact is that no "break" can do any more than give a guy a *chance to prove himself*. In other words, given that chance, presented with "the break"—from there on in, a fellow is on his own. He can't keep hoping for "breaks" to go on doing his job for him. If he does he's going to end up right back where he started from before he ever got his "break" to begin with.

Let me illustrate what I mean, by telling you now what my first real "break" was, and what happened as a result of it.

About the time Prohibition was repealed, there used to be a little musicians' hangout over on West 52nd Street called the Onyx Club. It had started out as a speakeasy, and now that it became necessary to buy a liquor license, the fellow who ran it, a man named Joe Helbock, got the idea of taking up a collection among the radio and recording musicians who frequented the place and making each contributor a "charter member" of this new, legitimatized Onyx Club.

At first the place ran strictly as a musician's club, where we used to drop in after work and sit in and play with other fellows. For a while, a few musicians were even hired to work there regularly, and, since this was a place where other musicians hung out, the musicians employed had to be damn good. But mostly, the best music in the place was made by the actual customers—those same jazz musicians who had to play that musical junk I've already spoken about, that was being played around the radio studios in which they made their living.

Pretty soon, the public began to find out about this little spot, and within a short while after it had opened Joe Helbock found himself with a small gold mine on his hands.

After a year or so, the Onyx Club became a kind of institution—and Helbock became a sort of unofficial jazz authority, merely by virtue of his acquaintance with most of the best jazz musicians around the business in those days.

I don't know how it finally worked out, financially at any rate, but for some reason or other the whole thing ultimately folded up, and the last I heard of Joe he was working at the Copacabana—as a bartender. Which is just about the same job he had when I first knew him, during the old days when the Onyx Club was a speakeasy—making this a rather tidy little example of the full circle type of life; although I can't say how Joe himself would feel about either the tidiness *or* the circle, let alone the life.

In any case, at about that same time the public was beginning to become interested in jazz music—on a large scale, that is—and the word "Swing" was being used to designate the aspect of American Jazz that later became a national, and even an international, fad.

At this point I can condense what happened, by quoting from an article which appeared in the June 29, 1951 issue of a magazine called *Down Beat*. This piece was written by a young English jazz critic named Leonard Feather, who was also around New York City in those days.

"In the summer of 1935," writes Feather, "Joe Helbock, then owner of the Onyx Club, decided to put on a concert featuring that red-hot novelty, 'swing,' at the Imperial Theater. Approached to participate along with a bunch of bigger swing names, Artie decided to do something different by writing a jazz piece for clarinet and string quartet."

This was the first time such a concert had ever been given in New York City. The whole idea was brand new, since up to this time American dance music had always been regarded as a sort of bastard child of "real" music—considered as a merely functional kind of music, good enough to be danced to but hardly to be taken seriously as anything to listen to.

Here, for the first time, as I say, there was this rather revolutionary concept—that "swing" music, as an American idiom, was something to be listened to for itself. Not the words, not the tune, not the popular melody—but the jazz idiom, as played by the musician who took the tune itself *only* as a point of departure for his own inventive, improvisational creativeness and embellished the melody, or else forgot it altogether and based his improvisation not on the melody but on the chord structure of the melody. The result was something entirely different from the kind of popular music it stemmed from (to say nothing of the words, which were, of course, completely forgotten, utterly meaningless in this new context), stressing the ability of the improviser, rather than the composer, and demanding an entirely different kind of audience from that which is interested in hearing popular music *per se*.

It's rather difficult to go into all this without using technical language. Perhaps I can leave it at this: Jazz, or Swing, or Bop, or whatever-you-want-to-call-it (since these words are all nothing but labels for something essentially pre-verbal, and no one has yet managed to define them so as to make any sort of sense for anybody who hasn't heard the music itself)—all these are rather complex idioms, musically; and so are the thousand and one factors that go to make them up, historical, sociological, psychological, even anthropological. The definitive treatise about this kind of music has certainly not yet been written; possibly may never be written. That's as it may be. As to what this whole idiom represents in the mainstream of music as an art form—well, that too is a pretty complex matter, far too detailed to attempt to deal with in the scope of such a book as this. For now, then, let's get back to this same "swing concert" of Joe Helbock's and I'll explain a bit more of what it was all about and how I came to get involved with it.

By the time the whole affair was organized, it had resolved itself into a benefit performance for the American Federation of Musicians, Local 802. As a result there was no difficulty in getting just about every big band in New York to appear.

The way the thing was to be run off was this:

In between each pair of big band performances, time was needed to break down one setup and get it off stage so the next big band could set up. Each performance was to last ten to twelve minutes. In order to kill the lag between big performances it was decided to lower the curtain after each performance and have the audience hear performances by smaller groups fronted by various top-notch instrumentalists. Although these instrumentalists had no "commercial" reputation what-soever outside the business itself—still, this being the sort of thing it was, the business of "big names" didn't mean as much as it might have under other circumstances.

The whole concert was to be more or less an inside affair, a kind of trade get-together, and even the audience itself was in some way related to the music business—if only in a distant manner, through radio, recording, publishing, etc.

Joe Helbock asked me if I would get together a small group for one of those in-between performances. Since many of these groups were going to be fronted by friends of mine, guys I worked with daily around the radio studios, I could see no harm in it. All it entailed was my calling up three or four musical acquaintances—a piano player, a drummer, a bass player, and maybe a guitar player—going down to the Imperial Theatre the night of the concert, and playing a few choruses of some jazz standard.

All we had to do was to fill in for three to five minutes at the most, Joe told me, so I said O.K.

It sounded like nothing very special, and on the whole it might even turn out to be some fun. That was all the thought I gave it, until about a week or so before the thing was to come off. Then one day I ran into a friend who was also going to appear with his own small group. He told me the instru-mentation he was going to use; it was exactly the same as what I had thought of. That same day, another fellow told me the same thing. It began to appear as if we were all going to do pretty much the same.

Of course, it didn't really matter. But for some reason I thought it might be a good idea if I were to dream up some-thing just a tiny bit different, just for the hell of it.

So I got what seemed to me to be a rather bright idea.

You see, from time to time during that period, I used to get together with a few fellows who had a string quartet, and spend an evening playing some of the clarinet-and-string-quartet literature—the Mozart quintet, the Brahms ditto, stuff like that. Now if you have heard either of these pieces you'll know they're pretty damn wonderful music of their kind. I happen to like the sound of clarinet and strings, and used to enjoy these little sessions enormously. In fact, it had at times occurred to me to try writing something in the jazz idiom for this combination. Now it suddenly occurred to me that this might be a good idea for this swing concert of Helbock's. At least I felt fairly certain no one else would show up with the same instrumentation.

Consequently, I dreamed up a little piece of music, a composition I entitled "Interlude in B Flat"—for the excellent reason that it was (a) an interlude, and (b) in the key of B flat. I got hold of two violin-playing friends, a violist, a cellist, and—adding guitar, string bass, and drums (for the sake of rhythm, since this was to be a jazz piece)—we ran the thing over. It sounded pretty good, and these fellows agreed to appear with me for my little stint at the concert.

The night of the concert we were all lined up backstage, waiting our turn. The longer we waited, the more dubious I became. The place was a madhouse. Those were the early days of this thing called Swing, and if you happened to be around at that time you may recall that such bands played in what could hardly be called dulcet tones. Those were the days when swing bands used to try to raise the roof, and some of them frequently did—or at least caused the roof to do some pretty ominous quivering at times.

By the time we were supposed to walk on stage my knees were knocking together like a pair of castanets. And with good reason. The band that had just finished, the particular big band we were following, was one of the loudest I had ever heard—with the exception of one other I'll mention in due time. And here I was, trying to follow it with nothing but a quiet little chamber piece for clarinet and string quartet—a combination hardly noted for its ability to produce great volumes of sound—plus an attenuated rhythm section, minus even piano, which I had left out for the sake of keeping the rhythmic aspects of the piece down to a subtle minimum.

Well, we got out there somehow, and somehow we managed to get started. And as I heard the first few notes of the introduction, I was pretty sure we might all just as well have stayed home, for all the benefit anyone connected with this clambake was going to get out of our performance. Still, there was nothing for it but to get through with it as best we could, so we went ahead.

There was a hell of a lot of racket going on out in the audience. I suppose all that loud music they had been subjected to up to this point had more or less deafened everyone; and now that they had to try to adjust to the comparatively puny sounds of an essentially chamber music instrumentation, they couldn't get with it immediately.

But in no time at all, much to my surprise, you began to hear people shushing each other all over the place. And in a few moments the whole theatre had quieted down. I was vaguely aware of people in the first few rows leaning forward and listening intently. The first few rows are about all you can ever see from a lighted stage anyway, so I couldn't tell what anyone else was doing; besides, I was too damn scared to notice much else, for it was time for me to begin playing, and after I came in and started in on the "jazz" part of the piece it seemed to me I heard some strange noise and it took a few seconds before I realized it was the audience applauding! I couldn't figure out what in hell was going on, for I had only just begun, and the only thing I was really consciously aware of, for my fingers were automatically coming down on the right keys and somehow making the clarinet do what it was supposed to be doing, was that I had to make *pipi* about as bad as I've ever had to in my whole life!

Somehow or other, we managed to get through the piece and

all come out together at the other end. At that point the only
thing I could figure out to do about it was to get the hell off
that stage as fast as I could. I think I tried to make some kind
of bow, or something I thought of as a bow; and then I ran. I
not only ran off stage, but I was ready to keep right on running,
out of that theatre and all the way home.

But Helbock was standing in the wings, along with several
other people I didn't know. Even if I did know them, I
wouldn't have recognized anyone at that moment. The only
way I recognized Helbock himself was when he grabbed me
by the arm and yelled, "That was *great*, Art—*listen* to them out
there. Go on out and take another bow."

I stared at him blindly.

"Go *on!*" he shouted, pushing me toward the stage.

I resisted him. I couldn't feel or hear or see very much of
what was happening.

"*Listen* to them!" he yelled at me again.

And all of a sudden I became aware of a noise. It was like
thunder. No, not like thunder—this seemed to *spray* the air
with a heavy thunderous *hissing* sound. I couldn't figure out
what on earth it was, and then all at once I realized it was
people still clapping out there. I began to hear shouting and
yelling and it sounded like "More, more, more," but I was too
dazed to be sure of anything that was going on; then suddenly, the next thing I knew, Joe Helbock had given me a
violent shove and I found myself out on the stage again.

The musicians in my little combination were still milling
around aimlessly out there. Apparently they hadn't even
come off stage at all.

I walked awkwardly out, and by the time I got to the center
of the stage, the theatre began to quiet down. Then there
was a long heavy silence, and I couldn't figure out what to do.
I looked over into the wings and saw Joe and those other
people grinning out at me, and I wished I could get out of

there and go somewhere where I could sit down and be by myself for a while.

I don't suppose I stood there for more than a few seconds at the most, but it seemed like hours before I finally heard someone from the wings whispering hoarsely, *"Thank 'em—tell 'em thanks."* Maybe it was Helbock, but I couldn't tell who it was.

I looked out at the theatre and saw a blur of faces out there, and the next moment found myself talking. I can't remember what words I said, but I remember thanking them and saying something to the effect that this whole thing was a complete surprise to me, that I'd had no idea that they might like the piece that much or I'd have written another one to play as an encore, but. . . .

There was another dead silence after this. I started to make a bow and get off when I heard somebody holler up from the audience, "Play the same one again," and all at once it seemed as if they were all hollering the same thing and I couldn't figure out what to do about that.

I looked over into the wings again. Joe Helbock was grinning all over his face now and nodding, as if to say, "Go *ahead*. Play it *again*. What are you waiting for?" I turned around to look at the musicians up there on stage with me. They were all grinning too. Somehow I must have got across to them that we might as well play the damn thing once more and then get out of there, for we started in once again, and this time we played the whole thing through in a deathly silence.

Not until then could I get out of there and go to the nearest toilet. I don't believe anybody has ever had to make *pipi* as bad as I did at that moment, as well as throughout the whole time I'd been out there on that goddamn stage of the Imperial Theatre!

And all my friend Leonard Feather can find to say about all this is, ". . . Artie's one number *Interlude in B Flat,* broke up the show." How do you like that?

Shows you how much you can trust a jazz critic. Why, if I'd had to stay out there for a few minutes more—just long enough to actually wet my pants—that's the time you might have seen a show *really* broken up.

"The best foundation in the world is money."

Chapter Thirty-Nine

WITHIN TWO DAYS after that Imperial Theatre shindig I learned I had apparently created a small furore. It seemed as if everybody in any way connected with the music business around New York had been present when I played that little *Interlude in B Flat;* and, although I hadn't thought it was *bad* when I wrote the thing, I certainly hadn't expected the kind of exaggerated reaction it actually got.

As a matter of plain fact, it really wasn't that good. All it was was a simple use of an ordinary enough jazz theme I had made up, scored for a combination of instruments which weren't traditionally associated with that kind of music—that's all there was to it. What seemed to have caught the attention of those who heard it was the enormous contrast between the combination of instruments I had used, as against what was being used around that time in jazz music.

In other words, although I had actually set out to do something just a trifle different from what might have been expected at an affair of that kind, I had had no idea that this slight difference (and at that only a difference in instrumentation rather than any real difference in the music itself) could have caused any such commotion as it did. I couldn't understand it at all.

The main factor, I suppose, is that, as I've mentioned,

"swing" music at that period was for the most part a fairly noisy business. The average so-called swing band in those days made a good deal of just plain racket. This doesn't mean that they did not at times play some forthright and honest music; for they did—the good ones at any rate. But for the average listener, even the informed listener, a small amount of this might go a long way.

So that, following right on the heels of some of the loudest bands in America, that little piece of mine had come as a rather distinct and, I suppose, welcome, contrast. Also, since jazz (or swing, if you prefer that term) had up to that time almost completely ignored string sections, this use of a traditionally pure musical combination had apparently intrigued the audience and caused a reaction exaggerated out of all proportion to any real merit the piece itself may have had.

However that might have been, and for whatever reasons, I received a phone call one day from the head of one of the large dance band agencies, who wanted to discuss the possibility of my forming a band of my own.

My first reaction was to turn it down. It seemed to me to be something I wasn't the least bit interested in. I was still trying to figure out ways and means of going on to what I had started out to do, to keep on studying and reading along the lines I had been, in order to get to the point where I might feel ready to try writing once more. That was my basic aim—although I will admit that I was a fairly confused lad at that stage of the game.

I couldn't very well go into all this with an agency executive who was proposing to book me as a bandleader with my own band, so I told him I would think it over and let him know within a few days what I had decided.

But before we finished talking, he asked me so many questions about why I was hesitating at all, that I tried to tell him about what was making it difficult for me to make up my mind. Not about wanting to try to write, specifically, but a few vague things about the kind of life I was trying to work out for myself, and that I could see no way of reconciling that with the kind of life a bandleader has to live.

In answer to all this, he said one thing that made a strong impression on me. He pointed out that whatever it was I wanted to do with my life, certainly a fair sum of money wouldn't do any harm. "After all," he added, "a successful bandleader can make himself twenty-five thousand bucks in a halfway decent year, and after you've made yourself a pile of cabbage you can always go on back to whatever you want to do, can't you?"

I couldn't argue with that. It made too much sense for me not to see the reason of it. At that same time I had already accepted an offer from the Brunswick Recording Company to make records for them with a combination similar to the one I had used at the Imperial Theatre, so I was now a recording bandleader in my own name anyway. I finally decided I might just as well go ahead and become a full-time bandleader with a regular band, instead of using studio musicians to make a few occasional records. It seemed worth a try, at any rate.

Accordingly I scouted around and eventually put together my first band. This took a few months, for since I hadn't enough money to buy arrangements with—and in any case wouldn't have been able to find many arrangers to write the sort of thing I had in mind for this combination of mine, which was altogether different from the usual dance band combination of those days—I had to set to work and make a library of arrangements myself, before I could be ready to accept a job.

Of course, I couldn't possibly make all the arrangements I had to have. The average dance band needs a library of at least forty or fifty arrangements to get through an evening without having to repeat too many; and it takes a long time to make that many, especially for a band of the kind I was putting together. For, since a string quartet is a rather delicate-sounding combination, you have to be quite careful about what you write for it to play in conjunction with the more traditional jazz instruments. Actually, once again avoiding too many technical details, what it amounts to is that this first band of mine was virtually two different types of musical combinations playing together as one. The problem was to write for the strings in such a way as to realize their particular kind of tone color, without interfering with the strictly jazz part of the band and yet adding something, so as to make an advantage of the string section without having to limit the jazz quality of the over-all musical effect.

So, not being able to afford the kind of prices I might be charged by arrangers skilled enough to do this sort of work, I had to get hold of some kid with at least a rudimentary ability, and train him along these lines.

One more thing: when it comes to solving this sort of musical problem, it's a whole lot harder to do it with forty or fifty arrangements (each of which must sound in some way different from the others, so as to avoid monotonous repetition) than it is to do it with one or two, or even five or ten. The whole thing took time—and not only time but a lot of damn hard labor and brain picking—before I was finally halfway satisfied with the library I had to have before I could even think of getting started on the band itself.

Eventually that part of the job was done. At that point I got some musicians together and started rehearsing. I had added several instruments to the original combination I had used at the Imperial Theatre, in order to give the band more flexibility and a greater range of tone color. And a few weeks afterwards, as Art Shaw and his Orchestra, I started my first engagement as a bandleader, at the Lexington Hotel in New York.

That was the summer of 1936.

I was now twenty-six years old, and on my way toward carrying out the practical decision I had made to get together "about twenty-five thousand bucks" and then quit the music business once and for all and "go on back" to my intention of making some altogether different kind of life for myself. This entire venture was to be one step toward the achievement of that goal.

It's really incredible, as I think about it now. Since that time, I've made that same "twenty-five thousand bucks" some hundred or more times over. Yet, somehow, I've kept right on going, continuing to make it over and over. Occasionally I've quit to try to find my way "back" to that fork in the road, but I've always been forced to go on, either by unresolved inner conflicts that drove me on, or else by realistic economic necessity involved in the way of life I ultimately got myself into out of the need for compensations for having to live the way I had to, in order to go on making the money I needed to live the way I had to, in order to go on making the money, etc., etc., and more etc.—on a kind of mad treadmill. By the time you've been going on and on like that for a number of years you can look back and see an enormous amount of energy that has been totally wasted; and after all the effort and worry and misery is over you're still right in the very same spot you were in before you started using the energy and making yourself miserable. That's when you realize you could easily have accomplished a great deal more by standing still and taking a good long look ahead at where you thought you were going before you took the first step that led you onto the treadmill to begin with.

And certainly it seems only fair that if a man *must* live on *some* kind of treadmill he should at least be entitled to pick one that travels at a pace comfortable to himself—shouldn't he?

However, long before I got to any point from which I could start looking forward or backward, I had to figure out how to meet the day-to-day problems involved in getting ahead without being *forced* to stop and go right back before I'd even got started at all. I had several rather basic fundamentals to learn about this new aspect of the business I had already been in for ten or eleven years.

Here's one of the first things I had to learn, all wrapped up in an Indian-nut shell. And, disillusioning as it may be, no one is going to get very far in any aspect of show business unless he has learned this and learned it thoroughly.

It doesn't matter what you do, or how good you are—as long as you can earn money for the fellow who hires you.

This lesson was given me by the manager of one of the first places I ever worked in as a bandleader. My new band had been in existence for only a short while at the time this happened. Now any band, particularly a band of that sort of unusual instrumentation, takes time to work itself into a good ensemble. A certain period is necessary before the men get the *feel* of each other and learn the music well enough to play freely and uninhibitedly. This is not only a musical question; it also has to do with the men getting to know each other, not only as musicians, but as people, men working together. They have to get to the point where they don't have to be polite with one another, so that—for instance—if the first trumpet player feels that the second trumpet isn't playing loud enough to fill up the chord the brass section is supposed to be making, he doesn't have to figure out how to tell him to play up without hurting his feelings. Once they know one another well enough, the first trumpeter can turn around and snarl, "Come on, for Chri'sake—blow!" Or "What the hell are you laying down for —let's hear it, what do you say?"

This new band of mine was just beginning to do this, to shake down and sound like an ensemble. Every night we worked, it got a little better. The rough edges were beginning to smooth out here and there, and it started to sound as if it might turn out to be a pretty decent little outfit by the time a few more weeks had gone by.

Then at one rehearsal I was told by my agent that the manager of the place where we were working had told him the band "wasn't doing a good job."

"What's he talking about?" I demanded. "The band's just beginning to sound like a band—listen to this thing we're rehearsing."

I ran the number down for him, and he nodded—although of course I knew by then that the average band agent doesn't necessarily know much about the music he sells. (In fact, as I've heard a number of these guys say from time to time, "I don't have to know anything about music—all I got to do is sell it.")

When we finished the piece I turned on him. "What the hell does he mean—not doing a good job? It's getting so it sounds better every night. The guy's out of his mind."

My agent shrugged. "I'm just telling you what he told me—I don't know anything about it more'n that. Ask him when you see him, if you feel like it."

I could hardly wait to get to him. That night when he showed up, I went to him during an intermission and told him what my agent had told me.

"I don't get it," I finished. "Let me play you a couple of things in this next set and then I'd like you to tell me what's wrong with them. Why, the band's beginning to sound better than it ever did. I can't understand what you're talking about when you tell people we're doing a bad job."

I was so indignant he had to cut me short. "Listen," he said. "You're telling me about music. I don't give a good goddamn about music. I don't know a goddamn thing about music. I'm paying you to play so we can get some goddamn customers in the joint and make some dough. What the hell do you think I'm running here—a goddamn concert hall or something?"

I tried to cut in again, but by now he was working up to a state of righteous indignation himself. "Listen. I'll tell you something," he continued. "Just take a look around and see how many empty tables there are in the goddamn joint. How do you expect me to run a joint like this and pay off my expenses and pay you and your goddamn band when you can't even get people to come in and *listen* to your lousy goddamn music—huh!"

"Well, what do you expect *me* to do about it?" I managed to put in now. "What do you want me to do—go out on the sidewalk and rope people and drag 'em in here? My job is to play the best music I can play for the people who do come in. I don't know anything about getting 'em in here. That's your problem."

"*My* problem, huh?" he said, his face red with rage. "Let me tell *you* something, Buster. You better make it *your* problem, you want to stay in this business long. You hear me? You better get yourself a name'll *bring* people in, or first thing you know you'll wind up passing a goddamn tin cup out on the sidewalk yourself."

I tried to break in, but he was going like a house on fire. And what he said next was the thing I have remembered.

"You listen to *me!* *My* problem is to get the dough to pay you and your goddamn band and all the rest of the expenses I got to pay to run this joint. *Your* problem is to get people in here. And if you want to take your pants down on that goddamn bandstand every night and take a crap up there, and if people'll pay to come in here and see you do it—*I'll* pay you to take a crap up there every night. That's how much I give a good goddamn about what kind of *music* you're playing—you hear me?"

So there it is—take it or leave it. It took me a few nights to decide for myself whether I would take it or not. In the end, I decided I might just as well go on with this racket I'd got myself into—after all, I still wanted that "twenty-five thousand bucks" and there was no law saying I had to stay on in this rat race after I'd made my twenty-five thousand, was there?

It says here in fine print. . . .

"Life is like playing a violin solo in public and learning the instrument as one goes on."

SAMUEL BUTLER THE YOUNGER

Chapter Forty

FOR THE NEXT FEW YEARS I ran what amounted to a peripatetic music school. I suppose that must sound rather peculiar, so I'll explain. In fact, right here is about as good a place as any to explain a number of things about the operational details of the band business.

The whole process of building a group of assorted musicians and welding this group into one unified stylistic ensemble is a complicated affair; and in order to accomplish this job, everybody connected with it has to learn a good deal about a number of things connected with it. Furthermore, all the time the job is being learned, there is the practical business of keeping the band together, working and getting paid from week to week, while the polishing job is going on. For intrinsically, even though the over-all problem of making a functioning unit out of a heterogeneous collection of inexperienced jazz musicians is to some extent a musical problem, the basic, fundamental problem is economic.

There have been a great many changes since the time I started out with that first band of mine; and as one change took place there were corresponding changes in the whole picture—musically and every other way. But that is far too involved to go into here.

So let's have a look at some of the problems as they existed and had to be met and solved at that time.

Top-notch jazz musicians are highly skilled men, and as a rule they get good pay. Now at the time I was starting out, I obviously couldn't command a very high price for my unknown outfit. Long before I could afford the kind of musicians I'd have liked to get, I would have to build up a "name" in my business.

So I had to start with relatively inexperienced youngsters, musicians who weren't good enough to demand high salaries, and who were willing to work for union scale. Nevertheless, since we had to compete with the top bands of that day, some way had to be devised to make these men sound good in spite of their inexperience.

This could be done only through constant rehearsing, through careful arranging, so the music would not make demands on the men which they couldn't meet; and, above all, through time. Time on the job itself. For no matter how much rehearsal a band gets, no matter how skillfully and carefully the arrangements are tailored to the abilities of the men playing them, there is still nothing that can take the place of appearing night after night after night in front of audiences. The very tension that results from being aware of an audience is one of the biggest single factors in smoothing out the rough edges and polishing the surface of a band.

There are no big successful bands that haven't undergone this process. Somehow the public senses this surface polish and reacts to it favorably. I can't think of a single band that has ever achieved and maintained success, where this surface polish has been lacking. In other words, in popular music, mass acceptance can't be achieved without at least a surface flawlessness.

This seems to me normal enough under the circumstances. We are on the whole a nation of craftsmen, artisans, engineers, rather than artists. So it isn't surprising that in all our popular art forms we demand this engine-turned, slick, flawless, shiny surface perfection. Look at the average Hollywood movie for example—look at the high degree of technical skill and craftsmanship involved in the making of even the worst piece of junk. And this is even more understandable in music. The mass American public is by and large musically illiterate; and as is the case with any uneducated group when confronted with a highly specialized, technically involved form of activity, there is always this engrossment with surface detail rather than intrinsic merit.

As for other examples of this sort of thing—well, take a good look at the average commercial illustration. Whether it is a story illustration or part of an advertising layout—either way it must have one quality, that same quality of slickness. If it hasn't that—with startlingly few exceptions—it isn't good commercial art.

Now I am by no means trying to say that slickness is the only thing needed. Far from it. There are all sorts of degrees in craftsmanship, any number of levels of actual creative work, up to the point of real artistry. However, when the criteria are those involved in interesting a mass audience—meaning a relatively uninformed group of people with little or no knowledge of the art forms used in these various commercial media—it is clear that the end sought is going to have to be a sort of lowest common denominator.

Aside from slickness, though, there are various other factors. Even under a slick surface, there is room for at least a certain amount of honest, straightforward, even "artistic" expression.

Which is why there *are* occasional honest and worthwhile movies made, even in Hollywood, even in spite of these slick-surface requirements; why there are also occasional damn good illustrations and paintings done, even *for* commercial purposes; and why some of the best American jazz bands have produced from time to time some of the most interesting indigenous

American music ever made, even in spite of having to maintain close contact with relatively uneducated audiences.

All this was something else I had to learn through personal experience. There was no other way I could acquire any real knowledge of what had to be done in this new realm of the music business in which I was now operating.

The next thing I learned was that this outfit of mine, this little band-built-around-a-string-quartet, was not going to work out the way I had originally thought it would. It was too far out of line with what was going on at that time.

There was no room for the sort of musical subtleties I was trying to create with this atypical little band. Those were the days of the tousled-haired, eye-rolling, gum-chewing drummers —those boys who hit everything in sight except the customers, and who would no doubt have hit the customers too if they could have got at them. A new fad had swept the nation. If a band couldn't play good music, it could always call itself a "swing band" and play *loud* music instead.

This fact was brought home to me forcefully during an engagement at the Adolphus Hotel in Dallas, Texas. We were supposed to go from there to New Orleans to play in another hotel in the Hitz hotel chain, of which this Dallas spot was one. However, although I had been promised the New Orleans hotel job immediately after this first one, business was so bad that the Hitz management decided not to go through with the promise. I had no contract, and the kind of band mine was couldn't make the amount of noise needed to fill the big barns you have to play in on one-night stands, so I had to transport the band all the way back from Dallas to New York City at my own expense. Which left me about as stony broke as I ever expect to be.

When we got back, we got a job at a spot in New Jersey, called The Meadowbrook, and that gave the band four more weeks to live. The manager of this spot (Frank Dailey, who had been a bandleader himself at one time) was crazy about the band from a musical standpoint—which, as I learned, was the only reason he'd booked me into his place to begin with—but the public made its indifference only too plain. So I saw, read, and accepted the handwriting on the wall—and at the end of that job broke up the band once and for all.

However, I was scarcely what you could have called "resigned" to the handwriting on the wall. I was a pretty angry young fellow. I was so disgusted that I made up my mind to give the public what it evidently wanted—which was, as I put it to myself at that time, "the loudest band in the whole goddamn world!"

It may sound crazy, but that's precisely what I did do. I got together a group of fourteen young musicians, scuffled around and picked up a batch of assorted arrangements. Some of them I got on credit, some had been pirated from the libraries of various bands around the country and peddled to me by a guy who used to hang around bands and make himself a buck that way. Then I started rehearsing that "loudest band in the whole goddamn world." And believe me, it was loud!

This band was called Art Shaw and his New Music, since the Brunswick Recording Company, for whom I was still making occasional records, wanted to make a distinction between this and the original string-quartet outfit I had started out with.

Our first job was at a little beatup joint in Boston, called the Raymor Ballroom. Some of the facts and figures about this job may give you an idea of the economics of the band business at the time.

This new band had, besides the fourteen musicians I just mentioned, a singer, a band manager, a bandboy to handle the gear, and an arranger—a young fiddle player named Jerry Gray, who had stayed on after the bust-up of the old band, in which he had played first violin and helped out with some of the arranging. Even this wasn't help enough for the job that had to be done now. We had to build up a whole new library to supplant those "pirated" arrangements we started out with. In other words, we had to build up a style which might eventually distinguish this "loudest band" of mine from some of the other loud enough bands which were also around on the scene.

So that made eighteen people who had to be paid, besides myself. Also, there was commission to be paid to an agent for getting us the job in the first place. And in the band business, by the way, commission does not come off the amount the bandleader earns, but "off the top," meaning off the amount paid for the whole band.

Now then. What was the amount I got, out of which I had to meet my payroll for this whole aggregation, plus agent's commission, and still manage to find something for myself to live on while trying to make a band out of this new outfit?

One thousand dollars a week.

Well, a thousand dollars a week may sound like a lot to you. But just try putting together even the worst band in the world, let alone any group of that size through which you can even distantly hope to get to the top of the band business. Try to go on operating from week to week, improving your band, constantly bettering the quality of the arrangements you'll have to have in order to improve the band itself. Then try to pay off nineteen people out of nine hundred dollars a week, which is what you're going to have left after you've paid an agent ten per cent of the thousand for getting you the thousand to begin with.

If you want to save yourself a whole lot of trouble, just take my word for it—it was tough enough to do in those days; today it couldn't be done at all.

We managed to keep going, after some fashion or other—and during the following two and a half to three years the process of transforming this Art Shaw and his New Music outfit into the high-priced, slick-surfaced, smoothly-functioning musical machine called Artie Shaw and his Orchestra—the metamorphosis of clarinet-playing bandleader into Cinderella Boy—was finally accomplished.

The whole story of what happened, how it happened, and even why it happened, is far too long for me to tell. However, I'll try to give you some idea, without going into all the endless details. Suppose we start by fading back to one of the thousand-and-fifty-eight rehearsals that were always going on in those days—in the cellar of some dance hall, or in the barn where we had played that night, wherever we could find a spot big enough to hold a bunch of inexperienced kids who had to learn their jobs as they went along. . . .

"This is the task, this is the labor."

VERGIL

Chapter Forty-One

IT'S LATE AT NIGHT—around one-thirty A.M.

We're in a big dark basement. Piles of junk are lying around here and there. Huge steel columns support the weight of the building overhead—and directly above us is the polished dance floor of the Roseland State Ballroom, a public dance hall in Boston, Massachusetts, located about a block from Symphony Hall.

Over at one end of the basement there is a piano, a set of drums, a cluster of music racks, a scattering of brass instruments and saxophones and clarinets, a guitar, a string bass, a number of straight-backed chairs standing around in random groups. A naked electric bulb hangs from a wire. There's no other light. Huge shadows dapple the dirty floor, sprawling in grotesque patterns.

Now we hear footsteps echoing on the stairway leading down here, and in a moment a Negro boy of twenty-one or so appears in the pool of light shed by the naked bulb. He starts arranging music racks and chairs into a kind of formation.

Four music racks down front, each with a chair facing it.

Three racks behind these chairs, each with its chair facing it.

Behind these three more racks, three more chairs.

The drums are set carefully to the right of this chair-and-music-rack formation, in the space between the formation and

[314]

the piano, which he has hauled into position some six or eight feet over to the right of all this.

Now he sets one other chair into the space between the drums and the piano, somewhat forward of both. He picks up the guitar, carefully lays it on the chair, and sets a music rack in front of it.

The string bass lies between the drums and the piano, behind the guitar chair. The Negro boy puts another music rack down in front of where the string bass lies, a chair next to that, another chair behind the drums, still another at the piano.

He goes around setting trumpets, trombones, saxophones, clarinets—each on its own chair. The front row of four, saxophones and clarinets; the next row back, three chairs, three trombones; the last row, one trumpet for each chair.

There's one more music rack, a taller one; this goes down in front of everything, toward the middle of the whole formation.

Now there is a tidiness about the whole setup, a kind of order, a neatly arranged pattern in what was just a short while ago a collection of assorted objects.

Only one thing is missing now.

The Negro boy goes up the stairs, and presently we hear footsteps again, this time many footsteps—and in a few moments men come straggling down the stairs.

They're young fellows mostly—ranging from eighteen to twenty-five or so. They're of every type and description; blonde, brunette, sandy-haired; short, tall, and in-between; thin, stocky, even fat. Some wear slacks and sweaters; others plain business suits. Some smoking, talking, kidding around with one another; others silent and alone.

They mill around aimlessly for a few seconds. One wanders over and picks up a trumpet; he blows it tentatively, quietly, then louder; finally a cascade of brassy sounds comes blasting out of the horn. A thin boy takes up a saxophone and plays a few arpeggios, the sounds competing contrapuntally with the blaring of the trumpet. Neither pays any attention to the other; each is intent on what he is doing.

Gradually others pick up instruments. The drummer sits down and tests the sound of a cymbal. He shifts his chair, puts his foot on the bass drum pedal and gives the bass drum a few loud thuds. He taps on the snare drum, then starts twisting the key that controls the snares, taps again, twists again, taps again, until he is apparently satisfied with what he hears. He bangs out a long roll on the snare drum, crescendoing to a loud crash on a huge cymbal dangling from a metal arm fastened to the rim of the bass drum. Now he puts down the sticks, lights a cigarette, and sits there dragging on it and staring somberly off into the darkened end of the basement.

By this time everyone has taken up an instrument. They are all at it now. It's bedlam. The blaring of trumpets, brassy, shrill, now and then ascending to a shriek, alternates with and overlaps the lower-pitched blatting of trombones resounding in the stuffy air; and over and through all this come the rippling scales of squawky-sounding alto saxophones, the sonorous throatiness of tenor and baritone saxophones. And far, far underneath—at occasional momentary ebbs in the din—there is the gurgle of the piano, the plunking thud of the guitar, the booming resonance of a string bass being plucked at random alternating with the wheezy scraping of the bow across the heavy strings.

A dark-haired boy of twenty-six or so comes down the stairs and strides over to the tall music rack down front. He looks around, then turns and yells over his shoulder into the darkness, "Hey, Gate! Where the hell's the music?"

The Negro boy shuffles back into the light. He says something but you can't hear him for the various instruments barking, screaming, groaning, chuckling, rippling, each clashing against and over the rest and flooding the whole place with noise.

The dark-haired boy nods and waits quietly while the Negro

goes over to a heap of battered-looking fiber cases lying over
to one side, opens one, picks out a large, queer-looking fiber
container, brings it over to the dark-haired boy's music rack,
and opens it up like a book. Now we can see the contents—
a thick stack of tattered, dirty music manuscripts, with ink
notes and pencil marks scrawled all over the pages.

The Negro has gone off into the darkness again; in another
moment he returns, dragging a high stool which he sets in
front of the dark-haired boy's rack. He goes off to one side,
opens up a small instrument case, takes out a collection of
sawed-off black wooden pipes, fits them one into the other,
adds a bell-like piece of black wood to one end and a mouthpiece to the
other end of the assembled collection, thus transforming the whole
into a clarinet. This he brings over and hands to the dark-
haired boy, who takes it, removes the shiny nickel-plated cap
from the mouthpiece, blows several notes, then lays it down
on his music rack across the ink-scrawled manuscript pile.

He sits on the stool now, shuffles through the stack of music
for a moment, carefully holding on to the clarinet meanwhile,
and finally, having selected a piece of manuscript from the
pile, lays it out on top of the pile. He stares at it intently for
ten or fifteen seconds.

All the time, the din is growing louder and louder as the
various musicians keep blasting and rippling up and down
the scales—here a long, loud ripping burst of shrillness explod-
ing out of the bell of a trumpet, there a throaty scattering of
notes from one of the saxophones, answered by an angry bel-
low from a trombone, all punctuated by the crash of cymbals,
the burbling of the piano, the smacking thud of the brass drum,
the booming reverberation of the string bass, the plinking of
one thin, delicate guitar sound now and then peeping through
the thick jungle of sound.

Suddenly the dark-haired boy puts down the piece of music
he has been examining, and shouts mildly, "O.K., fellas—
let's go!"

No one pays any attention.

"Come on—let's *go!*" he yells again.

One or two of the musicians stop now, but most of them keep blowing, tinkling, smacking.

"*Hey!* Come *on*. Break it up—let's get going, what do you say?"

There is a general slackening-off of noise and a general drift toward the chair-and-music-rack formation. The noise dies down more and more, and finally diminishes to almost silence, except for an occasional sporadic blast, as if someone had had a sudden afterthought at the end of a long and heated discussion.

"Come on, fellas—what the hell, we don't want to be here all night. Let's go, huh?"

And now there is only the sound of chairs scraping plus a certain amount of familiar small talk as the musicians take their places. These boys have been together a long time and know each other well—as people do who live together, travel together in broken-down buses and jalopies, share rooms in cheap hotels and tourist camps, eat together in diners and roadside hamburger and hot dog stands, work together in dance halls and amusement parks, barns and arenas, through month after month of barnstorming, one-nighters, occasional split-week or week stands, and an endless procession of rehearsals like this one now about to start.

"Yeah, yeah," grins one, "I hear you talkin'. Next time *you* get the broads, you're such a killer with the chicks."

"O.K., I will," says another, "At least they won't be dogs like these ones *you* come up with."

"Hey—throw me a straight mute, will you, Gate?" one of the trumpet players yells over to the Negro, who is quietly dozing over in a corner. "All right, all right," he mutters, laboriously getting up and going to another large fiber packing case, rummaging around in it, then picking up an aluminum mute and tossing it over the heads of the saxophones and the trombones, to the trumpeter, who catches it and places it in the wire-and-metal mute rack beside his chair.

"Get out number seventy-eight," the dark-haired boy calls out.

There is a rustling as the men reach into their music-books. A slight delay, as one trombone player mumbles something or other about not being able to find his part. "Here, George," he says, handing half his music to his neighbor. "Go through that, will you? Guess it got mixed up on the job tonight." His neighbor takes the pile of music, they both start thumbing through it, until suddenly the first boy says, "O.K., O.K.—I got it." He takes back the rest of his music, puts it back on his music stand, spreads out the piece he has been looking for.

"All set? Everybody got seventy-eight out?" asks the dark-haired boy now.

No one says anything.

"All right," he says. "Now look. Over at letter C, where the saxes come in under the brass and then saxes and trombones take it by themselves—see where I mean?"

The men look at their music.

"Let's just run that part down and I'll show you what I mean," says the leader.

He sets a tempo by tapping rhythmically with his foot. There is complete silence now, except for the foot-tapping. Tap, tap, tap, tap, tap, tap, tap, in regular rhythmic intervals—and then, over the tapping and in time with the tapping, he counts off, one number for each of two pairs of taps—"one," tap, "two," tap—and suddenly the musicians hit it at "letter C" at the point where count "three" should have come if the leader had gone on counting. Only now, instead of disorganized blaring and screaming and gurgling and groaning and bellowing and tinkling and thudding and plunking and plinking and booming, there is the sound of instruments fused in an organized, rhythmic pattern, brass blending into a sectional choir, floating over the rhythmic fusion of drums, piano, bass, and guitar, and resting lightly on the trombone-and-low-saxophone base. At last, the trumpets break off in abrupt cessation, the saxophone-and-trombone mixed-choir carry on above the rhythm-pulse in a low-voiced blend so interwoven that it is hard to tell which is saxophone and which trombone. The tune is an old one, of early jazz vintage, *Someday Sweetheart,* and at a certain point in the music, just before the melody soars to a high note, the leader cuts in with his clarinet, plays a crisp fill-in phrase, and suddenly takes his clarinet out of his mouth, shouting—"O.K.—hold it, that's the spot I mean."

The music straggles on for a moment, then raggedly peters out. The men look up quietly.

"See that place where we just stopped?" the leader says. "Right before letter D, where the brass goes off by itself away from the sax section—see where I mean?"

Several men nod, and one says, "Right there at a bar before D, you mean?"

"That's it," says the leader. "Now, you see what happens there? George and Les are doubling melody, and it comes out too heavy against the rest of the horns. What it should sound like is a heavy, thick chord—but all I can hear is that one melody voice. Come down a little in there, can you, George—and you too, Les. The rest of you blow up to them a little more. Let's see if we can't get it sounding like a thick blend, rather than just a melody with the rest of the voices accompanying. O.K.? Let's hit it again."

Once more the foot-tapping, then counting and tapping together, and once more the whole band hits it, and once more they're stopped at the same place.

"That's a *little* better," says the leader this time. "Only I think you can come down still more—Les and George only. The rest of you are about right now—just Les and George down a bit. Let's go—same spot."

Tapping again, then tapping and counting. Once more the same music. Once more the stop.

"That's got it," the leader says.

A couple of men start blowing their horns now. "*Hold* it, will you?" the leader shouts over the noise. The men seem not to hear. "*Hey! Chuck!*" the leader yells now, at one of the men, who puts his trumpet down. "George!"—and the other one puts down his trombone and looks up.

"Come on, let's quit fooling around and get this one over with," says the leader, mildly, now that he can be heard.

Silence.

"I want to hear another spot in the same piece," the leader goes on. "Over near the ending, about six or seven bars after letter L—where the whole band is supposed to build up to a big loud peak." Turning toward the drummer, "I think you'd better come in under that with a rim shot, Cliff, just to kind of accent it and underline the whole thing."

The drummer looks down at his music. "You mean that spot where the brass goes—" he sings a phrase and looks up questioningly. Several of the men grin. The drummer has a strange goaty voice, and his singing of the phrase has an odd sound, but he seems unaware of anything funny.

"Yeah, that's it," the leader says. "Mark it, will you? Sixth bar after L, fourth eighth-note of the bar."

"Who's got a pencil?" the drummer asks, looking around. The piano player hands him a stub of a pencil, he takes it, starts to make a mark on his music, and suddenly looks up. "Say, Art—what about the high-hat cymbals in that spot?"

"What do you mean—what about the high-hat cymbals?" asks the leader.

"Well—when we hit that spot I'm on high-hat, and now if I take both sticks to make the rim shot I'm going to have to get off the high-hat to do it."

"Well?"

"Won't that sound kind of empty? I mean, the beat'll sorta come to a pause, won't it?"

"The whole thing shouldn't take more'n a split second at

the most," says the leader. "And by that time we've got enough of a beat going to keep it right up there. Anyway, can't you make the rim shot with one stick?"

"Well, O.K."

"Let's try it and see," and the leader starts tapping again. Tapping, counting-tapping, and the band smacks in once more, this time a different sound altogether. They come to the spot, the drummer smacks his rim shot, the leader nods at him and waves the band to another ragged halt.

"That's it," the leader says to the drummer. "It needed that."

The drummer shrugs. "I guess so."

The leader nods.

They go over several other short sections of the same arrangement, and finally that one is put back into the pile of music. Another piece comes out and the whole process begins again—the same process we've just seen, with slight variations. After an hour or so, a sense of vague restlessness begins to permeate the whole group; the leader says, "O.K., fellas—take five."

The men lay down their instruments, get up, one or two stretching and yawning, light cigarettes, wander off in groups of twos and threes, talking, joking, laughing.

The leader sits on his stool, smoking and shuffling through the pile of manuscript on his music rack. Five or six minutes later, he looks at his wrist watch and shouts, "O.K., let's go, fellas. We've got a few more to run down before we start taking the new ones."

"What new ones we got, Art?" one of the saxophone players asks as he sits down.

"Couple of things—one original and a new arrangement of *Man I Love.*"

"What's the matter with the one we got on *Man I Love?*" another musician asks.

"Don't like the way it sounds," the leader answers abstractedly, shuffling through the pile of music in front of him.

He calls out another number, the men get out their parts, and they go through the same process as before. An hour or so later, another five-minute rest, then another hour or so of the same polishing-up rehearsal, and now it is three-thirty A.M.

At this point there is still another five-minute break. During the break two more people come in. The short, stocky one is the arranger, the other the band manager. The arranger is carrying two large manila envelopes. He comes over to the leader, who now gets off his stool and stretches lazily.

"Hi, Art," the arranger says.

"Hi, Jerry," says the leader.

The band manager is talking to the men over at one side of the band setup. He looks harassed. He is trying to explain about the time of departure for tomorrow night's job. The men are asking various questions about the bus, how much time it will take to get to the job, why they can't sleep longer and get started a little later, and so on and so forth, with everybody in on a discussion which grows more and more heated (since everyone has a different idea of what is the best way to handle the thing) until in the end the band manager hollers impatiently—"All *right*, for the love of Pete—shut *up*, will you, you guys? The bus leaves from the front of the goddamn hotel at two-thirty, and that's that. Anybody who doesn't feel like making it can get there his own way—period."

Grumbling, muttering, a bit of griping—but the matter is settled.

Meanwhile the leader and the arranger have been looking over the two freshly-copied new arrangements. They go over various parts of the music and then, the five-minute break over, the leader turns to the band manager. "O.K., Ben—get the boys together so we can get started on these."

The men have wandered off, some of them upstairs, others to the toilet, still others outside for a breath of fresh air. The air in here is now heavy and thick with shifting planes of cigarette smoke floating and eddying in the light from the one naked bulb.

The band manager goes off and returns several minutes later herding the men back down like a sheep dog worrying and snapping at the heels of a flock.

Everyone is finally seated in his place again, the new music is passed out, and this time the rehearsal starts in earnest. Note by note, measure by measure, phrase by phrase, section by section, chorus by chorus, the two new arrangements are dissected, explained, argued about, thrashed out, understood, played over a couple of times for good measure, numbered, and put into the books. Some hours later, when it is all over, the leader says, "O.K., fellas—that's it. See you tomorrow."

"So long," some of the men say. Others are busy putting their instruments away, getting their music numbered and put away before leaving the setup to be broken down by Gate, the Negro bandboy.

The leader hands his clarinet to Gate, says goodnight to him, and goes off with the arranger and the band manager.

Within five or ten minutes, they are all gone except Gate, who shambles tiredly from chair to chair, picking up music and putting the folders together into the fiber trunk in which they are carried from place to place as the band travels around the country. He folds up the collapsible music racks with the initials A.S. on them, breaking down the whole setup he put together only a few hours back. Once finished, he switches off the one dangling bulb, shuffles off by the light of a small pocket flashlight, and climbs wearily up the stairs.

In the morning he will be back to gather up all the paraphernalia and transport it to the bus before the men are picked up.

For tonight, one more rehearsal is over, and to Gate it's all part of the day's work. Right now it's time to catch some sleep. . . .

◇◇◇◇

There you have some idea of what this part of the job is all about. Just what *has* been accomplished?

Well, the band has learned a little more about several arrangements that were already in the books, which they will now be able to play that much more smoothly on tomorrow night's job. Besides that, they have two new arrangements which will be played in public tomorrow night for the first time—and these, if they still sound all right after a week or two of playing and re-rehearsing and polishing, will be kept in the books as a regular part of the band repertoire.

So much for rehearsals, then, and the part they play in the development of an organization of this kind. What else is necessary—what else is required? After all, we're aiming at the top. What other problems are we going to have to solve before we can get there?

Are they all musical problems?

Because if that were the case, all we'd have to do to make a successful big time bandleader would be to look around and find a good musician, a fellow who can play his own instrument well and/or arrange the music for his band so as to make them sound good—and there we'd be. . . .

"If by the people you understand the multitude, the hoi polloi, *'tis no matter what they think; they are sometimes in the right, sometimes in the wrong; their judgment is a mere lottery."*

DRYDEN

Chapter Forty-Two

THERE IS ONE big over-all and distinct difference between the bandleader and the musician who makes his living playing in other men's bands.

They are working for different kinds of employers.

Unless he understands that clearly, no musician can ever become a successful bandleader. For, whereas a musician working for other musicians has to deal essentially with other musicians and with musical values, the bandleader, on the other hand, must base his success intrinsically and fundamentally on public taste—and there the values are almost anything *but* musical.

In other words, the bandleader is a musician trying to sell a mass commodity; and in order to do so successfully he must accommodate himself to mass standards. Unless he can do this comfortably, sooner or later he is sunk. I say "comfortably" because at one point or another he may arrive at a state of development in which he is confronted by a rather difficult decision. How he deals with the decision, what choice he makes when it becomes necessary to make the choice at all— well, I suppose it depends on the guy whose choice it is. As I said earlier, most people never get close enough to what they started out after to be able to see what it looks like once they've caught up with it. So, as a result, there are relatively few people who are ever confronted with the kind of choice I'm talking about.

It took several years before I was able to catch up with the ambition I had started out to realize. And, during that time, it looked as if things were going to work out pretty well. It never even occurred to me that I had to do anything more than whip into shape the best band I could, in order to achieve success; and that being essentially a musical job, I was fairly well equipped to cope with it.

Of course, there were many problems I had to learn to cope with which were not musical at all. There are all sorts of personality problems involved in handling the kind of people who make their living at blowing horns, banging cymbals, plucking stringed instruments, singing, or what-have-you. I couldn't afford to hire the kind of professionals who had learned their business well enough to handle it with the minimum amount of temperamental display. So, since I had to deal with mostly young and inexperienced personnel during the first few years, things got rough from time to time.

Musicians showed up for work drunk. Singers couldn't manage to sing in tune. Men quit and went with other bands as soon as they got good enough to get jobs that paid more than I could afford to pay—and then I'd have to get new, young and inexperienced men and train them all over again and hope to keep them with me until somehow I could get to where I could pay them enough to compete with the next bandleader who decided to make a raid on my band.

Another big problem was transportation. Good buses cost money. I obviously couldn't afford to rent the kind of buses that could get us to wherever we were going without unforeseen difficulties of every description.

As for trains—they were out of the question. In the first place trains are more expensive than buses. In the second place, even if you can afford them, you can't get trains to lots of places you have to play when you're barnstorming around the countryside. And in the third place, even if you could, you'd still have to get cabs and trucks to carry your men and gear from the train to the night's job. So trains are out.

This whole business of transporting a band and its equipment, plus the personal belongings and luggage of the members of the band, is a good bit like what you're up against with a small circus. Only, unlike the average circus, it's not as well organized. So, you do the best you can—and for the most part it is hardly a luxurious way of life, even when you can afford the best.

As I say, I could not afford the best—and the worst became pretty rough at times. When things got really tough—as they did from time to time—we worked out ingenious methods of getting where we had to go. Some of the men in the band got hold of second-hand cars on the installment plan and I paid them so many cents a mile for transporting as many men as they could pile into their cars. I myself always drove, carrying as many as I could. And the equipment, luggage, and other assorted gear got there as best it could in a series of old beatup trucks that passed through my hands over a period of a couple of years or so. And speaking of trucks—I remember buying one second-hand from Tommy Dorsey and being too broke to remove his name and put my own on instead. So that for about a month my band would pull up at some barn of a dance hall and find the manager staring at our truck and trying to figure out whether he had made some mistake and booked Tommy Dorsey (who was then doing pretty well) for the same price as this Art Shaw.

At any rate, that was one part of the whole big scuffle. Another part had to do with the music we played.

Every big band is known by certain numbers—or at any rate by the way it plays certain numbers. In a sense, these numbers and the way in which they're played are actually what the band is. Which explains why many big bands go on year after year sounding pretty much the same as they always have, even though there may have been so many shifts in personnel that not one single musician is left of the original band.

Now, getting together such a library of arrangements is a long and arduous process. There is no way it can be figured out in advance. You never know what is or isn't going to be acceptable to the public until after you've tried it. Generally, as it works out, you have to do a lot more throwing out than keeping in. For every one arrangement that finally remains as a permanent part of a big band's library, there are probably anywhere from twenty to fifty arrangements that have been made, copied out, rehearsed, played in public, rehearsed and polished, played in public again—and ultimately discarded.

Of course, the process isn't *entirely* hit-or-miss. You don't work in a complete vacuum. Every time you try something new, you watch the response. And naturally, over a period of time you get certain hints. Still, when it comes to anything as imponderable as public taste on a mass basis, you're up against a tough thing to figure out in advance. Actually, you're damn glad if you can figure it out at all, let alone in advance.

During this period in which I was trying to build a library, I used to spend a good bit of time listening to what other bands were doing—on records, of course, for I was chasing around the country and obviously couldn't get to where these bands were. In fact, they were no doubt chasing around the country too. That's the one thing most bands have in common —successful or otherwise, whether they make lots of money or not. And sooner or later, most of them get good and goddamn sick of it.

As I said, I spent a good bit of time listening to what other bands were doing on records. This was during a time when I had made up my mind to sacrifice the small amount of revenue I could get by making records myself. I hadn't liked the records I had made thus far; and since I couldn't quite figure out what kind of records I did want to make I decided to quit recording entirely until I had made up my mind.

At this same time I also decided to scrap another whole library of arrangements. It had taken over a year to put it together, and much as I hated to start in all over again once more, I knew I had to. It was either that or quit. For nothing was happening—absolutely nothing. The public was completely apathetic; and after a year or more of barnstorming and scuffling along trying to make ends meet and keep this band together somehow, any-old-how, I knew something drastic had to be done.

So I made up my mind to replace this library, one arrangement at a time, until I had built up a new one. But this time I had some idea as to the kind of new one I wanted.

What I had been looking for was a common denominator. The records I had been listening to were mostly hit records—I hadn't selected them from any musical standpoint at all. All I was trying to find out was what *made* a hit—what was there about all these hit records, what did they have in common, what was it that the public had responded to in all these records, good or bad?

In the end I thought I had the thing I was looking for, the common denominator I had been certain must be there somewhere, if only I could get at it. And I finally wound up with a kind of formula.

At least one thing could be said for this formula of mine. It wasn't strict. There was no rigidity about it. What it amounted to was this:

There have been certain American popular composers who have over a number of years built up a body of music which bids fair to become a sort of folklore in popular music. Such men as Cole Porter, Jerome Kern, George Gershwin, Irving Berlin, Rudolph Friml, Vincent Youmans, Sigmund Romberg, Richard Rodgers, have written pop tunes which, in this highly commercialized field, have survived as "standards" out of the mass of junk with which the public is annually deluged. What I intended to do was to take the best of this popular Americana and arrange it the best way I could. That way I could be sure that, successful or not, I would at least wind up with a pretty decent-sounding band.

In other words, in making this decision I wasn't aiming at any so-called style. I wasn't interested in that. It seemed to me that the best "style" a band could have would come out of playing the best music it could. Each tune would more or less dictate the style of its own arrangement—and after that it was up to me and the men in my band to make each arrangement sound as good as we possibly could. Period.

Also, after having listened to and studied enough hit records, I had arrived at a few conclusions about what a *record* should sound like.

The thing that each of these hit records had, it seemed to me, was a crystal-clear transparency. Not only in the recording, but in the arranging as well. You could hear every single last instrument on the record. The arrangement itself was simple, essentially; as a result even a lay listener could (so to speak) see all the way through the surface of the music right down to the bottom, as when you look into a clear pool of water and see the sand at the very bottom of the pool.

That was the image that occurred to me. And from there on in, that was what I tried to get every arrangement to sound like, whether I made it myself or not. And if anyone brought in an arrangement which fell short of this criterion I had established for myself—that arrangement was out.

All this took a long time. Not only the arranging, but the development of a blend between the various sections of the band as well as the blend in the sections themselves—but by the time the whole thing was finished, the musical job was done. It was as simple as that.

That is, if anybody thinks it's simple.

It's actually about the toughest thing you can do. Anybody can work up a set of tricks. The toughest thing is always the least tricky, the least gimmicky, the least fancy, and don't ever let anybody kid you about that. And that goes for anything—not only music.

Anyway, after about two more years I had managed to get together a library of some two hundred arrangements. Out of these, forty or fifty were of the kind I'd had in mind when I started to work on this new formula-which-was-not-a-formula. And out of the forty or fifty, there were about eight or ten which seemed really right to me. So I signed a contract to start recording again, for by then the band seemed to be in about as good shape as I could hope to get it in at that time.

My whole life at that point was concentrated on this one job. To keep a group of musicians together, to replace those who couldn't take the life we had to lead in order to stay together, who drifted off one at a time either to go home and give up or to take jobs with other bands where they could make some money—to keep going long enough to build this band of mine to stand out from other bands in such a way as to *demand* attention from the public—to do all this in spite of the handicaps, financial or otherwise, under which I had to compete with other, more successful, already-famous organizations—this was the one thing into which I focused my entire energy, and all the drives that had been building up inside me since I had started in as a musician back there in New Haven.

I used to lie awake night after night figuring out ways and means of going on with this thing I had started, this band that had become an obsession with me. I worried and schemed, planned and connived. I fought with agents, quit agencies, signed up with others and fought with *those* agents. I argued with musicians, dance-hall managers, dance promoters—even dancers. When people came up to me during work and said something I didn't like, I told them to go to hell. If they asked me to play something I didn't like, I told them I didn't like it. If they didn't like *that,* I told them I'd be glad to give them their price of admission back. Some of them even took it.

None of this made any sense. It was against all the rules. It was even against reason.

It made no difference.

I was a wild man, a crazy man. I cajoled when I couldn't browbeat. I browbeat when I couldn't cajole. All I knew was that I had started something and I wasn't going to quit it until I'd either licked it or it had licked me. And I was going to take one hell of a lot of licking before I'd lie down.

In short, it was one big long battle, one big long rat-race—with me as the head rat.

And talk about tension—! At about that time I began to develop a little thing called migraine. But even that didn't matter too much. I learned to depend on aspirin—and later, when that got too weak to do the job, I began to keep large bottles of Empirin compound with codein in my clarinet case, right where I could get at it real handy.

Well, I signed a new recording contract—the old one with Brunswick had expired by this time—and went into New York City to make my first records on the Bluebird label under my brand-new contract with R.C.A. Victor. The first record we made was a slambang version of Friml's old *Indian Love Call,* with my old Aaronson band colleague, Tony Pestritto—now Tony Pastor—singing his own slambang version.

Everybody around the R.C.A. Victor studio thought we had a hit record. As it turned out, the R.C.A. Victor people were quite wrong. *Indian Love Call* had an enormous sale; but that wasn't because it was a hit. It just happened to be on the other side of a rather nice little tune of Cole Porter's, a tune that had died a fast death after a brief appearance on Broadway in a flop musical show called "Jubilee." I had just happened to like it so I insisted on recording it at this first session, in spite of the recording manager, who thought it a complete waste of time and only let me make it after I had argued that it would at least make a nice quiet contrast to *Indian Love Call*.

When this "quiet contrast" turned out to be what sold the record in the first place, what made it into a big hit record in the second place, and finally into one of the biggest single instrumental hit records ever made by any American dance band—well, naturally everybody was quite surprised.

I was as surprised as anybody else. For, although I *had* liked the tune I certainly hadn't thought of it as a hit possibility. Who would have picked a tune to be a hit after the public had already heard it in a show and apparently been perfectly willing never to hear it again? How could anybody in his right mind figure to make a hit record out of a dead tune with a crazy title like *Begin the Beguine?*

> *"How dreary to be somebody!*
> *How public, like a frog*
> *To tell your name the livelong day*
> *To an admiring bog!"*
>
> EMILY DICKINSON

Chapter Forty-Three

EVERY BUSINESS has its own kind of turning point. In show business generally, and in the band business particularly, this turning point can be, and quite often is, a sudden and rather dramatically explosive occurrence. So much so that the fellow to whom it's happening can be so bowled over by it that as often as not he'll go around in a fog for quite a while afterwards, trying to figure out just what hit him.

I was no exception. I disappeared into my own fog and stayed there for awhile; and by the time I emerged into the light of day again there had been a number of changes made— not only in me but in my world.

The recording of that one little tune, *Begin the Beguine*, was my real turning point. Once past that point I was transformed into something entirely different from the guy I'd been. And although it took several years before I could fully realize what had happened and was happening to me, I finally came to understand that this turning point, once reached, is a real point of no return. In other words, I had arrived at a new status, out of which I had to learn to function in a new way, so that in a very real sense I had to accept this new status and willy-nilly try to make myself over into a new person in order to go on living the new life that had been suddenly thrust upon me.

Overnight I found I had "arrived"—which in show business means a complete metamorphosis. I am not overstating at all when I say this occurs suddenly. One moment you're barely making ends meet—barely managing to meet your expenses, such as the payroll for your men, agency and management fees, publicity expenses, and so forth. The next moment you find yourself making thousands of dollars a week even after paying all these expenses, even after paying any number of other new expenses you've suddenly become saddled with.

All at once you're a new kind of creature, a totally different type of being from what you were a week ago. For some reason people begin to stare at you and treat you differently. You keep telling yourself you're still the same fellow you were last week; but it's no use. No one *else* seems to believe it. And finally you have to accept the fact that *something* has changed, although you can't quite figure out what it is.

For a while this can be terribly confusing unless, as I said earlier, you accept it as your due—in which case, as I've also said, there's something damn wrong with you. If on the other hand you continue to fight it and persist in trying to behave the same way you did before this weird sea-change took place, you're possibly healthier, but that's hardly a consolation; for you're still going to be stuck with this new attitude—if not on your own part, on the part of damn near everyone you have anything to do with. Even people you've known right along—for even they can't help being affected by the change.

Take, for instance, your relationship to the men you're work-ing with—the men in your band, those same guys you've been so close to for so long, with whom you've gone through all that scuffling. For example, before, one week during the early days, when the band didn't earn much money and you had only enough to give them half their week's salary. You gave them that and told them you'd give them the rest as soon as you could get hold of some more. At that time, these men and you had a relationship which made such a thing possible. You'd lived together, worked together, traveled around in buses and cars together—and you were friends, in a way. They took their half-salary and that was that. A few hours later, while you were on the way to your next job, someone started a crap game in the bus. You got into the game and got lucky, and started making pass after pass. You went through the whole band, one by one, until one of them got lucky himself and almost took *you* over. But you had too much luck even for him, and finally you cleaned him out too. At which point you had all the money in your pocket. And, since this was the money you'd just paid out, all you had to do now was to give it back to them and they had their full week's salary!

That was the sort of thing that used to go on. One more instance:

One night, going from some job up in the Pennsylvania mining district down to Washington, D.C., we were traveling in one of those rattletrap buses we used in those days. There had been heavy rainstorms during the past few nights, and we had been warned that the road was flooded out in several places along the way. However, the bus driver told me he knew the back roads, so we continued. We had to anyway, for we had a job to make the next day. So we all tried to settle down in our seats and grab a few hours of sleep. Sometime during the night I woke up, realizing I was being shaken.

The bus had stopped and it was still pouring outside. The bus driver was watching me. When he saw I was awake he said, "Come here and take a look."

I got up and went to the front, where he was sitting. I peered out through the rain-streaked windshield and saw, through the mist and murk, a wooden bridge ahead of us. In the light from the headlights I could see a sign over to the right of the bridge.

CAUTION

MAXIMUM WEIGHT LOAD

8 TONS

"Well?" I asked the driver.

"What do you want to do?" he asked me.

"What do you mean?" I asked.

"The bus weighs more'n that," he informed me. "And with all the men and gear and everything. . . ."

I looked at the bridge, then read the sign again. I looked back at the driver. Nobody said anything. Some of the men in the band were waking up now. I could hear them whispering back there in the darkened bus.

"Well, what do you think?" I finally asked.

"Search me," said the driver.

"Think we can make it?"

"I don't know. Sometimes those signs are cockeyed. Anyway, we're not too far overweight, and usually they leave a little leeway—know what I mean?"

"In other words, you think it's O.K.?" I said.

"I'm willing to try it if you want to," he shrugged.

"Shall we get everybody out?"

"Ah, I don't think it makes that much difference—one ton or so more. The sign is probably cockeyed anyway. I think we'll make it O.K."

By this time everybody in the band was awake. I turned and told them what it was all about. There was a good bit of jabbering going on all over the bus.

"Well? What do you say?" I wound up. "If you want to, we can take all the gear and get out and meet the bus on the other side of the bridge. Otherwise we can stay right where we are and take the chance."

"What does Joe think?" came a voice from the rear.

I turned to the driver. He repeated what he had just finished telling me.

Well, to cut it short, it *was* pouring, it *was* late at night, everybody *was* pretty beat after working all night and traveling several hours, and after all, Joe *did* say he thought we'd make it all right. We finally took a vote, and that decided it. The bus started to creep forward.

I was listening tensely to the tires rolling over the wooden planks of the bridge. Through the whoosh of wind and rain you could hear the wheels hitting the planks one by one—kalunk, kalunk, kalunk—and then we were out onto the bridge, still crawling forward, plank by plank, and pretty soon we were out on the middle of the bridge, and I was holding my breath, and now we were past the middle and we kept creeping forward, slowly, slowly, gingerly edging forward plank by plank, and, suddenly we were at the end and the front wheels were on solid ground and at that moment I let out my breath in a heavy sigh, and at the same instant everyone started talking and jabbering again just as if nothing had happened. And that was the first I had actually been aware of the dead silence of everyone in the bus all the time we'd been edging over the bridge. . . .

Anyway, that's the sort of thing that had gone on for the past few years with that band of mine. But now overnight things began to change.

At first it was fairly subtle. The men began to treat me more as an employer than as a friend of theirs.

I soon noticed that they were beginning to behave strangely toward me. I had occasionally gone out to eat with one or another of them when we were out on the road. Now I found a curious reluctance on the part of any one of them to be seen in public with me. There was talk about "apple polishing." Any one of the men who might show any intimacy with me began to be regarded with suspicion by the rest. And since he had to live and work with them, he was understandably reluctant to jeopardize his standing. So I learned to keep to myself and thus avoid embarrassment all the way round.

From then on I used to eat with the band manager, or by myself, up in my hotel room, whenever that was possible. But there was another reason why eating alone began to become an obsession. I tried going into restaurants by myself several times, but always sooner or later someone would spot me and then it would become a kind of side show. I'd sit there trying to mind my business, but unable to ignore the stares of people who had recognized me and were busily pointing me out and whispering about me to others.

This was pretty much inevitable, of course, since the towns we played in were always well plastered with billboards and window cards advertising our appearance and, naturally, my picture was prominently displayed on these cards and bill-boards; so it's not surprising that I should be recognized. Nevertheless it made things fairly difficult, if a fellow happened to want to limit his public life to those times when he was being paid for appearing on a bandstand or on a theatre stage.

I began to discover that this business of being a "big name" was a full-time job. People insisted that I was "different" and whether I believed them or not, I was going to have to accept this belief and the manifestations of it that were beginning to be thrust upon me wherever I went, publicly and even privately. I had become a sort of cockeyed celebrity. People began to point at me in the street, ask for my autograph, stare at me, and do all the nonsensical things people generally do with those they themselves have put up onto the curious pedestal erected for these oddities, these freaks, these public "personalities" who have achieved $ucce$$. The whole thing amounts to quite a routine to be put through.

The result was pure misery on my part. I simply couldn't adjust to it. I felt as if I were going around in a fish bowl with people staring and pointing at me and telling other

people who in turn stared and pointed and ogled and giggled
and whispered to each other and went on staring and giggling.
I began to feel like some sort of freak—and although I managed to develop an attitude toward all this while I was at work,
I couldn't get used to it when I was trying to go about my own
private business as a private citizen.

Of course, the main trouble was that I couldn't realize I was
no longer a private citizen. The truth is, I actually *was* a sort
of side-show freak—that was the essence of my so-called
celebrity. My big mistake was in thinking my status had
to do with music. I see that now—but at the time I couldn't
see it at all.

After a few months of all this, I began to develop a near-
paranoiac kind of behavior. Only, unlike a paranoiac, my behavior was based on the fact that people *were* actually following me around. Sometimes kids would get together in groups,
hop into cabs, and trail me to wherever I might be going. When
my band and I appeared out of town, there were times when
I had to be escorted by policemen who formed a square and
acted as a buffer between me and the mob of milling youngsters who wanted nothing more than to pull out my hair for a
souvenir.

At one time, during an appearance in the Fox Theatre in
Philadelphia, I was informed that on the first day of our
week's engagement there was such a drop in attendance at the
Philadelphia schools that the Board of Education lodged a
formal complaint with the police! After the first show, when
I tried to leave my dressing room to go out for a breath of air,
I started toward the stage door but was told by the doorman
that I'd better not try going out into the street. I asked him
why not, and for answer he opened the stage door just a tiny
crack, so I could look outside.

The whole street was jampacked with kids! Traffic was completely halted and there were half a dozen mounted policemen

trying to disperse this rioting mob of youngsters, with no apparent success whatsoever.

But there's no point in going into all these details. No matter how I try to understate this kind of goings on, no matter whether I try to play it down or not, no matter what I say—it's bound to sound exaggerated. All I can say is that if I deliberately tried to exaggerate some of the incidents that occurred to me during that period—I couldn't do it. The truth is far more insane than any exaggeration I could possibly dream up.

This insanity went right on, though, throughout that whole time. Meanwhile, I went around the country in my own private fish bowl, developing the loveliest set of paranoid symptoms you ever saw in your life. The plain truth of the matter is that throughout most of that year I was scared out of my wits!

I couldn't get myself to accept what was plainly going on. I was making so much money I couldn't believe it. There were many weeks when I would be told I had netted over twenty thousand dollars and several when the net figure was well over thirty! *Thirty thousand dollars*—do you know what that means? *In one week*, understand. And that was net—after paying all expenses, even transportation. Well, is it any wonder I couldn't take it? Is it strange that I couldn't adjust to it? How could any halfway sane person adjust to any such wacky state of affairs as that? What the hell could there be about *anyone* that would make him worth that much money? Not a single thing but—Publicity. That was all there was to it. But of course when you've said just that you've said a lot.

Anyway, for a fellow who has been going along on a more or less even keel (if anything connected with the band business can be called an even keel), all this crazy stuff going on day after day, night after night, week after week, and month after month, can have a devastating effect. Unless he happens to be a particularly well-balanced and well-adjusted person to begin with—in which case, Lord knows how he would ever have got himself *into* such a situation at all. Unless he *is* that, though, a guy is quite apt to flip his lid once and for all, as I've already seen it happen to more than one.

I was no exception. The whole story of how I flipped my own particular lid could have no real meaning to anyone but a psychoanalyst, but I'll try to give you a rough idea of what it's like when you're right in the middle of it.

In the first place, the thing is too sudden. Life is geared up overnight to a hectic, frenzied, feverish pace. You haven't had time to build up to it. One minute you're going along, trying to build up a band and get it to sound a certain way, and the next moment all that has become meaningless, it doesn't matter what you do or how your band sounds, or anything else. All you've got to do is show up somewhere and go through the motions, and the next thing you know people are throwing thousands and thousands of dollars at you and trying to pull your hair out or rip off your clothes in their enthusiasm. You feel as if you've suddenly become the focal center of a complete and utter lunacy. Nothing makes any sense at all. For you still feel more or less like the same guy you were a week or a month ago, when you were just scuffling along trying to keep things going somehow and barely doing that; but now, all at once, here you are, the same fellow you've always been, only now *you're* the dog who's caught the locomotive. In one sense only, though, for this particular locomotive hasn't stopped at all but is hurtling along at breakneck speed, and anyone who catches it is going to be taken for one hell of a frantic ride before it either stops or slows down enough for him to get off— or else throws him off altogether, which is more likely than anything else.

Everything is stepped up by a ratio of fifty to one. Where an ordinary person gets an ordinary salary—here you are getting twenty thousand dollars or more week after week after week. Which in itself ought to make you feel fine. But—it's all happening under tremendous tension. There is never any time to think. You can't get yourself set. You're on the go constantly.

If it isn't a theatre appearance you're getting ready for, it's a radio show. If it's not radio, it's records you've got to make. If it isn't any of these, it's a tour of one-night stands you're about to start on. And all through everything, there seem to be hundreds and thousands of crazy people pushing and shoving and crowding and milling around in mobs, shrieking for your autograph, or your picture, or something—or just plain shrieking for no reason on earth you can figure out. Your whole life has become a kind of wild nightmare. You're being hauled along to where you haven't the faintest desire to go; but you can't stay where you are either, because someone is hollering in your ear about the amount of dough you're going to make as soon as you get to wherever it is they're pushing and shoving and hauling you—and what the hell, you keep telling yourself, it *is* a lot of dough, isn't it?—more than you've ever dreamed you could possibly get your hands on, and you've got all the pressure of the whole world you've ever known weighing you down with fear that something might go wrong, so you've *got* to go on with it while you've got the chance, make the dough while you can, because how can you or anyone else tell how long this whole furious madness is going to go on before you suddenly wake up and find the whole thing was nothing but a wild and impossible dream?

. . . That's one side of it. The other side has vaguely to do with the thing through which you got here in the first place. Remember? You once started out to be a musician? Remember that? Music. . . . Whatever happened to that?

Well, something like this:

There isn't much time to rehearse nowadays, you know. There's all this work to do, all these appearances to make, all these records to be made, all these theatre and radio shows to play, all these one-nighters to get to, all this money to make, all this business to take care of—and so forth and so on, far into the night, night after night, week after week, month after month, with never a stop, year after year—you hope (at the same time that you also wish it could come to a stop for a short while anyway, so you could get a little rest, but then again at the same time you're also afraid that if it does it'll never start again and where'll you be then and where will you ever get another chance to earn the money you've now got almost in your hands?)—and where on earth, out of all this confusion and turmoil and madness, are you going to find time to even *think* about music? What's music got to do with all this stuff? All you've got to do is go on playing over and over and over again those same few tunes the public wants to hear you play—those *Begin the Beguines*, or whatever they happen to be—and if you *are* going to have to play something new— the hell with it, let your arrangers worry about making it sound halfway musical, because there just isn't time for you to take care of all the millions of problems and headaches connected with this kind of crazy life and still have any time left over for anything as vague and—well, immaterial, as music. . . .

As I say, I couldn't adjust to it. I tried to make some sort of adjustment, though, and the result was pretty abnormal, since it was an adjustment to a pretty abnormal set of conditions.

What it came to was that for a period of about a year or so, I went tearing around the country living what I fondly imagined to be the life of some bush-league steel baron—complete with entourage, stooges, and all the rest of it. Talk about money! The stuff was rolling in by the barrelful. At one point, I was pacing around in various hotel suites scattered around in cities from coast to coast, feeling like the guy in Saroyan's "Sweeney in the Trees" who kicks bushel-basketfuls of money lying around in heaps all over the floor. I can't argue that any of it made sense—and at this late date it would be fruitless to discuss the foolishness of my behavior. All I can do is tell you the facts; and one of them is this:

Throughout this entire year or so, while I went around in the midst of all this wild applause and adulation, I believe I was about as utterly miserable as a fellow can possibly be and still stay on this side of suicide.

And don't think the other side didn't occur to me quite frequently.

But I had long ago figured out a working method of dealing with that particular form of masochism; so all I had to do was to apply the method and keep on telling myself that at any time this kind of life became so unbearable as to make it completely worthless, all I'd have to do would be to realize that from that point on I had nothing to lose no matter which way I decided to go, and once that happened I could walk right out on the whole shebang and start doing anything I felt like doing. And that way maybe I could start having some fun again and enjoying life once more. At which point, of course, the idea of suicide becomes ludicrous. For anyone who has hopes of living in such a way as to derive some fun out of it is going to fight pretty hard to go on living. And while all this may sound pretty elementary and simple-minded, take my word for it, it's far from it. You can go a long, long way and do a whole lot worse than just having fun; and if you doubt that, ask the guy who isn't having it—or maybe yourself, if you happen to be one of those guys, which is possibly more likely than you're willing to admit, even to yourself. . . .

In any event, I kept on with the life I found myself living, and went right on living it the way everyone around me thought and told me I ought to; and along the way I began to understand what a fellow I'd once read—a quite un$ucce$$-ful guy named William Blake—had meant when he said, "You never know what is enough unless you know what is more than enough."

And then, a year or so later, when that whole treadmill I was on began to step up its pace to a point where I was unable to keep up with it any more without extreme personal discomfort—something happened that caused me to arrive at a rather important decision.

"It is easy to escape from business, if you will only despise the rewards of business."

SENECA

Chapter Forty-Four

AN ARTICLE THAT APPEARED in a publication called *Current Biography*, published by the H. W. Wilson Co., in the issue of May, 1941, more or less sums up what took place that year. It's accurate enough in its broad outlines, even though some of the factual details are incorrect. However, I can correct those as we go along, where they have any bearing on the over-all meaning of all this; and where they don't amount to anything much one way or the other I'll let them go. I don't know who did the article, but it doesn't actually matter. Let's take it from where it deals with the part of my story we've now arrived at.

"1939 was a bonanza year, despite the loss of a few weeks during the spring through illness. In New York he"—(This is that Artie Shaw guy again.) —"was stricken with *agranulocytopenia*, a usually fatal blood disease, and had to have several transfusions. Leaving his sick-bed to fulfil a Hollywood contract, he caught pneumonia and was again laid up for days"—(actually weeks)—"before he could get to work on his first feature-length picture, *Dancing Co-Ed*, starring Lana Turner. An Associated Press dispatch quoted Hollywood gossips as saying that they 'quarrelled endlessly throughout the only movie they had made together.'

"In November, 1939, Mr. Shaw got off his famous blast against jitterbugs. Although he denied its sweeping character, a large part of the press quoted him as saying that jitterbugs were morons. He recently corrected this impression by stating: 'It was the few rowdies who spoiled the whole thing for most of the kids who just wanted to listen or dance. . . . Anyway, I think that sort of music is on its way out.'

"That month he abruptly left his band and, on the advice of his physician, went to Mexico to rest. 'Even before his recent illness,' Alton Cook commented glumly, 'he was a tense, moody young man.' The musical world generally took the whole affair in its stride, regretting the inconvenience to musicians but in agreement with many of the criticisms Artie made of the music business at that time. It remained for the New York *Times* to see the incident in an heroic perspective. 'Any commentary that might occur to us,' the statement read, 'would be lost in the Shakespearean sweep of Mr. Shaw's exodus: the kind of spectacularly irreverent farewell to his work and former associates that even the timidest soul must occasionally dream of, a beautifully incautious burning of all his bridges behind him.'

"Shaw was already on his way to Mexico when the *Saturday Evening Post* published an article on which he had collaborated. In this he threatened to leave the music business before it had another chance to lay him low, and talked frankly of the musician in America, who 'hasn't only a financial and artistic problem with which to contend but must fight politics, corruption and a system of patronage.'"

That more or less sums up what took place in that first Year of The Big Boom of mine. And incidentally, the whole biography closes with the following: ". . . he keeps a notebook in which he records his impressions. 'I am using myself as a guinea pig,' he admits. 'My reactions to all this fame and excitement should be worth preserving.'"

Well, I'll certainly be in a good spot to know whether they were or weren't once *this* is published. As for notebooks, let me add, I didn't need them. What was going on was vivid enough so that I was pretty sure I wasn't going to forget the important parts of any of it in a hurry—and I haven't. In fact, although this whole thing I'm writing here has already added up to a fairly voluminous affair so far, I can say this much in all honesty—I haven't even scratched the surface. There's so much more that it could, and no doubt will, take the next ten or fifteen years before I've finally disemburdened myself of the entire story.

But—getting back to this, I'll take up some of the things I just quoted above.

First, there's one little item omitted, this new name change through which "Art Shaw" became "Artie Shaw." This was done by the Victor Recording Company, at the time they released my first recordings. For some reason, one of the Victor executives decided that the name Art Shaw sounded rather like a fast sneeze—and that when spoken rapidly it was difficult to tell whether the first name was supposed to be Art or Arch. (At least that's how I heard it; and since it didn't matter much to me one way or the other, I let it go at that and accepted the "ie" appendage which was consequently stuck on the end of my first name.)

So much for that.

Going back to our quotation once more, I have to make a rather trifling correction in regard to that illness. It was a strep throat at the start. After I left New York and went to California, the thing was finally brought to a climax by repeated overdoses of sulfanilimide, at that time still a new drug. In any case, I did end up with *agranulocytopenia*, and almost lost my life. In all, I was some six weeks recovering—after passing out cold right in the middle of an opening night before a record crowd at the Palomar Ballroom, at that time the largest in Los Angeles, in fact, one of the largest in the world.

During that six weeks of convalescence I had a lot of time. And I did a lot of thinking. And out of all this thinking I arrived at my decision that enough was enough. As soon as I could finish up certain contractual obligations, I was going to get out of the whole thing. After all, I had already made that "twenty-five thousand bucks" I'd started out to get; what was the point in going on making myself miserable in a kind of life I hated? What was the sense in remaining a side-show freak, gaped at and stared at and pawed at by thousands of "fans" wherever I went? Was this what I had set out to do? Was this where I had wanted to go? Was this any kind of answer to what I really wanted to do with my life? And if so–what about all that other stuff I had been trying to do when I went back to school so I could try to figure out a few things about myself and the world I live in?

I shuffled these questions over and over in my mind, as well as the various answers I could give myself; and in the end, my decision still remained. So that, by the time some months had gone by and I had come back to New York City again, my mind was made up.

I couldn't get anyone connected with me to agree, of course. Everyone told me I was crazy. My lawyer, my agents, everyone who had anything to do with me, said I must be out of my mind even to think of any such thing as quitting.

"Why," they said in essence, "you'll never get another chance like this as long as you live. Do you realize how many people would give their eyeteeth to have your chance to clean up? All you have to do is go on like you are for a few years, and you'll wind up a *millionaire!* Don't you realize that? What's the matter with you—you must be insane!"

And so forth. . . .

It was one of the loneliest times in my life. I had a few friends, people who were not in the music business, and with them I was able to be myself and still not be regarded as completely off my rocker. However, my working hours were scarcely conducive to maintaining any sustained relationships with people working more normal hours, so it was difficult to spend enough time with these friends to counterbalance all that well-meant advice and counsel I kept getting from business associates.

In the end I had to take matters into my own hands. This I did, one night at around eleven o'clock, in the middle of an engagement I was playing in New York, at the Pennsylvania Hotel. At the stage I was then in, any little thing would have been sufficient; and so, because of a slight unpleasantness with some idiot on the floor in front of the band, who was evidently trying to impress his partner by using me as a focal point for his witticisms, I suddenly decided I'd had it. Instead of kicking him in the teeth, I walked off the bandstand, went up to my room, and called my lawyer. When I got him on the phone I told him I was leaving.

"What do you mean, leaving?" he asked. "You've got a contract. You can't just walk out."

"I can't, eh? Well, that's what I've just done," I told him.

"Hold it, don't do anything till I come down, will you?"

I promised him I'd wait for him.

He arrived in an astonishingly short time, considering that he lived all the way out in Great Neck, Long Island. Still, I suppose that was the first time he'd ever had to deal with a client who'd suddenly gone berserk.

He came up to my room and tried to reason with me. I listened to him, and I must say he was quite good. Everything he said made complete, practical horse sense; the only trouble with it was that none of it applied to me as I was at that moment. When he was all through, my face must have shown him how little impression he'd made. At that point he asked if he could order up a few drinks. I told him to go ahead. By the time the drinks came up my agent showed up too.

He came storming and raving into the room. He is and was then the head of a large talent agency, and is usually a fairly calm man. But I've never seen him like he was right then. His face was red, his hair was all mussed up, and there was a mad glare in his eyes.

"What's this I hear?" he demanded as he burst in like a ball of fire.

I told him.

That tore it. He went into a tirade that lasted some ten or fifteen minutes before he came up for air. He stormed and stamped up and down the room, pleading his case like a great criminal lawyer, pulling out all the stops, leaving out nothing; and the gist of it all was that if I did this crazy thing I was threatening to do, I'd— I'd—well, I'd be cutting my throat at the absolute least.

"It's my own throat," I reminded him.

That only set him off again.

This time he turned to my lawyer and directed most of his arguments and pleas to him. My lawyer listened sympathetically enough, since most of these arguments and pleas were the very same ones he himself had just finished presenting to me.

The whole session lasted a long time—the rest of the night. There was one time when my agent begged me to allow him to bring up some person he swore by, who, he assured me, would bring me to my senses if anyone on earth could. However, when I learned that this "person" was a woman who performed her miracles with the aid of a mixture of Christian Science and astrology, I decided I'd have to draw the line.

In the end, of course, there was nothing anyone could do about it—for I had even ignored what my lawyer had told me about a number of lawsuits I might incur for nonfulfilment of various contracts.

I told him I was going anyway—contracts or no contracts, lawsuits or no lawsuits. I even went so far as to tell him that if I were really sued, I'd come into court and plead insanity; and that it shouldn't be too difficult to make a plea of insanity stick anyway, in the case of a man who is walking out on a fortune!

By the time daylight came, I guess they were too pooped out to argue any further. I arranged to leave the band in charge of one of the men, turn over my music library to them, and let them see what they could do without me. There was some talk of setting up the band as a co-operative organization, but I wasn't interested in the details. All I wanted to do was to get out of there—which I did the following day.

I had no idea where I was going. I had no idea of where I wanted to go. I was completely free, and all I wanted was to go someplace quiet where I could rest for a while and see if I couldn't find my way back to myself again, to get some idea of who and what I had become.

I got into my car and started driving. It was snowing hard, the day I left New York. I remember coming out on the Jersey end of the Holland Tunnel and suddenly realizing I was out from under all the misery and idiocy I'd been buried in for so long. The flood of relief that rolled over me made up for all the turmoil and trouble and talk-talk-talk it had taken to get out.

I was driving a big, heavy car, the heater was working, the snow was falling heavily outside, but it was warm inside the car—and that night I knew I wouldn't have to show up on a bandstand before a crowd of ogling strangers. That night I could check in at some hotel or tourist camp and be just plain Art Shaw again—Art Shaw, private citizen. I felt fine.

That was all I wanted at the moment, and because I had that, I was about as happy as I'd been miserable for the past year or more. And oddly enough, although it had taken me so many years to get to where I'd just been, I hadn't the slightest regret at having walked out cold on everything I'd always thought I wanted. For—as an old saying goes—there is only one thing worse than not having what you set out to get, and that's getting it.

Well, I'd had it, seen what it was like, and decided it was not for me. That's all there was to it, and when you come right down to it, that's enough. . . .

"His freedom was so vast that he was lost in it."

ELLEN GLASGOW

Chapter Forty-Five

ABOUT HALFWAY ACROSS the country I suddenly remembered something I had heard from a reporter who had once interviewed me during a week I had played in Detroit. The reporter had just come back from several weeks in Mexico and was so enthusiastic that some of his enthusiasm had rubbed off on me. And now, since I had no special place in mind anyway, and had spoken on the telephone to several friends out on the West Coast who had told me to stay away from there if I wanted the kind of peace and quiet I was looking for, it seemed to me Mexico was as good a place as any.

I stayed down there several months. I spent most of that time in Acapulco, in those days just a little dusty fishing village by the sea, with a local bistro on the central square, a place called the *Siete Mares*. I spent evenings sitting out on the terrace overlooking the plaza, having a quiet drink and watching the huge moths flutter through the arc light that cast a pale glow on the dusty leaves of the banyan trees, while the local *politicos* sipped their warm *cerveza* and played their endless games of dominoes. Daytimes I swam, fished, lay in the sun, loafed around, did absolutely nothing I didn't feel like doing—and had myself one hell of a good time imagining I'd settle down and stay put there for the rest of my days.

However, after a few months I began to feel an old familiar

restlessness creeping up on me again. I tried to fight it down, but it kept working in me, and pretty soon I saw it was time to move on.

But where to? Move on to what?

I owned a small house in Hollywood, but it was rented to the English actress, Flora Robson, and her lease had a short while to run—so that was out, I couldn't go there. Anyway, what was there for me to do in Hollywood?

Around that same time, I had an accident that sounds like something out of one of those "romantic" magazine serials.

I broke my leg. Nothing so extraordinary about that except that I did it in the process of pulling a young student of the Geneva College for Women out of the water. A heavy surf had knocked her senseless and was dragging her out in the undertow. I was the only one on the beach at the time who realized what had happened and I was the nearest person to her anyway. So I tore out to where she lay drifting, and started to pull her in toward the beach. At that moment an enormous wall of water rose up, broke over both of us, picked us up like a pair of tiny chips, and flung us down every-which-way. One of my heels came down hard on something and the next thing I knew, my knee had snapped. Somehow I managed to get the girl in to safety, and after that I must have gone out like a light. When I came to, all kinds of crazy stuff was happening. I found myself being treated like some sort of hero, with everybody making a big fuss over me; and all through it my leg hurt like the very devil.

Several days later I learned that it was broken and that I'd have to go to a hospital in Mexico City to have it properly set. Coming as it did, shortly after all the publicity attendant on my "walking out" on the music business, this was great stuff for the newspapers. They played it up quite big, with heavy accents on the "romantic" angle. . . .

While my leg was healing in Mexico City, I got a phone call from my lawyer in New York telling me about a deal he thought might interest me. This was a proposed film version of Gershwin's "Porgy and Bess," to be directed by Reuben Mamoulian and produced by a man named Boris Morros, whose name I vaguely remembered in connection with the old Publix Presentation outfit, with which I had got my first really professional job—at the Olympia Theatre back in New Haven.

A week or two afterwards, I flew to Hollywood, where I quickly learned that the "Porgy and Bess" deal had fizzled out. I eventually worked out some sort of arrangement with Miss Robson so I could move into my own house; and for a while I settled down out there in Lotus Land.

Some months later, my leg healed up altogether. Now I was all set again. But again—for what? I tried to find something to do that might be interesting, but the only thing any agents I spoke to could seem to come up with was the interesting suggestion that I get together another band. Starting in all over again on the same old treadmill was something I couldn't have cared less for; so I politely declined these offers and waited for something else.

Nothing came.

I was beginning to go a little batty just sitting around doing nothing; so, having several more records to make for that year on my still-existent R.C.A. Victor commitment, I decided I might just as well do that as nothing at all. I got together a crew of studio musicians and made six or eight records, using a large orchestra composed not only of the usual jazz band combination but a good-sized string section and a number of woodwinds besides.

Well-sir—what do you think happened?

The first record released was a little tune I'd heard and liked while I was in Mexico. The name of it was *Frenesi*—and all at once I found I had another big hit on my hands!

I found myself again besieged by agents offering all sorts of theatres and road tours, at all sorts of prices. All I'd have to do was put together a band and go back out on tour again. . . .

But all I wanted was to stay put in one place for a change, I kept telling these agents. Wasn't there some sort of job in the music business where I could earn, not fifteen or twenty or what-have-you thousand dollars a week, but a mere, say, thousand or so? Or less?

Apparently there wasn't. At least that was what the agents I was dealing with kept telling me. On the other hand, they would go on, if I were to get together a band and go out on tour. . . .

And so it went, round and round, like a merry-go-round gone crazy.

Looking at it now, I find it easy enough to understand their attitude. As I've explained, a band pays commissions "off the top," which means that the agent gets ten per cent for one-week stands or longer, and fifteen per cent for one-night stands or split-week engagements. So that the answer to this insistence on the part of the agents I was dealing with is simple arithmetic—ten or fifteen per cent of ten or twenty thousand dollars a week compared to ten per cent of one thousand dollars a week.

There was nothing I could do. I still had my old contract with the agency that had been booking me before I'd walked out; and although I asked for a release so I could try to get myself booked elsewhere, they of course refused to give it to me. So it was either feast on the road or famine at home. I tried to stick it out, but a great deal of that first bonanza year's earnings had gone for taxes; by the time several more months had passed, I saw I was going to have to get hold of some money somewhere. In the end, despite my determination never to go out on tour with a band again, I had to do just that.

And, although I put together a band that for the first time had in it what I'd originally wanted to have in a band—a large string section—still, there was only one basic reason why I went back into the band business again.

I needed the money.

And just to cut this whole thing down to a nub now—that is what has caused me to keep on going back time and time again, into a business I have no use for at all, then quitting it over and over again, and telling myself the very same thing each time I've quit—that I'd never under any circumstances go back.

I've been doing this zig-zagging back and forth for about twelve years now. And as I said way back at the beginning of all this, if the war hadn't come along and snapped me out of it—and if, after that, I hadn't gone through a long tussle with myself under the auspices of a couple of representatives of a fellow named Freud—I might easily have wound up as an old man with a long grey beard leading a broken-down jazzband in some backwoods dance hall.

Instead of that, because of all the stuff I eventually began to dig out of myself, I finally came to realize there must be something basically wrong with a fellow who tells himself he only wants enough money to keep going while he tries to do something he wants to do, but who for some reason never seems to be able to get together enough money to go ahead and do it; a guy who somehow manages to get rid of his money as fast as he gets hold of it, no matter how many times he keeps on getting hold of it; a guy who keeps insisting he *wants* to do something but for some peculiar reason seems unwilling, or unable to start *doing* it.

There certainly must be something wrong with a guy like that—wouldn't you say?

Well, there is. . . .

And in finding out what it was, I also learned a number of interesting things about what had been wrong with my attempts to solve some of my problems through one particular

Cinderella-solution I spoke of right at the beginning of this story.

I'm referring, of course, to that very common distraction, the legalized cultural institution known as Marriage—which is not as unrelated to the main theme of all this as you might imagine . . . just in case there *is* anyone who happens to imagine it is unrelated.

"The truth about women I will speak when I have one leg in the coffin; then I will quickly pull the other one in and clap down the lid."

TOLSTOY, TO GORKI

Chapter Forty-Six

LET ME MAKE IT CLEAR RIGHT NOW that I am *not* going to go into the intimate details of any of my various ventures into the marital state. But one thing can be safely and accurately said about all these attempts—I made an unholy botch of every last one of them. Of course, I believe I can also state, equally accurately, and with complete dispassion and objectivity, that I had a good bit of help in making these various unholy botches. After all, in each attempt I did have a partner in the enterprise; and while I would be the last to decry my own skill at botch-making, I must say I was either clever or lucky enough or maybe just plain stupid enough (in at least two instances) to have picked myself some pretty damn good partners when it came to gumming up the works.

Nevertheless, I can also tell you right here and now that I harbor no rancor toward any of these unfortunately misguided (but, both for them and myself, fortunately erstwhile) helpmates. Our big mistake, in every case, was in getting married to each other at all. Our divorces, in every last instance, made utter good sense all the way round. At least three of these ex-venturers are still friends of mine. As for the others— all I can say is that if they've succeeded in proving anything by the manner in which they've behaved at times since our divorces, it's been the necessity and inevitability of the divorces themselves. Which proof is, of course, quite valuable, and I would be the very last man on earth to minimize its importance.

But the main point here is not for me to discuss these various victims of our joint misfortune. All that could possibly come out of that would be more unpleasantness. And as anyone who has ever been through it can tell you, any divorce, even when it terminates a really bad marriage, is painful enough. Besides, there are several well-known public personalities among these gals. So what's the use of going into detailed discussion? No matter how objective and unprejudiced I might *try* to be, there's no telling how anyone else might feel about the other side of the story; particularly in stories of this kind, about which, to put it mildly, it's practically impossible for either protagonist to be entirely unprejudiced after all the bitterness involved in any such debacle as a marriage gone on the rocks.

But since a fellow can't possibly have gone through as many bouts as I have with this particular type of institution, without being forced to come to certain conclusions about it—I may as well pass these on to you.

First of all, when a fellow has been married as often as I have, there's one distinct conclusion that you must arrive at about him—he is seeking some sort of solution to his basic loneliness, trying to solve this problem within the established forms of the culture he happens to be living in. Without going too deeply into the psychodynamics of all this, that's really all there is to it. And since, of course, in this culture of ours, there is a realistic recognition of the many problems involved in making a workable and enduring marriage, we have evolved another institution designed to deal with marriages that *don't* work, an institution called Divorce. So that, when you come right down to it, the fact is I've behaved for the most part, whether misguidedly or not, in a decidedly conventional manner.

I've often marveled at the fact that there seems to be so much "humor" in this whole business of a man wanting to get married and have a normal life and never being able to work it out satisfactorily. Personally, I can't find anything specially funny in this picture—although, of course, I may be too deeply *in* the picture to be able to see it clearly. However, even when it comes to the numerous other men who have encountered this same problem, I still can't see anything particularly humorous about it. Not that I'm opposed to the idea of anyone's having a laugh wherever and whenever he can have it; for there is only too little real humor around these days and if anybody can find anything at all to laugh at he's got my best wishes. Still, a series of wrecked marriages seems hardly a laughing matter to me. And when the series happens to be one with which I have been so intimately connected, I don't believe anyone will find it difficult to understand this gap in my sense of humor.

However, regardless of whether humor is or is not justified, let me tell you a few things about this whole marriage game as I've seen it in my own experience and with other people I've known.

This kind of human relationship seems to me one of the greatest challenges any person can ever be called upon to meet. That is as flat a statement as I can make; and I make it out of intense subjective experience as well as out of a hope that I will somehow yet be able to meet this challenge and solve it in my own personal life. I honestly believe it is not impossible for me to do so, given what I have learned about my unbroken record of failures in the past, and the part I myself played in making these failures. In other words, I'm still an incurable optimist in this respect and I firmly believe marriage can work—even for me (which is saying a great deal, as I realize only too well).

However, *before* it can work—for me, or for anyone else— it seems to me pretty clear that the people involved in it have to be adults. And as I've intimated before this, an adult is a hard person to locate nowadays. The truth is, I've known only three or four real adults in my whole lifetime; and although your experience may be wider than mine in this respect, I doubt that anyone has ever had the good fortune to meet many more than that in his lifetime.

Of course there are any number of marriages which go on and on anyway—whether they work or don't. Everyone has seen examples of such relationships. The thing that keeps many marriages going, as a matter of plain fact, is the feeling that *any* known evil is probably better than an unknown one. It seems that people are so afraid of what they might have to do in order to live by themselves that they will put up with almost anything in order to go on having a lifelong sparring partner. Now this may be O.K.—if you happen to like sparring partners. I personally happen not to—so, rather than going on indefinitely with any such relationship as the so-called average marriage, I've simply given it up as a bad job at whatever time it has irrevocably and finally proved itself to be a bad job.

The capacity for going on with a marriage that has absolutely no value for either of the parties concerned, is a quality that has never ceased to astonish me. For example, to mention one man out of a possible hundred or more I know, who are in the same pickle:

This man and his wife have been engaged in one continuous unending dog-and-cat-fight for a period of twelve years now, that I myself know of—as to how long before that, I wasn't acquainted with them so I can't comment. This one long, un-interrupted, miserable squabble has become the whole pattern of their life together. The thing is actually so bad that I can truthfully say I have never spent an evening with them—nor do I know anyone else who ever has—which didn't end up in a complete bust for everyone else around.

What is their solution?

Every few years they have another child.

Now isn't that nice? Especially for the kiddies, isn't it nice?

One evening this fellow came up to see me, after another round in his long marital fight. He looked haggard, but after I'd given him a drink he settled back. "Listen, Art," he said. "You've been through this marriage racket a few times. What does a guy have to do to get away from a woman?"

"You're talking about yourself, aren't you?"

He nodded. "Yeah—myself and Florence. We can't go on this way much longer. But how does a fellow put an end to one of these things?"

"We-ell, let's see now," I said seriously, as if I were giving it a great deal of thought. "I'd say the first thing is to call a cab."

He stared at me.

"That's right. Call a cab—pack some things, and when the cab comes—well, get in and go away. That's about all there is to it," I told him. "Or else you can even walk—if you want to leave out the cab part."

"Listen—I'm serious. Quit the kidding," he said.

"I'm not kidding at all," I assured him. "In fact, that's the only way you can do it. You just get up and leave, that's all. As far as the details are concerned—hell, that's going to be nothing but headaches any way you want to look at it, and in any case you're going to have to get a lawyer to take care of that part of it, so. . . ."

He was looking at me as if I'd told him something he didn't know. He shook his head. Then he got up heavily and started pacing up and down the floor. "I know, I know," he finally said. "I know everything you say is true. . . . I just can't do it, that's all. I hate her, I can't stand her, I can't look at her without fighting with her. It's awful for her, it's awful for me, and it's even more awful for the kids—but what in the name of God can I do? I can't get back to any kind of civil status with her—it's gone on too long this way and we've gone too far ever to get back again. But. . . . I just can't get myself to make the break."

"Oh well. . . ."

"How in hell were *you* able to go through with it?" he suddenly asked me.

I shrugged. "It was different every time."

"Yes, I suppose. . . . But how does a guy do it? How does a fellow make up his mind once and for all?"

I told him this old chestnut:

A man is sitting in a hospital room, with his sick wife. She is dying and he knows it. The doctor tries to get him to go home and get some sleep, but he won't leave. He sits there, miserable and alone, watching his dying wife. Finally, she dies. When it happens he breaks down completely. He goes into such a spasm of uncontrollable grief that the doctor becomes alarmed.

"Get hold of yourself, my good man," he says soothingly. "After all, death must come to everyone sooner or later."

"Yes, I know, I know, I *know*. . . ." but the sobbing is still uncontrollable.

"Listen to me," the doctor now says. "I don't want to talk this way at a time like this, but I have to. You must get hold of yourself. This isn't the end of your life. Why, in a year, or maybe even less than that, you may meet someone else and fall in love again and at that point you can start building up a new life—don't you see that?"

"Of course I see it, doc," says the husband, pulling himself together for a moment. "But—but—"

"But *what?*" asks the doctor.

"But what am I going to do *tonight?*"

◇◇◇◇

. . . When I finished, my friend grinned wryly at me and said, "Boy, I sure know what *that* guy means, though."

"Yeah, it seems plenty of other people do, too," I said.

"Listen, I see quite a few of 'em myself," he said. "And you can say that again."

"All right," I said. "I guess plenty of other people do too."

He looked up at me again, and this time we both started laughing.

He went home after a while. This all took place quite some time ago, but he's still living with his wife—and still, by the way, fighting with her, just as ever. . . .

Another guy I know has worked out a different type of solution. He put it this way to me, one evening when we were having a couple of drinks and talking about this and that:

"You know, Art—you're a funny guy. Now take me and Joan. You think I don't get bored out of my mind with her? But does that mean a guy's got to go running off and upsetting the whole applecart every time he finds himself getting a little restless? After all, if a fellow wants to go off and get laid once in a while—well, what's so tough about that? You go off, find yourself a broad, get it out of your system, and then go home. At least you've got a *home* to come back to."

"But what's the sense of it? What's *in* it for you? Or for her? Or for your kids, for that matter?"

"Ah, you can't take it that seriously," he said. "After all, how many guys do you know whose wives are still interesting to them after eight or ten years?"

"Very few," I told him, honestly enough. "But there *are* some, here and there. There *have* to be—otherwise the whole thing would collapse."

He laughed. "Listen. I'll tell you something you don't know. . . . Joan and I don't even get along well in bed. She claims I don't satisfy her sexually. Now look—I've been around. I've never had that kind of problem before. Well, what am I supposed to do—worry my head off about *her* problems? After all, I haven't had any complaints with any other gal, so it can't very well be my fault."

I was appalled. "But what do you do about it?" I asked him.

"I ignore it, that's all."

"But how long can a thing like that go on?" I asked. "And after all, even if you haven't had any complaints from all these other gals you've chased around with—"

"And still do," he boasted.

"All right. Anyway, even if you *aren't* getting any complaints from these other gals, it still seems to me the important thing is the fact that you *are* getting complaints from the woman you happen to be married to. What good is it to *her* if you're able to function well with other women? You can't tell *her* that—"

"God forbid!" he laughed.

"—and even if you could it would hardly be any consolation to her," I continued.

"I didn't say it would."

"I know," I said, "but don't you realize what you're telling me? You're saying that in the first place you're bored to death with her, and in the second place you don't even have a good sexual relationship with her. What in hell *have* you got?"

He laughed again. "There you go," he said. "I don't know what you expect out of marriage, Art—you just don't seem to be able to make any compromises."

"Compromises?" I said.

"Well, what else would you call it?"

"I'll be damned if I can tell you," I said. "But if that's what you call compromise—"

He shook his head. "That's what I mean, Art—that's exactly why you've never stayed married."

"How long have you and Joan been married now?" I asked him after a short silence.

"Over ten years," he said proudly, as if that settled everything.

Well, maybe it does settle something. But it has very little to do with what I'd call a working relationship between two people. All you can say for it, at best—and at that you'd be stretching a point to just about the utmost any point can be stretched—is that it's a way of hanging on. But what for, and why? There I can't find any answer at all.

So there are two marriages I know of myself. Of course, not all marriages are as extreme as these—but still, they're not as unrepresentative as I'd like to believe. Both these men are quite successful in their respective professions, and are regarded by most of their friends and business associates as "happily married men." Which seems to me a fairly drastic commentary on the marriages of their friends and business associates.

No, I'm afraid it won't do. I've learned one thing about all this. It seems that many people go through life accepting all sorts of so-called compromises which are in reality not even worthy of the name "compromise" at all. Most of them feel so unresolved and incomplete as individuals themselves, that they're unable to believe it is possible to feel any other way. They cannot conceive of any other attitudes toward life except their own; so they accept these, on the basis that everyone else has the same attitudes. Now and then one of them tries to break out of his self-imposed hell, but for the most part the attempt is only half-hearted, therefore predestined to failure. And since they are always faintly aware of their own inner lacks as individuals, they seek some partner, necessarily also incomplete and unresolved, with whom they try to pool their own incompletion in order to make *something* out of two nothings, a whole out of two halves. The point is, of course, that we cannot function satisfactorily as people if we're going to accept the idea of being *fractions* of people—halves, thirds, or anything else. The big trick is to achieve wholeness *in our-*

selves, and *then* look for someone else who has also done a fair job of achieving wholeness. That way there is a good possibility. I say a good possibility—although it's hardly easy. But when you do see such a relationship—which will be rarely (since there aren't many of them around)—then you'll see something that can properly be called a marriage.

As for the millions of married couples who go on living together and deluding themselves that they have achieved a decent relationship simply because of an ability to "stick it out," and because of a capacity for further compromise long after the compromises themselves have poisoned everything else—for them, there can only be one over-all consolation. That is, that most of them seem to think it's the only way a marriage can possibly wind up anyway, so what's the point in trying to find anything better?

There's another story, which perfectly illustrates the real nature of this sort of sickness.

A man goes to see a psychoanalyst.

"What can I do for you?" the doctor asks.

"Well, Doctor," the man says. "You see, every morning, right after I get up and vomit and go downstairs for breakfast, my wife says—"

"Pardon me," the doctor interrupts. "Would you mind repeating that? Did you say *every* morning—every morning of your *life*—you get up and vomit?"

"Why sure, Doctor," says the man, looking up in surprise. "Doesn't everybody?"

The funny thing about that one is that everybody actually *does!* At least to some extent, anyway. The toughest thing on earth, it seems, is for a man to stop and take a good look at himself, honestly, with no self-deception, and then recognize what is wrong with the way he has been behaving. Most people never do. And even with those who do, there are relatively few who ever get to a point where they are able to do something about it.

For once you've gone off the main highway, it's a long, hard pull to find your way back. As I said before, I got good and lost myself, and I know.

So now let me tell you what *was* wrong and how I found it out. . . .

"The tragedy of not being able to be alone!"

LA BRUYÈRE

Chapter Forty-Seven

RIGHT AFTER PEARL HARBOR I broke up another band I was on tour with, and enlisted in the Navy. I was given three months to clean up various odds and ends connected with my business. After that I reported for duty at a mine-sweeper base on Staten Island, N.Y.

Shortly thereafter, I was transferred to Newport, R. I., where I remained for several months. By that time I had become a chief petty officer, and after making a trip down to Washington, where I spoke with Forrestal, then Undersecretary of the Navy, I was given orders to report to the Bureau of Personnel at 90 Church Street, New York City—where my duties were to recruit a group of men for overseas duty in the Pacific. This group was to be made up of musicians who would form a service band and perform as a unit touring battle areas all over the Pacific. This was the first such group ever sanctioned by the U.S. Navy—and no one had any idea as to how the thing would work out, least of all myself.

Eventually the group was organized, and we were ordered to report to the Naval Base at Treasure Island in San Francisco, there to await transportation to Pearl Harbor.

We arrived at Pearl Harbor on Christmas Day, 1942. After several months there, we embarked on the North Carolina, one of the huge new battleships just then recently commis-

[372]

sioned and put into action. In a few weeks we disembarked at Noumea, New Caledonia, from which base we set out on a "tour" of the New Hebrides, the Solomons, etc.

After hitch-hiking our way from island to island, we finished up at Guadalcanal, then went back to Noumea; from there we were sent down to New Zealand for a month or so, and finally to Australia. At that point, the whole outfit was beginning to show signs of wear and tear. We stayed on in Australia, however, and traveled up and down the entire continent for some months more before the whole band, including myself, began to come apart at the seams. By then our instruments were being held together by rubber hands and sheer will, having survived any number of air raids and damp spells in fox-holes; and the men themselves were for the most part in similarly varying states of dilapidation. The Navy had a term for this type of exhaustion—they used to call it combat fatigue, or operational fatigue, depending, I suppose, on the doctor who was doing the diagnosis.

The men in my outfit had a far more descriptive phrase for this state—"I'm beat, man."

When it finally became absolutely impossible for us to go on any longer, we were all shipped back to the United States. A month or so later I was in the Naval Hospital at Oak Knoll, California, a few miles outside of Oakland; and there I remained until I was finally discharged, three or four months later.

I was pretty much washed up.

This was in 1944, and at that point I wanted nothing more than to lie down somewhere in a deep hole and have someone shovel enough dirt over me to cover me. I was *really* beat—not only physically, but completely. The war was, of course, still on; but I was out of it, and now, after the hectic pace at which I'd been going for the past several years, winding up with the big crescendo of the past year and a half down in the Pacific—well, I couldn't make it, that's all. I had no idea what

I wanted to do, what I could do, what would make sense for me to do—and I wasn't in any state to do any constructive thinking about it.

In short, I'd had it—or, as the psychologists would say, I was in a state of dysfunction. As I would put it, I was nowhere. For a while I hung around Hollywood, hoping I'd snap out of whatever I was in—but nothing happened. Nothing would have happened right up to this moment, I guess, if I hadn't somehow, from somewhere inside myself, summoned up enough energy to see someone about what was going on with me. The someone I went to see was a psychoanalyst—period. Or, perhaps I should say, colon—new paragraph.

As I said earlier, it's futile to talk about this particular method of self-investigation. The whole process is almost completely incommunicable. Not that there's any mystery about it —it's only that the process is a distinctly different process for each person who goes into it. So much so, that even a doctor who wants to become a psychoanalyst himself must, among other things, undergo an analysis himself in order to gain a subjective understanding of the process before he can start treating others—and although this type of psychoanalysis is called "didactic" there is practically no real difference between a didactic or any other kind of psychoanalysis, aside from the individual, subjective differences which would be there in any case.

However, leaving out any attempts at detailed description, I can at least discuss some of the actual results I got from the year and a half I put into this thing at that time, on a one-hour-a-day, five-days-a-week basis.

Now that's a long time to spend talking about yourself—which is essentially what you do throughout most of this treatment. By the time a fellow is through putting in that much time discussing it, he ought to have learned at least a few interesting things about the way he ticks.

I certainly did. And in fact, I'm still digesting some of the stuff I had to swallow about myself. Out of it all, I did succeed in assembling an over-all picture of myself and the way I had been functioning all my life—and by the time the pattern began to emerge, I started to get myself into focus.

Of course, there were other, realistic, pressures on me also, and after a year and a half I had to do something about meeting those. I had to suspend further self-research for a time in order to get back down to earth and hustle up a few bucks again. My mother still had to be supported. I had recently been divorced and had to get out and earn some alimony money. There were a number of other expenses to meet and there was only one way I could dig myself out of the financial hole I had buried myself in.

I went out on tour once more.

After the tour was finished, I went back to California and started my analysis again. But financial pressures still continued. I tried various dodges—even writing a picture scenario and selling it on option, which, once the option was picked up, I was to produce—but in the end I decided to get out of Hollywood altogether. For by that time I had been stricken with the deadly virus that overcomes people who stay out in that fantasy factory too long. Fortunately I caught myself in the nick of time and managed to escape with at least a semblance of sanity. I came East and settled in Norwalk, Connecticut.

At this time I was again married—to a lady novelist whom, for purely quixotic reasons of my own, I prefer to leave nameless; although, I might mention that she is almost anything *but* "nameless."

However that is an altogether different story. Sticking to my own story for the moment, I may as well tell you what I did for the year and a half I lived in Norwalk.

I wrote.

That's right—I finally got all the way "back" to the one thing I had been trying to give myself an opportunity to do for fifteen years or more since I'd started out to earn that "twenty-five thousand bucks"!

Now I'm quite well aware that this whole thing of my "wanting to write" must sound rather exaggerated to anyone reading what I've written so far. The fact is, it may well be altogether exaggerated; certainly, so far as any importance anything I may ever write has in regard to the rest of the world. I'm not enough of a fool to delude myself about that, no matter how much of a self-deluded idiot I may still be in regard to a great many other things. The point is, it's important *to me*—and that's enough for me.

You see, during that year and a half I spent talking with that psychoanalyst out on the West Coast, I'd learned *how* important it was to me. I'd also learned some of the things I had to know before I could start *doing* this thing that had such importance for me. Possibly the most valuable thing I learned was how to go into a room by myself and stay there long enough to meet myself. In other words, I'd learned how to be by myself.

There's nothing very startling about that, is there? But then, you see, a lot depends on the person who has to acquire this particular ability. You'd probably be completely flabbergasted at how relatively few people there are who can actually perform this simple feat.

Remember all that stuff about distractions and Cinderella-solutions? Well, that's one problem; and that one alone is enough to defeat most people. There are any number of others —and not the least of them is that little matter of having to meet oneself when one is alone; and *that* is enough to defeat the few who are left over after having come past the distractions. For most of us are ready to seek any distraction, to do just about anything but meet ourselves face to face, all alone in a quiet room. Somehow, it's a painful process. There aren't too many people who are willing to admit, even to themselves, how little real respect they have for themselves. So most of us generally manage to avoid actually spending much time examining ourselves.

Now then, when you come to this thing called writing—good writing, that is, by which I don't necessarily mean clever writing, or skilled writing, or money-making writing, or any other kind outside of simple, honest, aware, nonself-deceptive writing—that can be a terribly painful job for a man who is trying to escape either from himself or from a true realization of what he is as a human being, limitations and all. . . .

That's *one* of the big lessons I learned—and as a result of learning it I began writing during that first bout with psychoanalysis.

So. . . .

What's so important to me about writing? Why do I feel it's more important for me to do than, say, playing a clarinet or leading a band? And what bearing can any of this possibly have on the problems of anyone else anyway? Well, let's see.

Let's go back to the theme we started with and see where we are now.

The whole point of this book I've written, the principal purpose of all the stuff I've told you about myself, the only thing about it that can possibly have any meaning to anyone outside myself—is this:

Any man who sets out to achieve a goal is apt to end up right where he started, unless one thing is straight. The one thing is *the nature of the goal* he sets out to achieve.

If the goal is static, if it is money, $ucce$$, fame, "security"—there's no use. For, whether you get money or not, whether you do or don't $ucceed, whether you achieve fame or not—the one thing you can't find anywhere on earth *unless you find it in yourself* is "security." Money isn't security—although it'll help you to find yourself, if you use it to eliminate, rather than procure, distractions. Fame won't do it either—for the famous man is almost invariably far more insecure about hanging on to his fame than the man who never achieved fame. The

$ucce$$ful man is almost never secure—for, having climbed to a high pinnacle of $ucce$$, he is for the most part far more worried about falling and breaking his neck than the guy who was never able to climb that high to begin with. And so forth and so on.

Well, then—what kind of goal is left? What is there to aim at that does make sense?

Just this:

Anything at all, providing it gives you a chance to go on growing and developing as a human being. Anything at all that interests you and absorbs you creatively—whether it is writing a book or building a better mousetrap, whether it is painting pictures or constructing model airplanes—anything at all, *just so it does not have an end.* Just so it doesn't lead to a final stop. Just so you can keep on with it, keep on working at it, keep on perfecting yourself in whatever you're doing. Just so you can never arrive at the place *where you have to stop developing,* growing, working, being absorbed, learning, planning, thinking about it, trying to get better at it. In short, anything that doesn't bring you to a point where you have to stop and say—"Well, that's finished."

For if you ever do have to stop and tell yourself you're finished—well, at that point you may as well lie down, because, whether you know it or not, you'll have stopped living.

In order to achieve success in a mass business, producing a mass commodity, you have to please masses of people with what you do.

This necessity imposes a brake on you. For if you want to keep getting better at what you do there is apt to come a time when your audience says, in effect:

Whoa! That's far enough. We like what you're doing now, and we'll pay you to keep on doing it—but don't go any further, because if you do we won't understand what you're trying to do and we won't pay to hear it.

You see?

Take Irving Berlin, for example. There's a man who writes popular music and does a damn capable job of it; with the result that he makes millions of dollars, pleases masses of people, and has a good enough life–so far as I can tell.

Now everything seems to make good enough sense there, doesn't it? But–just for the sake of supposition–what would happen if Mr. Berlin had gone on developing himself as a composer to the point where he was now writing, say, operas or symphonies? Or, if operas and symphonies sound a little too highbrow for you–what would happen if he started developing himself as a composer to a point of specialized musical development where a mass audience could no longer understand and enjoy what he was composing?

The answer is obvious enough. Mr. Berlin had better not.

Now as I've pointed out several times before, this might be O.K.–if he just happens not to want to develop himself along such lines. In which case, everything is hunky-dory for Mr. Berlin, and we can leave him to enjoy his life. But let's not forget that there are any number of people, and damn capable people at that, who *do* want to go on developing, and not only want to but must, for some people are built that way– and if they don't go on developing to the utmost of their capabilities, such people are apt to get very, very sick. And of course, there is always the other side of this picture–which has to do with the audience itself, which, if it stops such people from going on and developing their crafts, is only depriving itself of the benefits (and they're real enough!) of what such people could give if allowed a halfway decent break–instead of being penalized for wanting to go on and develop to their fullest creative extent.

Besides all that, there is the matter of "appearing" in public, which involves, in the music business, almost everything but actual musical ability. And since the music itself is, for me, the only real reason for any musician's appearing at all, since that is what any self-respecting musician wants to get paid for when he does appear—it's become impossible for me to take seriously all the other stuff that goes with appearing in public for audiences conditioned to pay more attention to the way a man is dressed, say, or his so-called "personality," than to his actual performance of the music he is there to perform.

The basic truth is that popular music has little or nothing to do with musical values at all. It's fundamentally functional—just one more form of "entertainment"—and the music is only incidental. A man who makes his living leading a dance band hasn't too much time to concern himself with musical values. His main problem has to be whether the dancers are able to dance to his music. If so, good. Of course, if they happen to be also pleased by the music he plays for them to dance to—well, so much the better. But basically, all that has nothing to do with musical values. And if a man happens to be the kind of guy who *wants* to play real music, he's likely to get into serious trouble. Far more so than the man who regards music as a strictly business matter and goes about it in a businesslike way and unemotionally and detachedly gives his customers what they let him know they want.

In other words, if you happen to be built in the shape of a musical businessman, you're right in step, everything is O.K.—and the chances are nine out of ten that your name is Guy Lombardo, or Sammy Kaye, or any one of a number of fellows who continue year after year giving the public an honest return in dance music for the money the public pays them.

But—and don't forget it—there's no point in confusing entertainment (which is all that this stuff I've been discussing basically is) with any such self-expressive and highly emotionally surcharged art form as music.

So. . . . Given that a fellow is built in such a way as to demand *some* form of self-expression, and that he happens to be unable to function comfortably in crowds of people; given that a fellow wants to spend his time learning more about the world he lives in, and about himself as a creature living in his world; given that he has developed an ability to spend time alone for the purpose of getting at himself; given that this is, to him, enjoyable and constructive as an end in itself; given all these things plus the things I've already told you about this fellow who happens to be writing this stuff you're now reading—well, I ask you, wouldn't you say that almost anything *but* leading a band would be better for a fellow like that to do?

The only wonder, actually, is that it took me so long to come around to knowing it myself. For the fact is, I must have recognized all this a long, long time ago—only, you see, there was that other damn problem, of wanting "all those people behind all those windows" to know my name! Dear God! You'd think a fellow would know better, wouldn't you?

"One's real life is so often the life that one does not live."

Chapter Forty-Eight

AT THE VERY BEGINNING, I made a comment on the meaninglessness of the term "progress" as it is ordinarily used. There are a great many such terms commonly tossed around in discussions of human affairs. Good and Evil, Progress and Retrogression, Advancement and Recession—all these words represent ideas and concepts which will remain pretty fuzzy unless they are formulated in terms of workable criteria.

Now it's simple enough to find criteria when it comes to the simple matter of "progressing" from one place to another; it's quite another thing to establish acceptable criteria for such matters as where we are going as human beings, or what we ought to do with our lives, either as individuals or as a society. And this whole question of criteria becomes increasingly complex the larger the group you're trying to set them up for; until, when you start on such a huge question mark as is presented by our entire World-group Society as it exists today (as you must do sooner or later if you want to try to arrive at any kind of realistic understanding of the world you live in), you are up against an enormous set of problems indeed.

This is one of the large problems in the form of government known as Democracy. It is of course an even larger problem (particularly for minority members) in any other form of government thus far evolved. So, all things equal, we are no doubt better off even with a faulty democracy (as long as we keep it evolving and don't allow it to freeze in one place) than with something that might work out far more efficiently in a machine manner but far less flexibly regarding such important matters as the possibility of criticism, and consequent improvement, from within. .

Now while it isn't always possible for an individual or a group to know exactly where it is heading, it is at least a workable possibility to examine the road ahead and ascertain where we do *not* want to go. At least this could be one *form* of progress in that we'd at least not be "progressing" backwards or sideways. There is a distinct probability that "events repeat themselves," not necessarily in exactly the same way, but on different levels. The trick, then, would be to determine (insofar as is possible from past performance and experience) what *has* happened in the past, and then try to directionalize and channelize existent, recognizable, known forces toward what we agree are "good," useful, constructive ends—rather than those we already know to be "bad," impractical, and destructive. And in order to manage this, we are going to need a good deal of skill, experience, and applied wisdom.

If a man is willing to experiment, he can easily enough learn what ways of life are of no use to him. Bringing all this down to the personal level, I may as well point out that my entire life up to now has been nothing more or less than my own attempt at self-exploration and orientation.

So that this otherwise egoistic exploration of the island, or series of islands, constituting my inner self is in the end only one more attempt at communication for the purpose of understanding; and insofar as any writing is done for that purpose it seems to me a worthwhile enough pursuit. I can now also say that while I may not be entirely clear as to where I am going or how I am going to get there (or even what I'll find if or when I do get wherever I'm going) I can in any event be quite clear about where I do *not* want to go, what I do *not* want to do, what I am *not* interested in achieving.

I've spoken of various aspects of the business I've been in, and the life I've led in this business. And although I've said a number of disparaging things about the business itself, let me make it clear that I have nothing against the music business as a way of earning money. I've earned several million dollars—and that's a conservative estimate—since the time when my band first got into the chips. I said "earned," not "made" or "kept" or "deserved." I'm only too aware of the difference between these various words. All I mean is that *it has been profitable* for those people who have hired me and paid me these large sums, to do so. If they *hadn't* made money with me, they wouldn't have hired me—or else they wouldn't have paid me as much as they did. It's as simple as that. So, in spite of the fact that it's customary for people in my business to go around modestly disclaiming their right to make the kind of money made by headliners in show business, or else being ever-so-grateful because everyone is being "so nice"—in spite of this, let me say right now that I see nothing to be coy about. When I say I "earned" that amount of money, I mean just that. Economically speaking, I was "worth it"—in terms of what I could make for those who employed me. Or, as Sam Goldwyn is supposed to have said about an untalented actor who nevertheless was a valuable box-office attraction: "Sure he's overpaid, but he's worth it."

The main point is that all this has nothing to do with music or whether I can play well or even whether my band is or was any damn good or not. It is nothing but a matter of enough people being curious enough (or what-not enough) about me to pay money to come to wherever my band and I were appearing.

Well, then. . . .

What's the matter with a business that enables a fellow to earn that kind of money?

One big thing. For me, that is. Simply that there is far more business connected with it than there is music—or self-satisfaction. Market-place values dominate to such an extent that musical ones finally cease to exist.

I have already pointed out that the running of a successful dance band is not a matter of music. The music itself is entirely incidental to that ability which enables a man to appraise and understand his market and go on selling his product at a profit. That's all there is to it. Whether it's music or beans you're selling—as long as you're selling enough notes, or vegetables, at a profit—you're in business.

In order for a bandleader to go on maintaining popularity year after year, he must be willing to forget about music and concentrate on the business details involved in selling his commodity. I don't mean that he has to do it all himself. He can hire a whole corps of lawyers, agents, managers, advisers, bookkeepers, accountants, etc., etc., to handle all the details of contracts, payrolls, commission fees, taxes, and so on. But in the last analysis the bandleader has to supervise all this planned activity or else he has to learn to delegate authority in the same way as any other business executive who wants to continue in business.

The trouble with all this is that I never set out to be a businessman. I was railroaded into it—out of my own inner weakness and Cinderella wishes. Primarily, I have always tried to play music that would satisfy me, within the limitations of the fields I've worked in. True enough, I haven't always succeeded in carrying out my best intentions, but I've tried. In that respect, at least, there are good enough precedents. Given the imperative necessity to please enough people to continue making enough money to be able to pay good enough musicians to play the kind of music I felt more or less satisfying—given these distinct limitations, I have done the little best I could.

But judging from any strictly creative viewpoint, I have

never actually been a musician at all. In my opinion, no public performer in any mass medium can ever be creative in any real sense. At best, a performer can only *re*-create, interpret, modify, seek—and sometimes find—new values in the creative work he is interpreting, performing, re-creating; but the fact of the creating itself, *the making of something where nothing existed before,* this is the domain of the composer, and the composer only—when it comes to making music. In the same sense as it is the playwright who makes the theatre, the writer the book business.

Now whether you agree with that or not, the fact remains that it is my point of view and whether I like it or not I'm not going to try to fool myself about it. I've long ago got past whatever form of self-deception a man needs to convince himself of his own creativity when the plain truth is that he may never have created one single thing in his whole life.

But enough of that. I've gone into it at so much length only to establish the way I feel about all this, in order to clarify the rest of what I have to say.

Creating music, then, or creating anything else for that matter, has for me one enormously important implication. Any man who wants to do it must be prepared to spend his life at it—if he wants to do it well, or even as well as he can. This is a matter of self-dedication. If you're going to do something to your own absolute limit, you're going to have to dedicate yourself to it completely. And that means you're going to have to accept whatever way of life it entails.

All of which is fine, if you happen to care for the way of life, but it can also be utterly miserable if you happen *not* to care for it.

Essentially, the popular musician in America must learn that his basic job is to entertain people, to make them forget their sorrows for a moment or two; in the same sense that any popular art form must aim at the same distraction value. Any such job as that is basically a young man's business. It takes a young man's energy to go traveling around the country, night after night in a different place, prancing and cavorting around in front of mobs of people all out to try to forget their problems for an evening. And for a young man it can be a good enough way of life, if he happens to like it.

I happened never to like it—and I've already explained most of why. I've also tried to explain why I stuck with it for as long as I did—since I couldn't learn what I had to know about myself in order to begin doing the sort of thing I do like.

So. . . . Here we are, and if you've come this far with me you've now got a good-sized chunk of my life in your hands and in your head.

Where does all this lead?

And how does it apply generally?

"And we are here as on a darkling plain . . ."

MATTHEW ARNOLD

Chapter Forty-Nine

I KNOW A MAN who is a world-famous social scientist, a highly successful psychiatrist, and the author of several important treatises in the field of cultural anthropology, in which he is a recognized authority.

During a recent conversation we had, he mentioned that he was becoming increasingly aware of a sudden sharp intensification in the anxieties of the large majority of his students and psychiatric patients. Ever since the rapid expansion of international tension beginning with the Korean War, he went on to say, there seems to be a growing hopelessness and bewilderment pervading the minds of most of the people he deals with.

"One at a time, at some time during the past few months," he told me, "I've seen people walk into this office shaking their heads, all saying pretty much the same thing."

"What's that?" I asked.

"It could be summed up in these words," he said. " 'What the devil am I doing? I try to make myself go about my business as usual, but every once in a while I find myself stopping and asking myself what's the use of it and who am I trying to fool?' " He stopped and looked at me for a moment. Shrugging his shoulders, he continued, "The terrible part of it all is that here I am, the man they're coming to for help with their problems, and what on earth am I supposed to tell them?

What *is* there to tell them? How do I know where any one of us will be this time next year? I can't even be certain *I'll* be here practicing my *own* profession. Whether there will even be a New York City, for that matter. How on earth can anyone tell anyone anything in a world like this, where the future is so unpredictable that no one can even be certain he *has* a future at all?"

"But you can't very well tell patients what you've just told me, can you?" I asked him.

He smiled. "Hardly. . . . Still, I can't very well lie to them about objective realities either. I couldn't get away with it if I tried. Many of them know a good deal more than I do about what is actually going on in tne world. What I have to do is to deal with their tensions and anxieties on a clinical level. But today even that becomes terribly difficult at times. The reason is, of course, that it's becoming increasingly difficult to separate the real outer problems from those that are inner, personalized properties of the patient himself."

He went on to discuss this whole matter for a while after that. And what came out of the discussion is something along these lines: that although all this is indeed frighteningly true, it is also true that this particular type of tension and uncertainty raises more hell with one kind of person than with another.

Now I am certainly not intimating that it can ever be easy on anyone; but the fact remains that a great deal depends on the life-situation of the person involved.

Take, for instance, a man who has spent his life building up a successful business, say a law practice. Let's assume that he originally decided to study law because it seemed to him a sound, stable profession, through which he would have as good a chance as any other to achieve the kind of life he wanted.

What are his principal aims? Well, for one thing, he wants to accumulate enough capital to take care of himself and his family, to have enough to provide for them when he gets old enough to think of retiring. These are normal enough aims, if by "normal" we mean "average"—which I'm afraid most of us do, although they're far from the same.

At any rate, that is how it works out for most people—or at least that is how they want it to work out. There are relatively few people who predicate their behavior on other principles. For most of us the aim is to get together enough money to "provide" for a time when we are either unwilling or unable to go on earning money. This is basic, and anyone who digs deep enough will find something of this sort as the mainspring of most people's activities. With startlingly few exceptions, that is the way we live, and for the most part—given the sort of training most of us get—it's the way we damn near have to live.

However, it is not necessarily the only way. By and large, it may be the easiest. It is always easier to follow long-established lines of least resistance, and it is terribly difficult for a man to acquire enough knowledge of himself and his true needs, and also retain enough of that old-fashioned thing called integrity, to branch off onto a line of greater resistance and make for himself a new way, a life of his own choosing, and one not necessarily either understood or approved of by his contemporaries.

But today, even the line of least resistance is becoming less and less easy to live with. It might be well enough if it worked. There may have been times in the past when it did work—although I doubt that it was ever more than just barely tenable as a way of life in any period of history at all—but the simple fact confronting us *today* is that it will no longer work *now*.

It seems quite clear to me that we have arrived at a point where there is no longer any question as to the easy way or the hard way. It's either the hard way or—well, quite possibly no way at all. Unless we manage to clarify ourselves, unless we learn to think and reason and communicate and behave as *social creatures,* rather than mobs of greedy, grabbing, frightened animals, we're all going to wind up face to face with a little thing called catastrophe much sooner than we even realize. "Enjoy yourself, it's later than you think"—run the first words of a pop tune. Well, that's no use either. Too many of us have been concerned with enjoying ourselves for too long now. This whole business of enjoying ourselves and letting the devil take the hindmost is one of the main reasons it *is* later than we think. And precisely because it is so late, it's damn well high time we started pulling the fat out of the fire before it's all burnt to a crisp and ourselves along with it.

Getting back to my sociologist-psychiatrist friend and the anxieties and hopelessness of his students and patients—let's see how what he says applies to our main theme. Of course there are hundreds, perhaps thousands, of personal factors on the clinical, individual level. But even overlooking these, there is one big generalized, all-important factor we can discuss.

Anyone who has been high-pressured, through outer and/or inner pressures, into setting up his life along lines that have no particular meaning for him except as a means to some security-end—anyone who functions that way today is going to find himself in a fix. What kind of "security" can a man look forward to when the whole of civilization as we know it is shaken to its foundations? As my friend asked, "How can anyone tell anyone anything in a world where the future is so unpredictable that no one can even be sure he *has* a future at all?"

In other words, what's going to happen today with a man who is spending his whole life, putting in all his time and energy, on a gamble that he will achieve some sort of static "secure" future out of what he is doing? Anxieties? Tensions? Hopelessness? Well, what else can he expect?

No, it's no use. Without a set of clear values to live by, no one can escape hopelessness today. The future we face is one that only a fool would bank his *entire* present life on.

So there is only one valid choice. As I said, it is by no means an easy choice, given the kind of training and conditioning most of us have had, but it is either this choice or the alternative—some degree of hopelessness, the degree depending on the sensitivity of the person involved.

We must learn to live meaningfully. Our lives have to have value *in the present,* as well as in terms of the future. We must learn to live in such a way as to derive some measure of personal satisfaction out of what we do from day to day. *We must begin to examine ourselves and our lives in terms of social, rather than individualistic, meaning.*

Certainly there is need to be realistically concerned about the state of the world. *But the concern of a man whose life has real, day-to-day, social meaning is quite a different thing from the anxiety and tension of the man who lives only for the possibility of what he hopes to get out of some dubious future.* For, whatever the future may or may not be, whether The Bomb is or is not used to wipe out this "world we never made"—at least we can each do what we must do, in whatever time we have to do it. And, oddly enough, there is no other sane way to guarantee ourselves a future at all.

What all this adds up to is simply that we must learn to regard the realities of our time with different eyes. The following sentence comes out of an editorial published in England shortly after the death of G. B. Shaw: "G.B.S. always held that life is unbearable if one thinks of it in terms of individual success or suffering, but fascinating if one analyzes biological and economic change." Bringing that into this context, we must stop thinking of change as terrifying and understand that it is inevitable.

For my own part, I am no longer looking for happy endings, or Cinderella-type solutions. It's all very well to fool around, as we did when we were making little plot points and blessing Cinderella with offspring for the sake of the story line. But the truth about this Cinderella gal is that, among her numerous other drawbacks, she has one outstanding fault. She's sterile.

"And I would find myself and not an image . . ."

WILLIAM BUTLER YEATS

Conclusion

I STARTED ALL THIS BY TELLING YOU about a road I'd been
traveling for a long time, and that I'd come to a wide open
space with lots of other roads radiating off in all directions
like spokes in a wheel. Well, in one sense, we've both come
to that kind of open space now, and from here on our roads
diverge.

Very well—you've probably got your own picked out. But
possibly along the way we've come together I may have
influenced you a tiny bit in regard to your choice.

As for myself. . . ?

The real purpose of my existence (which I must assume to
be a reality, since I can't very well see how I could even
doubt it if I didn't exist) is to me a matter of absolute confusion. When it comes to final values, I add to the punctuation
of the world one tiny question mark. In the vast enigma of
the entire universe, I flaunt the childish riddle of myself and
my own trifling self-preoccupations. My life is just one more
ridiculous toy in the littered cupboard of the spinning galaxies
that wheel unendingly through an infinity of time and space.
The whole miraculous chain of organic development from pro-
toplasmic slime to steel-girdered skyscraper has, through a
whim called evolution, contrived my meager mind as an im-

perfect mirror in which Nature can regard herself with wonder. . . .

Question: What is it that has seven legs, six arms, five eyes like telescopes and four more like microscopes, and behaves like an isotope of hydrogen?
Answer: I don't know—what is it?
Question: Oh, I don't know either. I don't know any of the answers. All I do is make up the questions. . . .

Coming back, then, to that question of which road I'm taking from here on in—well, I can't tell where it's going to end up. Actually, it doesn't really matter. All that does matter is that it be whatever road will lead ultimately to the highest degree of *awareness* I'm capable of achieving.

Where does awareness lead? That, of course, is a question without any final answer—but this much can be said:

It leads to wherever a man has to go in his own development as a human being. And as I said way back at the start of all this, basically it's a trip a fellow has to make by himself.

I've finally made my own choice. In fact, I've just finished taking my first stumbling step along the road I'm going to travel from now on.

This is the first step—this book. . . .

Picardy Farm
Pine Plains, N.Y.
December 1950—February 1952